Kirsty McLeod is the author of a number of books and was a publisher's editor before becoming a full-time writer. She was also a regular reviewer on the *Yorkshire Post* for ten years, a columnist for the *Daily Telegraph*, and is a Commissioner of English Heritage.

BATTLE ROYAL

This is the story of the two eldest sons of King George V — David (who became, briefly, Edward VIII) and Bertie (later George VI). It tells how two brow-beaten boys emerged into adulthood, the one confident and self-indulgent, the other hesitant and insecure. One married Wallis Simpson, the other Elizabeth Bowes-Lyon, two strong and fiercely opposed women who shaped their husbands' fate and that of the monarchy. The book follows the swing of the pendulum which left David an exiled, rootless socialite, while Bertie grew into kingship and earned the love and respect formerly bestowed on his older brother.

KIRSTY McLEOD

◆

BATTLE ROYAL
Edward VIII & George VI
Brother against Brother

Complete and Unabridged

CHARNWOOD
Leicester

First published in Great Britain in 1999 by
Constable and Company Limited
London

First Charnwood Edition
published 2000
by arrangement with
Constable and Company Limited
London

British Library CIP Data

McLeod, Kirsty, *1947 –*
Battle Royal: Edward VIII & George VI:
brother against brother.—Large print ed.—
Charnwood library series
1. Windsor, Edward, Duke of
2. George, VI, King of Great Britain
3. Large type books
4. Great Britain—Kings and rulers—Biography
I. Title
941′.084′0922

ISBN 0–7089–9180–7

Published by
F. A. Thorpe (Publishing)
Anstey, Leicestershire

Set by Words & Graphics Ltd.
Anstey, Leicestershire
Printed and bound in Great Britain by
T. J. International Ltd., Padstow, Cornwall

This book is printed on acid-free paper

For Christopher
who shares in this book

Acknowledgements

I should like to express my gratitude to the *Institut Pasteur* in Paris for their authorisation to use copyright material relating to the Duke and Duchess of Windsor. I am grateful to others who have given me permission to quote from material still in copyright — in particular Mrs David Hankinson, Mr David Metcalfe, Mr Nigel Nicolson and the Trustees of the literary estate of Lady Diana Cooper. I have made every effort to contact owners of copyright material used in this book. If I have inadvertently missed any of them I apologise.

Many of the pictures in this book come from the remarkable Hulton Getty collection, and I am grateful for the help of its researchers. Mr Michael Bloch generously gave me permission to reproduce a photograph of the Duke and Duchess of Windsor from his collection. Jane Mays kindly arranged access for me to the *Daily Mail* picture archives. I owe a great debt to Clive Dickinson, and also to Philip Ziegler for his advice. His *King Edward VIII* was an invaluable reference source, as was Sarah Bradford's *George VI*, and Michael Bloch's *Wallis & Edward: Letters 1931 – 37*, together with his studies of the Windsors' peregrinations in the early months of the War. Any mistakes or misinterpretations of events are of course mine and mine alone.

My agent Gill Coleridge was a tower of strength throughout the passage of this book. Carol O'Brien, my editor at Constable, has also been wise and encouraging and positive, and her assistant Alexandra Gruebler coped very efficiently with the practical side. Finally I should like to thank David Elstein, whose inspiration it was to compare the two royal brothers, and whose enthusiasm helped the project on its way.

1

YORK COTTAGE

A fortnight before her first wedding anniversary and three weeks into an extended stay with her parents, May, Duchess of York dutifully brought her first-born son into the world. 'At ten o'clock this evening, May gave birth to a sweet little boy,' the Duke of York and future George V announced with paternal pride in his diary. The date was Saturday 23 June 1894. 'I imagine,' the sweet little boy was to observe drily as an old man of seventy, 'that this was the first and last time my father was inspired to think of me in exactly those terms.'

The birth of the eldest son of the eldest surviving son of the eldest son of the Queen Empress Victoria was to have taken place, fittingly, at Buckingham Palace. However, the stifling heat which lay like a pall over the capital forced the expectant mother to retreat to White Lodge in the green shade of Richmond Park. Cool and airy it may have been among the trees outside, but inside White Lodge was a high-Victorian *domus horribilis*, every square inch of it muffled with shawls, dotted with potted plants and crammed with dark, gloomy furniture. No wonder the Yorks' first son and heir grew into what his mother, contemplating the two-year-old toddler, described as a 'plain' and 'jumpy' child who in later life, as Edward VIII, was determined to cast off the suffocating mantle of his inheritance.

The birth — 'of course it is a great bore for me and requires a great deal of patience to bear it, but this alas is the penalty for being a woman' — was followed for May by a family argument. Queen Victoria took it for granted that any great-granddaughter would be named after her, while a great-grandson would take the name of her dear departed husband Prince Albert. The Duke of York had to break the news to the Queen that the name he and his Duchess had long set aside for their eldest son was in fact Edward, after 'darling Eddy', the Duke's older brother, who had died of pneumonia two years before. 'This is the dearest wish of our hearts, dearest Grandmama, for Edward is indeed a sacred name to us, and one which I know would have pleased him beyond anything.' But Victoria, Queen of Great Britain and Ireland and Empress of India, was not in the habit of being gainsaid. 'You write as if Edward was the real name of dear Eddy,' she rebuked her grandson, whereas Eddy had in point of fact been christened Victor Albert. After a struggle, the baby prince was burdened with the names Edward Albert Christian George Andrew Patrick David, and thereafter known to his family as David.

With the birth of her first son *The Times* credited May, Duchess of York with a notable royal hat-trick. She had ensured, for a further generation at least, the direct line of succession

2

for the House of Saxe-Coburg-Gotha, providing the reigning sovereign, for the first time in history with three male descendants in the direct line of inheritance, and consolidating 'the close family affection which binds together every branch which issues from the parent stock.' May must devoutly have wished that this last statement, in particular, were true. That it wasn't, and that her husband's family took cruel pleasure in reminding her that she had been grafted from inferior stock, ensured that almost from the start the newly married Duchess of York began to withdraw behind a frigid reserve — what her life-long friend, Mabell, Countess of Airlie, was to call 'the hard crust of inhibition.'

In the eyes of many she had achieved the unique privilege of hitting the regal jackpot twice, by becoming engaged to both the sons of the heir to the British throne. But her path had not been an easy one. Admittedly her mother's side brought the robust blood of King George III to shore up her fragile royal credentials. But the Tecks had been dragged into disrepute by a morganatic marriage. May's grandfather Duke Alexander of Wurttemberg's reckless union with an obscure Hungarian countess ensured that his son, Prince Franz, Duke of Teck, had to make do with the title, not of Royal Highness, but of Serene Highness, which relegated his family to the lower divisions of European royalty.

In this caste-conscious limbo, May endured an uneasy childhood with her impoverished parents. Her mother, Princess Mary Adelaide,

3

weighed in at seventeen stone and indulged in extravagant and lavish expenditure which far out-stretched the £5000 a year she was granted by Parliament. Her father, nervous of lowering his already precarious status by penny-pinching, did nothing to stem the financial haemorrhage. Indeed he did nothing much at all, apart from gardening and trying his hand briefly at soldiering in the Egyptian campaign of 1882. Victoria's Prime Minister Benjamin Disraeli suggested that Prince Franz might assume some minor royal post, possibly as Viceroy of Ireland, but this was vetoed by the Queen. The Tecks were considered too poverty-stricken even to occupy the throne of Bulgaria. And when the family did move abroad, it was writs from creditors rather than the treasures of the Renaissance which prompted them to spend a couple of years exiled in Florence.

Dismissive as Queen Victoria might have been about the Duke and Duchess of Teck, she saw far greater potential in their earnest and level-headed daughter. As her biographer James Pope-Hennessy was to remark, May was 'too Royal to marry an English gentleman and not Royal enough for Royalty' — but Queen Victoria brushed aside this minor impediment when the need arose to find 'a good sensible wife with some considerable character' for her grandson, Prince Eddy, Duke of Clarence, eldest son of the Prince of Wales.

It would have been an unhappy marriage. Successor to a Crown and Empire which

4

included one in four of the world's population and almost a quarter of its land surface, Prince Eddy was unstable, dissolute, sickly and so slow-witted that many observers maliciously excused it as softening of the brain brought on by his rumoured syphilis. A well-known alcoholic, he was linked to a scandal involving a homosexual brothel, and his name still surfaces on the wilder shores of speculation about the identity of Jack the Ripper. Fortunately, no sooner had Queen Victoria arranged the young couple's engagement, at the beginning of December 1891, than Prince Eddy caught flu, developed inflammation of the lungs and died.

Within a matter of weeks, May found herself in the running again, with a substitute. Prince George, Eddy's younger brother, was now the Prince of Wales's heir and, like Eddy, the one significant hurdle in his pathway to the throne was his lack of a suitable wife. Eddy and George had been born within a year of each other and, in accordance with a curious royal practice, had been raised virtually as twins in their nursery. Although smaller and younger, George took it upon himself to watch over his taller, languid and increasingly dissipated elder brother; it was one of his first self-imposed duties in life. As they grew up, the royal brothers shared the same tutor, joined the same naval training ship and shared the thrill of being tattooed. On shore they shared the same girl they kept and bedded in St John's Wood. What was more natural in the circumstances than they should share the same fiancée?

The Queen was in favour. Her subjects approved. The Duke and Duchess of Teck who had seen their winning ticket cruelly torn up in front of their eyes could scarcely believe their luck. Even the young couple shyly concurred. Only Alexandra, Princess of Wales expressed misgivings, but then Eddy and George had also shared her suffocating maternal affection. Increasingly isolated by her deafness, her eldest son cruelly despatched to an early grave, and her husband's affections long since diluted by a succession of mistresses, Princess Alexandra staked out her claim to her remaining son, writing to him, 'There is a bond of love between us, that of mother and child, which nobody can ever diminish or render less binding and nobody can, or ever shall, come between me and my darling Georgie boy.'

And nobody did. Even after her son's marriage, Alexandra continued to sweep proprietorially and unannounced into his new home, York Cottage, Sandringham, showing it off to friends, taking it upon herself to rearrange the furniture, interviewing and employing a nurse when her daughter-in-law was pregnant. For the Duke of York, life at York Cottage was undemanding and uncomplicated — his mother saw to that, but then the house had been her wedding present to her son. Living in the grounds of his 'Dear Old Sandringham, the place I love better than anywhere else in the world', and where he had chosen to spend his honeymoon, 'Georgie' was only an umbilical cord away from his 'dearest little Motherdear', who treated York Cottage as

6

an extension of the nursery she had ruled over when 'Georgie' was a child. Nor was George ever allowed to drop the flirtatious attitude he had had to adopt towards his mother which may have signified an unconscious attempt to compensate for his father's scandalous treatment of her. Alexandra knew how to keep her son subservient by gently tweaking his insecurities at the first sign of independence from him. Even after her son's marriage, his was the male company Alexandra demanded and craved. Emotionally short-changed by his father's bullying and disinterest, George was bonded to Alexandra by a fear of complete parental rejection that prevented him from ever breaking away from her.

Even a princess as steeped in veneration for the British royal family and the constitution as May was, must have been unnerved by so demonstrative and possessive a mother-in-law. Certainly these were traits May would never display towards her own children. No doubt the material rewards which now came her way, after years of relative poverty as a branch-line royal, helped to offset any doubts she may have had about this second rather hasty engagement. Married in July 1893, the Yorks received fifteen hundred wedding presents valued at £300,000, with personal gifts of jewellery adding a further £1 million to the sum, and a trousseau for May which included forty outdoor suits and fifteen ball gowns.

Now that she was married to Prince George, May might have been expected to look for

7

companionship among her three royal sisters-in-law. If she did, she did not find it. The princesses Victoria, Maud and Louise were a close and mutually adoring threesome, who proved jealous of the interloper. May was self-reliant and accomplished, which made them envious. She was shy and diffident, which they chose to interpret as aloofness and arrogance. Their brother's new wife needed all the steely determination instilled into her from childhood to withstand the steady erosion of her self-confidence by her husband's family. 'Poor May, with her Wurttemberg hands,' commiserated Princess Louise, typically resorting to her sister-in-law's morganatic lineage as the ultimate slur. May, like Princess Michael of Kent eighty years later, determined to be queenlier than any of them.

Besides, once her baby son was safely delivered, the Duchess of York had become the mother of a future King — an Emperor indeed, on whose global empire the sun never set. She never forgot to what she owed her new status. By marrying her, Prince George had in a stroke satisfied her lifelong yearning for security and respect. Henceforth, her husband was to be her world. She obeyed him, deferred to him, revered him, and colluded with him, even against their children. To George she owed everything, and in consequence, George came first.

The new Duchess of York had displayed a rare flash of independence in insisting that she give birth to David away from her marital home. After enduring six hot summer weeks at Richmond, Prince George made sure that the arrival of the rest of his children would cause him as little inconvenience as possible by demanding that they were born at York Cottage. For eighteen months baby David was cock of the walk in the royal nursery while his mother prepared for her second confinement.

The arrival of a second son in the small hours of Saturday 14 December 1895 should have been greeted with joy; instead it brought disappointment and disquiet. Prince George had been hoping for a daughter: his wife had failed him there. Worse still, she had given birth on the blackest day in the royal calendar, Mausoleum Day, the double anniversary of the deaths of Queen Victoria's Consort, Prince Albert, and of their third child, Princess Alice of Hesse.

Queen Victoria's eldest son, the baby's fifty-four-year-old grandfather, the future Edward VII, was still sufficiently in awe of his mother to remark, 'Grandmama was rather distressed that this happy event should have taken place on a darkly sad anniversary for us.' After thirty-four years of regularly having to troop off to the hideous mausoleum where Albert had been laid to rest, the Prince of Wales had rather hoped that his son George's news might break the spell. And indeed, naming the baby Albert (to the family he would always be Bertie) and asking Queen Victoria to be his godmother, helped win the old lady round.

From the start, Bertie suffered by comparison with his elder brother. Beside the column-inches in the press devoted to David's birth, the

9

coverage when Bertie was born was scant. Then his christening had to be postponed to make way for the funeral of his great-uncle, Prince Henry of Battenberg, who had caught malaria on a military expedition to West Africa and died on the voyage home. Even when Bertie did make it to the font, he was upstaged by David who screamed so loudly he had to be removed to the vestry. For the next five years the Duke and Duchess of York continued to fill the nursery at York Cottage. Mary, the long-awaited daughter, was next to arrive in 1897. She was followed three years later by Henry (the future Duke of Gloucester) and in 1902 by George (the future Duke of Kent). Their last child, John, an epileptic who played little part in family life, was born in 1905.

'Until you have seen York Cottage, you will never understand my father,' David, as Duke of Windsor, told Harold Nicolson when Nicolson was working on his official biography of King George V. Sir Harold did see it half a century later, and was dismissive of the 'glum little villa' which had been built to house guns invited to shoot on the Sandringham estate. Outside, York Cottage was pebble-dashed and 'enlivened by very imitation Tudor beams'. Inside, Nicolson found the cramped rooms indistinguishable from those of any Surbiton or Upper Norwood terrace house. Indeed, the rooms were small, but there were enough of them to accommodate (as they do today) five sizeable flats, as well as store-rooms and offices for the Sandringham estate. Besides, Prince George felt at home in small rooms which reminded him of happy days spent living in his cabin on board ship. The rooms were too small for entertaining, moreover, which spared him the social obligations that otherwise would have been expected of the son of the Prince of Wales. George was not smart and was never at ease with the raffish society his father enjoyed. When his father offered to rent the nearby mansion of Houghton for him, he turned it down in a trice. 'Very nice to be in this dear wee house again,' he wrote in his diary on returning to York Cottage.

Inside, knowing or perhaps caring nothing about his future wife's taste, Prince George, accompanied by a man from Maples, methodically worked his way through the rooms of his future family home, imposing a bland and gloomy orthodoxy. Only his study showed any individuality: there he covered the walls with the same red cloth from which the trousers of French infantrymen had been made. 'It is almost incredible that the heir to so vast a heritage lived in this horrible little house,' the royal biographer recorded in his diary.

Throughout his life, the future George V remained stubbornly impervious to his heritage. With one of the world's finest collections of furniture and works of art to draw upon, he preferred to surround himself with reproductions and fakes. Like his father, George had too much time on his hands and too little education to make profitable use of it. Edward and Alexandra had themselves both received minimal schooling and this was mirrored in the upbringing of their children. 'The melancholy thing is that neither he nor the darling Princess ever care to open a book,' Lady Frederick Cavendish noted of the Prince and Princess of Wales. Only May, when she became Queen Mary, gained for herself something of a reputation as a collector and connoisseur. However, as her biographer, James Pope-Hennessy pointed out, her interest sprang initially from portraits and miniatures of the royal family. She was seventy-seven when she first saw a performance of *Hamlet* on the stage and even older, eighty, when she first dipped into Tolstoy and Dostoevsky. None of her children ever read a book for pleasure. David, the eldest, at least had a quick, enquiring mind and he could turn a phrase, but later in life he was to complain to Harold Nicolson that, 'I am completely self-educated.'

The Duke of York opened only two kinds of books with any enthusiasm. There were the game books in which he recorded the seasonal slaughter of the tens of thousands of birds, deer, rabbits and hares that confirmed his reputation as one of the finest shots in the country. And there were the shelves of stamp albums in which he obsessively sorted and re-sorted his magnificent collection of British Empire stamps — tributes paid (in postage duty) to his family from every corner of the globe. In his brief naval career, George had sailed to some of these far-off places. At York Cottage, immersed in the solitary world of his stamp albums, he could revisit them and, at the same time, vicariously impose his own authority and order over them.

Later on, when he became King George V, he would enjoy the narcissistic pleasure of seeing his own image appear on virtually every postage stamp of the British Empire, reflecting the vast territories with their millions of subjects over whom he ruled.

Watching him settle into his stolid, philistine life as a Norfolk squire dismayed Harold Nicolson as he set about his official biography. About the time he visited York Cottage, he confided to his diary, 'I fear I am getting a down on George V just now. He is all right as a gay young midshipman. He may be all right as a wise old king. But the intervening period when he was Duke of York, just shooting at Sandringham, is hard to manage or swallow. For seventeen years he did nothing at all but kill animals and stick in stamps.'

Bluff, unimaginative and practical, with a strong sense of propriety, George was ideally suited to the kingdom which awaited him.

The Duke added to York Cottage as he added to his family. By the time he had completed both tasks, the outside of the house was all gables and hexagonal turrets and beams and tiny balconies. Inside, it had become a rabbit-warren of narrow passages and boxy rooms, into which were squeezed the Duke and Duchess, their six children, ten footmen, four pages, three wine butlers, assorted equerries, ladies-in-waiting, private secretaries, valets, and kitchen and domestic staff. There was also the nanny, closeted away with her young charges in the two small rooms that had been designated the nursery. During the day, she shared one room with the three children in her care, the space so cramped that there was little room for toys, apart from a small rocking-horse. By night, nurse and children slept together in the other, only marginally bigger room. It was in this night nursery that the children also took their baths in tin tubs filled with water carried upstairs by a servant.

Apart from brief formal visits to their parents, the York children's world was centred on nanny and nursery. In this respect their lives matched those of every other upper-class child of the time. Their particular misfortune lay in the choice of their first nanny. Mrs Green, barren, neurotic and deserted by her husband, turned out, not surprisingly, to be incompetent and neglectful. What could not have been foreseen, though it should have been swiftly recognised, was that she was also a sadist who showed perverted affection for David and almost total disregard for Bertie. She adored David with as much passion as she was jealous of his parents, so that when she took him on his regular tea-time visit to see them in the drawing-room she pinched him painfully or twisted his arm, making him scream and bawl as he was presented to his mother and guaranteeing that he was swiftly passed back to Nanny.

Bertie, at her hands, soon began to experience the neglect he was to suffer as the younger son of his parents for the next thirty years. When his nurse did remember to feed him, it was often during a ride in an exceptionally bumpy carriage, with the result that Bertie developed chronic stomach problems which were to cut short his war service and bedevil him well into adult life. If Mrs Green's legacy to Bertie was a debilitating gastric condition, she may well have produced in David a distorted association of love with pain which was to colour his life to an even more devastating effect. It took three crucial years for this appalling mistreatment to come to the notice of the Duke and Duchess of York, and then it was only when Mrs Green had a nervous breakdown after working non-stop without a single day's holiday in three years. It says a great deal about the scant attention paid to the children that in a household crammed to bursting point with attendants and servants of every description, not to mention their parents, this constant abuse was allowed to go undetected for so long.

The York children differed from their peers in one important respect: the deadening hand of majesty reached into every corner of their lives. As adults, both David and Bertie recalled never being alone with their two parents. Always there was a lady-in-waiting or some other supernumerary with whom they had to share their parents' attention. Then there was the royal treadmill of official engagements, in particular the lengthy foreign tours, which deprived the children of their mother and father sometimes for months on end.

Majesty and her allegiance to the Crown governed May's life. Motherhood need not necessarily have proved incompatible with all this pomp and splendour. Queen Alexandra was the most regal of figures, yet managed to combine public formality with a demonstrative interest in her children. If May had married some minor German princeling, the natural warmth and even girlishness which some old friends occasionally glimpsed in her might have been allowed free rein. As it was, she felt it incumbent upon her to be majestic both in public and in private. Both the babies' grandmothers were not averse to rolling up their sleeves and bathing the children from time to time, but their mother, stiff, unbending and painfully reserved, found no pleasure in such intimate contact. When her baby son screamed as soon as he was put into her arms, her natural reaction was to have him instantly removed; any attempt to comfort him seems not to have crossed her mind. The general opinion of those who knew her well throughout her life was that she was very cold and stiff and unmaternal — confirming the widely held belief that 'Queen Mary had nothing of the mother at all.' In fact May wanted to be valued and needed by her children, but not at the cost of irritating her husband, who actively disliked small boys and wanted as little as possible to do with them.

Instead, she clung to a strict regal etiquette which, as she judged it, required her children's love as part of their princely duty towards her. Her rules of correct behaviour made no concession to small children. 'What a curious child he is,' she wrote in her diary of her eldest son. 'David was 'jumpy' yesterday morning, however, he got quieter after being out.' That

David was only two at the time and could not be expected to exercise the desired self-control seems to have entirely escaped her. He did better, however, on another occasion which prompted his mother to write, 'Baby was delicious at tea this evening, he is in a charming frame of mind . . . I really believe he begins to like me at last, he is most civil to me.' Children, in other words, who behaved like little adults with charm and civility were rewarded with her approbation. Those who fell short, made demands or gave way to childish tantrums or moods, were cold-shouldered and handed over to others for improvement. Such narcissism made Mary both an exacting and a distant mother.

Duty was her touchstone and she never questioned that her first duty was to her husband to whom, after all, she owed her extravagant jewellery, the clothes she adored and the *objets d'art* with which she surrounded herself and which, not infrequently, she scavenged from aristocratic friends. Queen Mary, as she became, was the most bejewelled monarch to occupy the throne since Elizabeth I, draped in ropes of pearls, ringed, braceleted, encased, for state banquets in diamond stomachers and covered in orders and decorations. Jewels fed her sense of self-worth and represented a value she could understand — one she believed to be rightfully her birthright, but which she had been denied in her childhood. Unlike sobbing, clinging, damp and messy children, these regal trinkets were passive and immutable. They complemented

17

her role as Prince George's wife and future Queen Consort. She herself knew the score better than anyone, chillingly rationalising the distant relationship she and George maintained with their children as they grew up: 'I have always to remember that their father is also their King.'

With a father like Prince George, the children needed little reminding of this. His relationship with his own possessive mother had made him determined that he would not have to share his wife with his children. For Lady Airlie, a family friend for many years with close inside knowledge of the royal couple, 'The tragedy was that neither had any understanding of a child's mind.' Nor did either George or May make any effort to develop that understanding. In its place ruled ritual and dogma, masking the insecurity which had shaped their own childhoods.

As a child, Prince George's own father, the Prince of Wales, had been made to suffer 'for his own good' by Prince Albert and Queen Victoria. When the young prince was still only six, the diarist Charles Greville noted that 'the hereditary and unfailing antipathy of our Sovereigns to their Heirs Apparent seems thus early to be taking root, and the Q. does not much like the child.' With only his own unhappy experiences of parenthood to draw on, Prince Edward had little option but to pass on the same legacy of neglect and stern indoctrination to George and his siblings. George, like his father, was not his parents' favourite child and throughout his formative years he compensated for the fear

18

of rejection with unquestioning obedience and overt displays of affection. Despite this, his father gave every impression of having little time for him. As a compensation perhaps, George became obsessed with punctuality and, when he was King, kept all of his father's clocks at Sandringham thirty minutes fast.

Tongue-tied and inhibited, George and May both had great difficulty in saying what they felt. Even to each other, they always found it easier to express themselves on paper. 'It is so stupid to be so stiff together,' May wrote to George not long before their marriage, '& really there is nothing I would not tell you, except that I love you more than anybody in the world, & this I cannot tell you myself so I write it to relieve my feelings.' Her husband-to-be replied in similar vein on the same day, again by letter. For their young children, not yet able to read, this embargo on displays of affection during those early years when the security of parental love is so crucial for healthy development, presaged serious consequences.

When they *were* old enough to read, the messages from their father usually carried thinly disguised threats or reprimands. Prince George, possibly as a reaction to his own upbringing in the company of the dissolute Prince Eddy, wanted, above all, children of proper moral character and a dutiful sense of purpose. On his fifth birthday Bertie received a characteristic greeting from the Duke of York: 'Now that you are five years old I hope you will always try to be obedient & do at once what you are told, as you will find it will come much easier to you the sooner you begin. I always tried to do this when I was your age & found it made me much happier.' Perhaps also, in writing this, he was recalling a similar message he had received from his grandmother when he had been a couple of years older than Bertie. Queen Victoria had sent young George a watch, 'hoping that it will serve to remind you to be very punctual in everything and very exact in all your duties . . . I hope you will be a good, obedient, truthful boy, kind to all, humble-minded, dutiful and always trying to be of use to others.'

It is no wonder that children used to receiving presents with greetings such as this were far happier when the giver was away, as George frequently was during the shooting season. In his absence the atmosphere lightened and, more importantly, the children had their mother to themselves. 'My father was a very repressive influence,' David later told James Pope-Hennessy. 'When he used to go banging away for a week or two at some shoot in the Midlands, and my mother never would go to those things, we used to have the most lovely time with her alone . . . she was a different human being away from him.' And indeed, others observed that the Duchess of York seemed to shrink and recede in her husband's presence.

Their all too brief moments of naturalness with an otherwise stiffly formal mother must have confused the children even more, nor can it have done anything to improve their relationship with their father when he was at home. They were allowed occasional visits to her boudoir in the hour before dinner, when the Duke was in his study reading the paper, or poring over a game book or stamp album in what was absurdly called the Library. Holding court in her private domain, her children seated dutifully around her, May gave them her attention for a short spell while she read improving extracts from the classics, or royal history. Even in these times of intimacy, duty was never completely abandoned: May used the opportunity to teach her children how to knit woollen comforters to be sent to one of her charities. For David those fleeting moments when he felt close to his mother remained among his most precious childhood memories. When, years later he was Duke of Windsor, ricocheting giddily back and forth across the Atlantic in a life of restless socialising and continual travel, the one object he always asked for before leaving on a journey was the rag-doll chimney sweep his mother made for him as a child. The same doll recently sold at auction to a collector in New York.

In these early years the children's one consistent source of affection was their new nanny, Charlotte Bill, who had come as a nurse to Princess Mary and took charge of the little princes after the reign of terror of Mrs Green had come to an end. She did her best to act as a surrogate mother, but even by that early stage much irreparable damage had been done, and both of the older boys suffered from nervous stresses which were to manifest themselves in Bertie's stammer and David's constant fingering of his tie. 'Lalla' Bill, as she was known, must sometimes have been compromised in the children's affections when her duty to her employers required her to impose their discipline. It was her responsibility to make sure that outside the nursery the children behaved like the small adults their parents wanted to see: running in the corridors, for instance, was strictly forbidden. She was also responsible for their appearance and deportment, which must have been as nerve-racking for Lalla Bill as it was for her young charges. Throughout his life the Duke of York was obsessed by his sons' appearance and seemed to relish every opportunity to humiliate them over the smallest detail. When one of the little princes had the impudence to be spotted with his hands in the pockets of his sailor suit, it was poor Lalla Bill who was ordered to sew up the pockets of all their suits to prevent it happening again. Even on holiday at Balmoral there was no respite. 'I hope your kilts fit well,' his father wrote to David not long after his ninth birthday; 'take care and don't spoil them at once as they are new. Wear the Balmoral kilt and grey jacket on week days and green kilt and black jacket on Sundays. Do not wear the red kilt till I come.' Sometime in the excitement of the summer this strict protocol became confused. Edward and Bertie wore red faces, if not the red kilt, when their father arrived and delivered his dreaded reprimand.

George V, the sailor King, has been typecast over the years by forgiving biographers as a flawed but fundamentally decent man, bluff rather than brutal. Of his dealings with the outside world, this is probably correct — but at home he was a lamentable parent. He was at his worst with his sons, whom he alternately scorned and neglected. Princess Mary he indulged and, though always dutiful and obedient, she grew up comparatively carefree. Poignantly, it was only when his sons were babies that Prince George could enjoy tenderly entering into their world of babyhood. When chickenpox broke out in the nursery, it was the sick children's father who took time to write a comforting yet playful letter: 'I hope none of you have grown wings and become little chickens, and tried to fly away, that would be dreadful, and we should have to go up in a balloon to catch you.' Yet, typically for the kind of insecure, unimaginative man he was, as soon as the princes began to grow and reason for themselves, his need to dominate them grew. A very different kind of parent emerged — an insensitive, blinkered martinet, prone to outbursts of uncontrolled explosive rage.

Prince George's inability to curb his temper terrified his offspring. Even at the age of seventeen Prince Harry, summoned to his father's presence after accidentally knocking off balance a footman carrying a tray of silver, fainted dead away from fright as he entered the Library. Ever eager to catch them out, the Duke of York would set traps for his two eldest sons, drawing on his detailed knowledge of military decorations. The young princes, noted Mabell Airlie, Queen Mary's observant lady-in-waiting, 'showed the utmost forbearance'. 'The House of Hanover,' the royal librarian Owen Morshead observed, 'like ducks, produce bad parents.' How so? 'They trample on their young.'

Once they were out of babyhood, the royal children lived on edge, in terror of their father's retribution. Serious misdemeanours resulted in a summons to the Library. 'Just as my mother's room came to represent a kind of sanctuary at the end of the day,' David (as Duke of Windsor) was to write in his memoirs, 'so the Library became for us the seat of parental authority, the place of admonition and reproof.' The thrashings their father gave them there can have done little to foster a love of books or learning in the young princes — though here too the Duke of York was following established Hanoverian royal practice. Prince Albert, Queen Victoria's beloved Consort, was even-handed in whipping his daughters as well as his sons; any kind of noise from the nursery especially annoyed him. By the time he was four, Albert's eldest son, the Prince of Wales, had developed a stammer and would fly into uncontrollable tempers. Half a century later, his grandson, Bertie, inherited both these traits.

If the children found their father's explosive quarter-deck anger hard to cope with, the Duke could be just as disconcerting on more benign occasions. When Prince Henry was born, his father recorded, 'David of course asked some very funny questions. I told him that the baby had flown in at the window during the night, and he at once asked where his wings were and

I said they had been cut off.' David was six at the time. It is not surprising that among his many insecurities, fear of the dark shadowed him into adult life.

When Edward VII at last inherited the throne on Queen Victoria's death in January 1901, the Duke of York became Prince of Wales and heir to the throne, and looked to the years ahead with an even grimmer determination to be dutiful. His sons were expected to march to a brisker tune as well. The first they knew of this was their sudden removal from the warm embrace of Lalla Bill. From now on they were to be under the care of the former nursery footman, Frederick Finch. Finch was, in the Duke of Windsor's words, 'handsome, stalwart, muscular'. Fortunately, both boys grew devoted to him, for as a male nanny-cum-valet Finch looked after their clothes, made sure they were properly washed, nursed them when they were ill and tucked them up in bed at night, after kneeling beside them as they said their prayers. Less fortunately, David again became the favourite. Bertie's self-esteem dropped another notch as the man who was the closest he knew to a natural father fell, like so many others, for his older brother's charm. When David went to Oxford, Frederick Finch went with him as his valet; when he became Prince of Wales, Finch served as his butler.

Other changes to the young princes' familiar routine were soon to follow, as their father supervised what he deemed to be their education. 'The Navy will teach David all he needs to know,' declared the new Prince of Wales, who had himself been in the Senior Service since adolescence, and had learnt there, according to his elder son, 'a gruff blue-water approach to all human situations'. The royal family harboured a deep-seated suspicion of intellectual attainment. There were also grave doubts about the moral threats posed by boarding-schools. 'I have a great fear,' Queen Victoria had written, 'of young and carefully brought up Boys mixing with older Boys and indeed with any Boys in general, for the mischief done by bad Boys and the things they may hear and learn from them cannot be overrated.' David and Bertie's father shared his grandmother's misgivings: he decided his sons would be taught at home until they were old enough to join the sort of rigid naval establishment that had helped shape his own character. By keeping his sons at York Cottage, Prince George could continue to impose his stern authority over them, whilst also ensuring that they would not outstrip him intellectually.

The man selected to begin the education of two future kings fulfilled all Prince George's narrow requirements. Henry Hansell was a thirty-nine-year-old bachelor, the son of a local Norfolk gentleman. A six-handicap golfer, an accomplished rifle shot and a keen sailor, he was the ideal man to instil the precepts of muscular Christianity. He had an Oxford degree in history, but his intellectual aspirations were modest enough for the new Prince of Wales not to feel intimidated by them. Even a man as uninspiring and unimaginative as Hansell could see the limitations of keeping the young princes at home. He urged their father to send them to a preparatory school, where they would have benefited from mixing with boys their own age. The Prince of Wales scotched the suggestion out of hand and Hansell was left to do the best he could.

If the boys couldn't attend a school, a school would have to attend them. So with the earnest dreariness that he applied to the princes' education, Hansell set about creating a schoolroom similar to those in which he had taught during his time as a prep school master. His pupils were given wooden school-desks with hinged lids and chairs attached — hard and straight-backed. There were school textbooks, a blackboard and maps on the wall. He provided a prep school timetable too: a rigidly inflexible routine which began at 7.30 a.m. with three-quarters of an hour of prep before breakfast. The princes then spent a morning hunched over their desks, punctuated by an hour's break, then some fresh air after lunch before getting down to a final hour's work until tea. Their day rounded off with a formal visit to the drawing-room to see their parents. Hansell also collected a modest staff of additional teachers, appointing himself as unofficial headmaster. No doubt the Prince of Wales approved of his choice of colleagues in the 'common-room' — three of them had taught *him* in his youth. May's old governess had also been drafted in to help with the early education of the young family. Until Hansell's arrival, the

27

children had received rudimentary schooling in the nursery from Mademoiselle Bricka, a portly Alsatian lady. The shortcomings in her tutelage were soon apparent to all concerned as Hansell set to work to help the princes reach the standard of their prep school peers.

It was an uphill struggle from the start. Neither boy was a natural scholar, and Hansell had neither the commanding presence of their father to control them, nor the inspiration of the gifted teacher to stimulate their minds. Plodding turgidly through his curriculum, he recorded their daily progress (or the lack of it) in the report book he wrote every night for their father's inspection. It made gloomy reading. 'Both boys must give a readier obedience. I often describe them to myself as obedient boys at the second time of asking,' he noted in the autumn of his first year. Almost a year later there was little sign of progress. 'The work in simple division sums is most disheartening,' Hansell wrote of eight-and-a-half-year-old Bertie. 'I really thought we had mastered division by 3 but division by 2 seems to be quite beyond him now.'

Bertie's struggle with mathematics was only one of the symptoms of the crippling insecurity which was enveloping him. Sandwiched between his older brother who caught everyone's eye, and his sister who was unquestionably her father's favourite, he felt unloved and overlooked. The trauma of leaving the nursery for the schoolroom had affected him deeply, pushing this sensitive and highly-strung little boy further into himself. By now Bertie had already acquired his stammer, which under Hansell's regime grew noticeably worse. Bertie was a natural sportsman, and like many natural ball players he was left-handed. To the Prince of Wales this was sinister in every sense of the word, and in accordance with the accepted practice of the time, Hansell was instructed to force him to write with his right hand. This helped to demolish Bertie's already shaky self-confidence. It made him even clumsier with pen and paper. And his stammer worsened — a direct result of what psychologists now recognise as the link between stammering and forcing left-handers to become right-handed.

Bertie became as physically incapable of expressing himself as his parents were emotionally uncommunicative. Indeed Prince George, who did not like to see what he considered weakness in his second son, was impatient and unsympathetic when Bertie was literally stuck for words. 'Get it out,' he would bellow as the boy struggled to speak. Lady Airlie, always a sympathetic observer, thought that Bertie's intense sensitivity over his stammer caused him to 'take refuge either in silence — which caused him to be thought moody — or in naughtiness.' As a result, 'He was more in conflict with authority than the rest of his brothers.' And yet, as late as his teens, Bertie would sit by himself in a dark room rather than draw attention to himself by asking one of the innumerable servants to light the gas.

For a child battling to make himself understood in his native language, the strange words and pronunciation of a foreign language must have been doubly difficult. Nevertheless French lessons formed part of the curriculum for the royal children, given in the first instance by Princess Mary's spiteful French governess, Mademoiselle Dassau. She loathed small boys and enlisted Princess Mary in a conspiracy to have her brothers regularly summoned to the Library. She also made the children speak French whenever she was present at meals. These were glum, monosyllabic get-togethers, which can only have aggravated Bertie's stomach troubles and certainly turned the brothers against French for good. David always showed a preference for German. Even in later life, when he had been living in France for many years, he used to talk to his gardeners in German, having discovered that one of them came from Mademoiselle Bricka's German-speaking Alsace. 'I am a good boy,' he boasted to his father at the age of five. 'I know a lot of German.'

Whether he did or not, David managed to give an impression of easy confidence with the language when he and his brothers and sister were called on to give public displays of their prowess. It was a family tradition that, on the birthdays of their parents or grandparents, each child had to copy out a set passage of verse, learn it by heart and then recite it in front of the assembled grown-ups and their guests. To begin with, the passages were chosen from the English classics. Once French and German were added to their studies, poetry from these languages joined the schoolroom repertoire. David shone on such occasions, even winning grudging praise from his father for his delivery and confidence. All Bertie got was a black look and an embarrassed ripple of rather forced applause after he had stumbled and stammered through his set piece. The horror of these ordeals gave him a dread of public speaking for the rest of his life.

Bertie's response to these frustrations and humiliations was to explode in frequent ungovernable fits of rage — the so-called 'Hanoverian spleen' he had inherited from his namesake, Prince Albert, and from his father. 'I am very sorry to say that Prince Albert has caused two painful scenes in his bedroom this week,' Hansell reported, a month after Bertie's eighth birthday. 'On the second occasion I understand that he narrowly escaped giving his brother a very severe kick, it being absolutely unprovoked & Finch being engaged in helping Prince Edward at the time.' Years later, David complacently asserted, 'I could always manage Bertie.' Yet when Bertie was at his most vulnerable, in these traumatic childhood years, Hansell described the brothers as being like a 'red rag' the one to the other. David's smug superiority blinded him all his life to his brother's potential for breaking free of his control. The irony was that Bertie's father frequently upbraided him for his bursts of anger. 'You really must give up losing your temper when you make a mistake in a sum. We all make mistakes sometimes.' Yet the Prince of Wales made no effort to curb his own temper within the household. Looking back over his

31

childhood, the Duke of Windsor was to confide to James Pope-Hennessy that, 'Off the record, my father had a most horrible temper. He was foully rude to my mother.'

It was not Bertie's tantrums alone which concerned Prince George. While Hansell was forcing the boy into right-handedness in order to conform to current orthodoxy, his father spotted that Bertie's legs showed signs of becoming knock-kneed, like his own, and set about correcting them as well. (In fact four of Prince George's sons had knock-knees; only David was spared the disfigurement.) The treatment to which Bertie was subjected by his father's doctor reduced him to tears at times. For several hours a day he was strapped into a set of splints which were supposed to straighten his legs.

'This is an experiment!' he wrote bravely to his mother. 'I am sitting in an armchair with my legs in the new splints and on a chair. I have got an invalid writing table, which is splendid for reading but rather awkward for writing at present. I expect I shall get used to it.' What Bertie found hardest was having to wear the splints in bed every night. But when Finch did give way to his sobbing protests one evening and left the boy's legs free, he was confronted by a furious Prince of Wales. Pulling the royal trousers tight against the royal legs, Prince George revealed his own knock-knees to Finch and yelled, 'If that boy grows up to look like this, it will be your fault!' In the end the splints did their job, but the psychological scars of such treatment lingered also.

Knock-kneed or not, Bertie was always a better sportsman than David. He was a better shot, as fine a shot as his father. He was a more talented horseman — though David himself was considered a demon at polo and on the hunting field. Bertie became a tennis ace, who played in the doubles of the 1926 Wimbledon championships. And he held a unique cricketing hat-trick, dismissing in three consecutive balls, in a game of garden cricket, three consecutive kings: his grandfather (Edward VII), his father (George V) and his brother (Edward VIII). But despite Bertie's superiority in the field, David took the honours on the rare sporting occasions when the princes appeared in the outside world. Occasional games of football were organised with pupils from a nearby school. In the team photograph David was naturally enough the captain, Bertie just one of the other players.

Walter Jones, the headmaster of the school at West Newton which supplied the football team, understudied Henry Hansell when he was away on holiday. Jones was a dedicated naturalist, whose self-acquired knowledge of the wildlife and ecology of Norfolk commended him to the Prince of Wales and his sons. Unlike poor Hansell who failed dismally to engage David's enquiring mind or harness Bertie's quiet determination to learn what interested him, Walter Jones used to take both boys on fascinating rambles through their grandfather's estate. To Jones, Bertie owed his lifelong love of the Norfolk countryside and especially

Sandringham, the home where, in spite of miserable childhood memories of York Cottage, he was happy to die.

During his childhood of course, Sandringham was his grandparents' home, as extravagant and gay as York Cottage was pedestrian and dull. Sandringham, the big house across the park, all luxury, light and laughter, was the dazzling pinnacle of Edwardian society. When their grandparents were in residence, the young princes were allowed to run across to the big house after tea to catch a glimpse of King Edward's court at play. After the monotony of Hansell and their schoolroom, the sound of Gottlieb's orchestra playing Lehar or Strauss, the heady smell of scent and cigars, the sparkling array of jewels and tea-gowns and the buzz of animated conversation must have seemed another, unattainable world. 'Dickens in a Cartier setting,' was how David when he was Edward VIII recalled the lavish Sandringham Christmas, highpoint of the Sandringham year. To add to their enjoyment, David and Bertie were lovingly welcomed into this glamorous adult circle. Their grandparents doted on them, indulging them with the love and affection the children lacked at home. Edward and Alexandra liked children to be 'romps'. It amused them to undermine their son's and daughter-in-law's stuffy authority. The little princes were always firmly instructed to be back at York Cottage by seven after their tea-time visits, but their grandparents frequently succeeded in delaying them, so that their brief excursion to King

34

Edward's magical realm ended with a dressing-down in the Library for being late home. If his father had had no time for him, Prince George was damned if the old man was going to be allowed to make up for it now by squandering time and attention on his grandchildren.

After Queen Victoria's death in 1901, George and May went on a tour of Australia. For the near on eight months they were away, the York children were in the care of King Edward and Queen Alexandra, who spoiled them horribly. They encouraged their grandchildren to tear about wherever they liked, even in the dining-room and among the guests. Lessons with Mademoiselle Bricka took second place to fun and games. When they arrived home, the new Prince and Princess of Wales were appalled to hear about such licence. Even May, who was accustomed meekly to obey her in-laws, complained to Queen Alexandra that David in particular had been distracted from his lessons. The Queen answered *inter alia* that in their opinion David was becoming too bossy, 'laying down the law & thinking himself far superior to the younger ones'. Alexandra blamed the time he was spending with Mademoiselle Bricka for turning him into 'a single child' and ultimately 'a tiresome child'.

Certainly David showed none of his father's awe for Edward VII. So easy did he feel in the King's company that he once interrupted a conversation he was having at table. The little boy was admonished smartly but waited imperturbably until he was finally allowed to

35

speak. 'It's too late now, grandpapa,' he then said. 'It was a caterpillar on your lettuce but you've eaten it.' Edward VII's status as King Emperor rested lightly on his eldest grandson. During a stay at York House, the family's London home, a tailor's assistant arrived outside the nursery with a suit for David to try on. She was waiting in the corridor when the young prince rushed out. 'Come in,' he told her, 'there's nobody here.' The assistant demurred, wondering if perhaps it was not convenient. 'There's nobody here,' David reassured her. 'Nobody that matters, only grandpapa!'

To a small boy it must have seemed that King Edward held all the cards. He stormed and raged as much as Prince George did, but his fury washed over his grandson. When he did bellow, however, servants appeared and the King got what he wanted. As far as David could see, his grandfather was free to do whatever he wanted and nobody seemed to mind, except possibly his own father the Prince of Wales who, wondrous to observe, could do nothing about it. The King also chose his own friends, with the result that there were always plenty of pretty women to amuse him, only one of whom happened to be David's grandmother.

For twelve of David's first sixteen years his grandfather's mistress, much in evidence at Sandringham, was Alice Keppel. Mrs Keppel was a regular guest at Sandringham, although she was married to George Keppel and the mother of children who never lost their deep love for her. She was adored by the King, tolerated by the Queen, admired by everyone at court and, it seems fair to suppose, must have been a source of some puzzlement to the little boy. In Alice Keppel's light-hearted presence, David experienced fun, laughter and pleasure, none of which were qualities associated with the married woman he knew best, his mother. As a quick-witted boy, he must also have worked out that 'Mrs K', as his parents darkly referred to his grandfather's mistress, was bitterly disapproved of at York Cottage. 'We've seen enough of the intrigue and meddling of certain ladies,' George V observed with tight lips after his father's death. 'I'm not interested in any wife except my own.'

What was David to make of it? Whose lead was he to follow? His grandfather (whom he would closely resemble as the young Prince of Wales), who seemed to do whatever he pleased and get away with it? Or his hectoring, high-minded father, whose sole preoccupation appeared to be his duty and destiny? Lord Esher who as a trusted friend of Edward VII maintained a close interest in David for many years, spotted the Prince's growing awareness of what lay ahead even while he was still quite young. A few weeks before David's tenth birthday, Esher was staying at Windsor Castle. 'I have been walked off my legs, and pulled off them by the children,' he wrote. 'The youngest is the most riotous. The eldest, a sort of head nurse. It was queer looking through a weekly paper, and coming to a picture of the eldest with the label 'our future King'. Prince Albert at once drew attention to it — but the eldest hastily brushed his brother's finger away and turned the page.' Despite living in his older brother's shadow, Bertie looked up to David with the kind of uncritical admiration David could regularly command. Indeed, eighteen months later Lord Esher was back at Windsor telling his diary, 'Prince Edward develops every day fresh qualities, and is a most charming boy; very direct, dignified and clever. His memory is remarkable, a family tradition; but the look of *Weltschmerz (sic)* [world-sorrow] in his eyes I cannot trace to any ancestor of the House of Hanover.' Lord Esher's eerily prophetic observation was borne out when David was older. Lord Louis Mountbatten, his cousin, who knew the Prince as well as anyone did 'soon realised that under that delightful smile which charmed people everywhere, and despite all the fun that we managed to have, he was a lonely and sad person, always liable to deep depressions'.

However stoutly they upheld the traditions and reputation of the British monarchy, Prince George and Princess May managed to produce two sons who showed themselves either unwilling or unsuited to play their parts in the dynastic saga. Their eldest son self-consciously turned away from the prospect, displaying a winsome but stubborn detachment from pomp and panoply, and in particular the hated role of 'princing' which was supposedly his destiny. His younger brother had meanwhile been reduced to a stammering, knock-kneed invalid, nursing chronic abdominal trouble and plagued by an uncontrollable temper. At no time did George and May appreciate the part that their parenting had played in all this. In 1907, blindly following the only precedent he knew, George brusquely packed off young David, poised on the threshold of puberty, to find his feet in the outside world. Ill-prepared and hopelessly out of his depth, he was seized by the royal press-gang and hustled into the Royal Navy.

Thirteen years earlier, in the week of David's birth, *The Times* in its Parliamentary report had carried the famous prediction of the first Labour MP, the member for West Ham South, Keir Hardie. In opposing the motion that a humble address be presented to Her Majesty to congratulate her on the birth of a son, Keir Hardie addressed the House on behalf of those who disowned any allegiance to hereditary rule. To a background of cries of 'Order!' and shouts of outrage, he questioned 'what particular blessing the Royal Family has conferred on the nation'. Then he turned his fire on the new-born child who would be called upon someday to rule over the Empire. 'We certainly have no means of knowing his qualifications of fitness for this position,' the MP declared. 'From childhood onward, this boy will be surrounded by sycophants and flatterers by the score and will be taught to believe himself as of a superior creation. A line will be drawn between him and the people he is to be called upon some day to reign over. In due course, following the precedent which has already been set, he will be sent on a tour round the world, and probably rumours of a morganatic alliance will follow, and the end of it all will be (that) the country will be called upon to pay the bill.'

Keir Hardie sat down to universal cries of 'Shame!' from a House of Commons which, forty years later, would as unanimously shout down Winston Churchill's efforts to prevent Edward VIII from fulfilling these dire predictions. In 1894, the House passed the humble address with only Hardie's one dissenting vote, and business moved smoothly and predictably on to the next item on the order paper. By 1907, when the tearful thirteen-year-old was packed off to Naval College, most of the fears and antagonisms which would ultimately bring about the abdication were already ingrained in him.

2

REGIMENT

To George, Prince of Wales, his sons were The Regiment. (The idea of the family firm, with its demeaning association with trade, was to be left to a later, less secure generation.) David, Bertie, Harry, George — and even briefly poor little John until he was certified as unfit for active service and banished from the mess — played raw subalterns waiting to be knocked into shape by their father whose role was an amalgam of colonel and sergeant-major. As such, he saw it as his duty to instil in them the cardinal principles of royalty: patriotism, obedience, self-discipline and service.

Had his elder brother Eddy stayed the course, Prince George would still have been happily ascending the promotional ladder in the Navy as Edward VII's second son. His naval training was never intended to prepare him for the constitutional role into which Prince Eddy's death had forced him. As King George V, he recognised these early shortcomings and with glum determination struggled during adult life to make up the deficit. His efforts were largely unavailing. He spoke virtually no German, despite the plethora of German-speaking relatives dotted round the courts of Europe. His French was little better.

41

He had no knowledge of politics, economics, international affairs, social history, or even classics in which many of his contemporaries had been schooled. His mind had been filled instead by the narrow, technical disciplines of navigation, seamanship, naval warfare and the etiquette expected in an officer of the Royal Navy.

It may have been some consolation for him to remember that Prince Eddy, who *was* destined for the throne, had been subjected to the same blinkered upbringing in his teenage years. Like David and Bertie, Eddy and George had been very close as brothers. Indeed it was this brotherly bond that landed Eddy in the Navy in the first place. Their tutor, Canon Dalton, was to blame. He knew better than anyone that Eddy showed little sign of the moral or physical attributes expected of a king, so he suggested sending him with his younger brother to have a spell in the Navy where he could acquire 'those habits of promptitude and method, of manliness and self-reliance, in which he is now somewhat deficient'. Dalton's opinion, backed by the boys' father, Edward, Prince of Wales, prevailed over the inclination of Queen Victoria to send them first to public school where she thought they might receive a less narrow-focused, jingoistic education. So Eddy and George found themselves aboard the training ship *Britannia*, anchored in the River Dart, in Devon.

Prince George was short for his age, as even his doting mother Alexandra felt obliged to point out to him — 'Victoria [George's sister] says so old and so small!!!' she wrote to him on his fourteenth birthday. 'Oh, my! You will have to make haste to grow, or I shall have that sad disgrace of being the mother of a dwarf!!! But let me wish you happy returns of that dear day, which we ought to spend together.' Humiliation and homesickness in three brisk sentences — the letter is a masterpiece of insensitivity. The *Britannia* was a survivor from the Navy of Nelson's day and schooled its cadets in the same traditions. 'It never did me any good to be a Prince, I can tell you, and many was the time I wished I hadn't been there,' the elderly George V told his librarian, Owen Morshead. 'It was a pretty tough place and, so far from making any allowances for our disadvantages, the other boys made a point of taking it out of us on the grounds that they'd never be able to do it later on.'

From *Britannia* Eddy and George, with Canon Dalton still in tow, went to sea for three years aboard HMS *Bacchante*. In the course of this they saw a good deal of the world, had an eerie encounter with the phantom ship *The Flying Dutchman*, acquired the tattoos they bore for the rest of their lives and left the ship with the gaps in their education more conspicuous than ever. Prince George had at least acquired the brusque salt-water manner which never left him; though his tutor recognised that in other respects he had matured little. In particular, in Dalton's words, 'Prince George's old enemy is that nervously excitable temperament which still

43

sometimes leads him to fret at difficulties instead of facing them.' If Dalton and Hansell had ever compared notes on their respective charges, they would have found many similarities between George and Bertie at this age.

His immersion in the Navy produced no noticeable improvement in Prince Eddy, who was packed off to Cambridge in a vain attempt to lodge something of value in his mind. George, left free to pursue his naval career, was in due course rewarded with his own command. It was a lonely existence: the Prince was quarantined by his royal minders from mixing too freely with the rest of the wardroom, and was still snagged in the net of his mother's possessiveness. As soon as he was old enough, Prince George took refuge behind the full-set naval beard from which the open face of his childhood would never re-emerge. Brought up to command a ship, he suddenly found himself, after his brother's death, destined to rule an empire. It was against this background that George, as Prince of Wales, concluded that the Navy would teach his son and heir all he needed to know, and instil the respect for tradition, hierarchy, and authority, not to mention punctuality, needed to be a successful monarch.

David was a few weeks short of his thirteenth birthday when he was dumped at the Naval College at Osborne on the Isle of Wight in May 1907. This first taste of naval life would have been daunting for a boy coming from a loving, caring home and used to the company of other children of his own age.

For David, the shock can only be imagined. The contrived games of football with the boys from West Newton, occasional dancing classes with carefully screened partners, and even rarer parties with the offspring of courtiers, was the sum of his experience of other children. At Osborne he suddenly found himself surrounded by strangers day and night. There were thirty other boys in his dormitory. From six in the morning, when they were woken by bugle, his day was spent in a bewildering frenzy of activity. Everything had to be done at the double, from brushing his teeth to saying his prayers, against a backdrop of constant barracking and reprimands from the senior cadets.

'There is Nothing The Navy Cannot Do' read the Osborne motto in the main hall of the college, quoting Nelson. As far as David was concerned the first thing it did was to cut the future King down to size. His head was shoved out of a window and the sash slammed down, pinning him by the neck, as a reminder of the fate of his predecessor King Charles I. On another occasion red ink was poured over his head and down the front of his clean white shirt. For boys who had become inured to this sort of treatment at prep school, such examples of ragging and bullying were familiar; for a royal prince, experiencing them for the first time, they were demoralising and isolating. At a juncture when the pressures to conform and fit in with your peer group are all-important, when anonymity seems essential for your happiness, everything about David made him stand out from the rest.

In time his perseverance, good humour and forbearance in pulling rank were rewarded with a nickname. Perhaps this was an encouraging sign that he was following his father. Prince George had been Sprat. His son was Sardine. He followed his father as well in failing to make close friends. His lack of companionship amongst his peers (the mystery of majesty had to be protected in these increasingly democratic times) did at least spare him from the knowledge that discipline at Osborne was much tougher than that at most ordinary public schools. One particular episode in the institutionalised brutality must have shocked and unnerved him. Not long after his arrival a fellow new boy, who had collected a string of reprimands from minor offences, was sentenced to six official cuts — a beating administered with a bamboo cane by a PT instructor while the culprit was strapped to a gymnasium horse. David and his fellow cadets were drawn up to witness the scene, which was made all the more horrifying by the fact that the victim's own father, the head of the college, had ordered his son's public thrashing.

It was hardly surprising that David burst into tears when he was summoned to the Library after his father had received his report at the end of his third term. In fact this report was acceptable and no punishment was forthcoming, but the mere prospect of incurring his father's displeasure was now enough to make him blub like a baby. This was not the behaviour of a

46

naval officer, as his father brusquely told him. At home, as at school, it was made plain that David was failing to live up to the role in which the colonel of the family regiment had cast him. More convivial were the bunting and banners hung out when this particular Osborne cadet returned home for the holidays. 'Vive l'amiral!' the banner read.

Not that there was any point in seeking feminine comfort from his mother. At the start of his first holidays from Osborne she decided that her duty lay in Germany, where she remained on a visit for the first two weeks David was at home. Throughout these sensitive years when her eldest son was stepping gingerly away from childhood to find his feet as a man, Queen Mary remained as uninterested as ever in her son's state of mind. 'I hope that we will have great fun together when we do meet,' she wrote to him in the tone of a pen-friend lacking a good command of English. She chose not to look behind the brave false jollity of David's first letters home. 'He has fallen into his new life very quickly,' she wrote complacently to her aunt, 'which is such a blessing.' Many years afterwards, Lord Harewood, Queen Mary's grandson, remembered, with some understatement, that his grandmother 'didn't find it easy to discuss vital things, crucial things — to show warmth to people'. George VI's official biographer, Sir John Wheeler-Bennett, noted that she would 'seldom stand between them [her children] and the gusts of their father's wrath'.

James Pope-Hennessy's explanation for this was that Queen Mary 'believed that all should defer to the King's slightest wish, and she made herself into a living example of this creed. Outwardly this was not a spectacular part to play. Inwardly it required a constant and dramatic exercise of imagination, foresight and self-control.' When she did venture an opinion, it was often to close associates rather than to her husband. She had little faith in the boys' tutor Hansell and complained to Lord Esher, among others, about his limitations, but she dared not interfere with her husband's prescribed regime. Bertie's prospects worried her, too. With one eye on family history and another on the future she told Esher, 'Albert ought to be educated also. Look at William IV — he was a long way from the throne, yet he succeeded.' Prince George would probably have argued that the future William IV had also been sent to sea with the Navy — but if May had stood up to him on behalf of her children, how much happier and more fulfilled the barren years of David's and Bertie's childhood and adolescence might have been.

Henry Hansell's inadequate tuition meant that David had a constant struggle to catch up with the rest of his class. In his written exam he had failed by a few points to reach the minimum entry requirements to the Naval College. His oral was a different story. Free to present himself verbally, his marks in the *viva voce* were said to be equal to the best of the three hundred candidates. If David drew any comfort from going to Osborne, it would have been that he had talked his way in, relying on his own personality and judgement to succeed where the regime imposed by his father had so demonstrably failed.

Poor Bertie, who followed his elder brother to Osborne two years later, could not even call on these powers of communication to ease his passage. 'You must look after him [Bertie] all you can,' the Prince of Wales, always more fatherly on paper, had written at the start of the term to his older son. David was in his final year when Bertie arrived and the strict demarcation that divided the terms meant that he could do little to help his younger brother adjust to the spartan regime and the unwelcome notoriety that he had suffered. Hansell had recorded that the brothers had quarrelled constantly during their final months together in the schoolroom at York Cottage, but at Osborne these squabbles were forgotten in the face of their combined isolation and unhappiness. At pre-arranged meetings on the playing-fields, David offered what comfort and reassurance he could. Bertie stoically followed his elder brother's example, suffering silently through the loneliness and homesickness — and the bullying too. He was once trussed up in a hammock and dumped outside the mess hall after breakfast: though he became in the end generally more popular than David.

Both brothers struggled with the curriculum. Maths was a particular nightmare for Bertie, whose stammer prevented him from pronouncing the f in fraction with any confidence. His constant silences on these occasions were interpreted as stupidity. Prince George might have tolerated his sons' inabilities but he had no truck with idleness. When Bertie's tutor pointed out continuing problems with his work, his father warned, 'I am sorry to say that the last reports from Mr Watt with regard to your work, are not at all satisfactory, he says you don't seem to take your work seriously, nor do you appear to be very keen about it. My dear boy, this will not do, if you go on like this you will be the bottom of your Term.' In choosing to play the disappointed parent Prince George might just as well have handed Bertie the dunce's cap. When he sat his final exams at Osborne, he fulfilled his father's grim prediction and came 68th out of 68. Nevertheless he was still allowed to follow David to the second stage of their naval education, the Royal Naval College at Dartmouth.

By the time Bertie arrived at Dartmouth in January 1911 he had become the son, no longer the grandson, of the King. Edward VII died shortly before midnight on 6 May 1910. Alexandra, magnanimous in grief, had sent for Mrs Keppel to attend the deathbed. The following morning, as Bertie and David were dressing, Finch brought the message that their father wanted to see them downstairs. 'My father's face was grey with fatigue,' David was to recall as Duke of Windsor in his memoirs, 'and he cried as he told us that Grandpapa was dead.' David replied that they already knew because they had seen the Royal Standard flying at half-mast over Buckingham Palace. At first his father seemed not to take this in as he described their grandfather's deathbed scene. Then he paused, and asked sharply, 'What did you say about the Standard?'

'It is flying at half-mast over the Palace,' David repeated.

'But that's all wrong,' muttered the new King. Repeating to himself (as the Duke of Windsor was to write) the old but pregnant saying 'The King is dead. Long live the King!', he sent for an equerry and ordered in peremptory naval fashion that the Standard at once be transferred to the roof of Marlborough House. At his insistence, his wife May, at the age of forty-three, rechristened herself Mary and so left the last emblem of her childhood behind.

One month into the new term at Dartmouth, the Naval College succumbed to an outbreak of mumps and measles. Two Dartmouth cadets died, and the epidemic reached such a serious level that bulletins on the well-being of the two princes were sent to the press. Both David and Bertie were isolated in the commandant's house as soon as the outbreak was identified. However, both boys developed measles and, more seriously, mumps. As adolescents they were at their most vulnerable to the complications which may arise from mumps — in particular orchitis, a swelling and inflammation of the testicles which can lead in the most extreme cases to sterility. History, and his two daughters, show that Bertie escaped unscathed. History and his lack of children in or out of wedlock suggest

51

that David probably did not. Although sexually enthusiastic as a young man, his relative lack of body hair, and the delicate references by courtiers to something having gone 'wrong with his gland' when he was in his early teens, indicate that his attack of mumps may have left him incapable of producing children. As Sarah Bradford writes of him in her biography of George VI, fear of sterility can prompt the sufferer in the direction of a promiscuous sexual life. And when, a quarter of a century later, David pondered abdication, the knowledge that he had little chance of leaving an heir may have helped persuade him to hand the Crown on to his brother.

At Dartmouth Bertie would have detected a subtle change in the way that his classmates behaved towards his elder brother. David was now the heir to the throne. This made him Duke of Cornwall and the inheritor of a vast fortune derived from property in London and the West Country. His grandfather, Edward VII, had bought and improved Sandringham with the revenues from the Duchy estates that had built up before his coming of age. Whatever else it brought with it, David's destiny promised to make him a very rich man. He was also Prince of Wales, which probably appealed to him less. There was no money in the title, and his father was insisting upon an investiture ceremony which David had no desire to undertake.

The children of King George and Queen Mary attended the coronation. David, in charge of his younger brothers and sister, had his work cut out to supervise them as they fidgeted and fought in the state carriage taking them to and from the ceremony. In Westminster Abbey, dressed in his newly acquired Garter robes, David led the peers of the realm in paying homage to his father. The new King was deeply moved by the sight of his eldest son kneeling before him, swearing to become his liege man of life and limb and of earthly worship. Now God, too, had been enlisted on the side of parental authority. Others among the privileged few in the Abbey noted in David's face what the *Morning Post* described as the bashfulness of youth and the serious thought of a man called to a great destiny. The world at large would become familiar with that wistful look in the years to come.

All David's English predecessors, with the possible exception of Charles I, had managed to acquire the title of Prince of Wales with the minimum of fuss. David was not to be as lucky. The Chancellor of the Exchequer, David Lloyd George, saw the chance to make political capital out of the event and, as he also bore the title of Constable of Caernarvon Castle, concocted some arcane traditions and arranged for David to be invested among the hastily patched-up ruins. The King acquiesced, and the investiture took place in July 1911, a month after the coronation. By this time David was already beginning to be established in the public eye as a Prince Charming out of fairytale. Slim, blond, blue-eyed and soft-complexioned, he was almost girlishly good-looking. His awareness of this made him particularly sensitive about dressing up in royal finery. He had tolerated the Garter costume because of its illustrious pedigree, but the investiture costume was more than he could bear. A fanciful creation of white satin breeches and mantle and surcoat of purple velvet trimmed with ermine, it would not have been out of place in a pantomime and caused what was politely referred to as a family blow-up. 'What,' he railed at his parents, 'would my Navy friends say if they saw me in this preposterous rig?'

He was prevailed upon to do his duty and won from his father the ungrudging diary entry on the night of the investiture, 'The dear boy did it all remarkably well and looked so nice.' Nevertheless it confirmed in David's mind that he was not cut out for the role of a dutiful Prince Charming. Although for the time being he was prepared to go along with the trappings and show of kingship, he had no stomach for the displays of personal adulation that went with them. Being invested as Prince of Wales had only made him 'desperately anxious to be treated exactly like any other boy of my age'. He was to recall later that it was at this time that 'I made a painful discovery about myself. It was that, while I was prepared to fulfil my role in all this pomp and ritual, I recoiled from anything that tended to set me up as a person requiring homage.' Lala Bill put it more bluntly when she wrote, in a mood of high emotion to commiserate with Queen Mary after the abdication. 'Do you remember, Your Majesty, when he was quite young . . . he never wanted to become King.'

54

As David well knew, all the other boys of his age at Dartmouth were at sea on the cruise that marked the end of their time at the college. His father's coronation had forced David to miss this and as a consolation he was sent for three months to serve as a midshipman aboard the battleship *Hindustan*. While he sailed off for a brief taste of life as a real sailor, Bertie was left floundering at Dartmouth, alone and ever more conscious of the comparisons being made between him and his elder brother. As David took more of the limelight, the shadows over Bertie darkened. He loved and revered his brother, but his nagging inferiority complex produced in him a growing resentment that he should constantly be put in the position of coming second best. In 1937, when he had been King only a few weeks and relations with his brother, the ex-King, were preying on his mind, he revisited some of this, pouring out his heart to Mrs Baldwin, the Prime Minister's wife. Confiding to her that his brother had always outshone him in everything, he went on to admit that 'there had been times when as a boy he had felt envious that eighteen months should make so much difference'. David with his winning charm and blond good looks easily outshone the withdrawn, gawky and physically undistinguished Bertie. One contemporary from their naval days noted that it was like comparing a cock pheasant with an ugly duckling.

Nor was the relationship between the two brothers ever again to be quite so exclusive as in the days of their boyhood. When Bertie came back to a crowded York Cottage for the 1911 Christmas holidays (his grandmother, Queen Alexandra, was still regally installed at Sandringham), David was at home, yet again under Hansell's tuition, mournfully cramming for a spell at Oxford. George V had finally come to the conclusion that the Navy was too specialized; so once more David faced a change of direction for which he was ill-prepared. The one benefit derived from an otherwise bleak winter was the close friendship he had developed with his much younger brother, Prince George, in whom David discovered 'qualities that were akin to my own; we laughed at the same things . . . we became more than brothers — we became close friends.' Prince George, the fifth of George and Mary's six children, was by far the most self-confident of them. He shared David's charm and good looks. He also grew up to be amusing, intelligent and as dissolute as his late Uncle Eddy, with a talent for attracting entertaining and clever people. For the next twenty years George was closer to David than anyone, until he too was shut out of his brother's life by David's obsession with Wallis Simpson. Bertie must have recognised the affinities between David and George without being able to share in them. Although Prince George was also forced into the Navy by his father — where, according to Bertie he 'kept up the best traditions of my family by passing out of Dartmouth one from bottom, the same place as I did' — that was one of the few things he and Bertie had in common.

Bertie's generally low self-esteem took no account of the genuine strides that he made at Dartmouth once David was out of the way. Having survived Osborne, Dartmouth had few fresh horrors in store for him. His supervising officer encouraged him to develop his sporting talents, which boosted his confidence. He joined in the general skylarking, being beaten once — with sixteen others — for the less than heinous crime of setting off fireworks on 5 November. Even in the classroom he showed greater application and aptitude for lessons which were now directed more towards the day-to-day work of a naval officer, with less emphasis on purely academic subjects. The complete opposite was true for David. He had no wish to go to university — and certainly, thanks to the wretched Hansell, had no interest in furthering his studies. (In later life he maintained that he had learned more history from looking at pictures than from reading. His grasp of English literature was shakier still. David's private secretary in the 1920s, Tommy Lascelles, recalled him remarking of a present he had received one weekend, 'Look at this extraordinary little book which Lady Desborough says I ought to read. Have you ever heard of it?' Lascelles had — the little book was *Jane Eyre*.)

George V placated his eldest son with the promise that his vacations would be spent on trips to France and Germany to learn the languages. It was scant comfort. When Bertie told David how much he envied him,

David complained that his only wish was to be 'back quietly in the only service — the navy'. Reluctantly he knuckled down to his Oxford preparation, and evidently tried to stay in his father's good books by writing to him enthusiastically about the shooting he was enjoying at Sandringham. As usual he struck the wrong note. The King-Emperor during the winter of 1911–12 was on a state visit to India for his coronation Durbar, and was missing the shooting season back home. He wrote back snappishly, accusing his son of spending too much time shooting and not enough time riding. 'Judging from your letters and from the number of days you have been shooting there can't be much game left at Sandringham, I should think.' Father and son appeared incapable of seeing eye to eye. As a rule, any letters the children received from their mother and father while they were abroad on state visits were perfunctory and detached in tone. In return, the children were expected to write regularly to their parents to say how dreadfully they missed them.

Not long after the King and Queen returned from India, David was sent abroad to spend three months in France, ostensibly to improve his French. Although he failed in this, he did profit from the visit by getting to know something about French history and politics. He also charmed everyone from the British Ambassador to the officers of the French Mediterranean fleet, with whom he spent the happiest week of his visit. With nostalgic memories of that all too short spell at sea, he came home and began packing his bags for the next posting ordered by the Colonel of the family regiment — a spell as an Oxford undergraduate.

The lure of Oxford — even 'Oxford, that lotus-land' of Max Beerbohm's *Zuleika Dobson*, which had been published the previous year — failed to seduce the Prince of Wales. True, he was hardly in a position to make the best of the city. Having insisted, as he had at Osborne and Dartmouth, that the heir to the throne was to be treated just like his fellows, King George laid down conditions which immediately set him apart from every other undergraduate. The Prince of Wales went up to Magdalen, Hansell's old college, accompanied by Hansell himself. In itself that would have been enough to cramp David's style, but for good measure the King sent along Finch as his valet and William Cadogan to act as his equerry. Cadogan had no more interest in scholarship than did the Prince. His job was to get David to hunt: the King still harboured a concern about his eldest son's riding. Wanting to make sure that David mixed with the right sort of company, George V arranged for his old friend Lord Derby to send his heir, Lord Stanley, to Magdalen as a chum for the Prince of Wales. In David's eyes he was yet another of his father's courtiers sent to spy on him and report his misdemeanours, and his reaction was to keep Lord Stanley at arm's length for the two years they were together as undergraduates. Later, in the Army, they did become close friends — but then it was of David's choosing and on David's terms.

The early weeks at Oxford were as discomfiting as the early weeks at Osborne had been. Many of the other freshmen had come up with friends from school, swapping one set of draughty, bathless buildings for another. David hankered after the Navy which was all he knew. 'The junior common room is something like a gunroom,' he told his diary forlornly. As at Osborne and Dartmouth he forced himself to mix with people, and gradually broke down the barriers of reserve. 'It was impossible not to like him,' recalled a Magdalen contemporary. 'He was clean-looking and jolly, with no side at all.' The Prince got drunk, played a few silly pranks, made a few friends and grudgingly sat through the tutorials and personal lectures laid on for him by some of the most eminent teachers the university had on offer. Unfortunately, the President of his own college, who took it upon himself to teach humanities to his royal pupil, was a snob of the first degree. In the Edwardian undergraduate vernacular (in which he was the Pragger) the Prince of Wales would have called Sir Herbert Warren coshy. Every week he was obliged to read an essay to this awful old toady, and it must have reinforced his loathing of formal education. The high point of his work at Magdalen was an essay on Captain Scott, based on a month's laborious reading of *Scott of the Antarctic* during a vacation at York Cottage. This heroic tale of failure and obstinate determination by a fellow naval officer, ill at ease with himself and with a lot to prove to his contemporaries, plainly appealed to David, whose essay on Scott received much exaggerated praise.

Home on vacation for the Christmas of 1912, David might have hoped that his parents would adopt a less authoritarian attitude towards him, now that he was at university. But such a thought evidently did not occur to them, for they even removed from their son the small pleasure of finding his own Christmas presents for them. That year the King had set his heart on a gold soup bowl, and to avoid any disappointment ordered it on David's behalf. It cost £150. 'I only hope you won't mind,' wrote Queen Mary, who that spring had bought a couple of charming old Chinese cloisonné cups (price £12) for her son to give her as a birthday present.

King George may have been anxious lest any Christmas present David chose would reflect his personal tastes, which at Oxford had begun to diverge markedly from the King's. Both Edward VII and George V were sticklers for correct dress, as the royal princes knew to their cost, and it was significant that David developed a particular obsession with clothes which could not have been less formal or severe. He liked bright colours and bold patterns, vulgar in his father's eyes but marking the Prince out as a trend-setter to the fashion-conscious. During their buttoned-up childhood, the King's sons spent their days chafing in starched Eton collars, and never removed their coats. The King, like others of his generation, donned a frock coat whenever he was in London. If David dined with his father, he was expected to dress in white tie and tails adorned with the Garter Star. No wonder that at Oxford he revelled in flannel bags, fashionable turned-up trousers and casual sports coats. It was the beginning of a lifelong interest in clothes, which became the theme of a book he published in 1960, *A Family Album*.

The one aspect of his time at Oxford of which his father appeared wholly to have approved was David's growing enthusiasm for riding. Thanks to Cadogan's encouragement, David took up hunting and gradually came to enjoy the exhilaration and thrill of the chase. He never became a really good horseman but he was fearless and energetic. As far as the King was concerned, his eldest son could at least be relied on not to make a fool of himself on a horse in front of his subjects. Otherwise the Oxford term held few attractions for David. He acquired a car, went beagling, played for the Magdalen second football XI, and took himself off on punishing cross-country runs under the ludicrous impression that he was getting fat. Early in 1913 he had dinner with a new friend whose judgement would later play a critical part in his life. On this first meeting the Prince of Wales marked down Walter Monckton, President of the Oxford Union, as a very nice man.

During that Easter vacation David toured Germany, doing the rounds of his many relatives there. Driving with Cadogan, Finch and a jolly academic named Professor Friedler, the Prince visited several of the kings and scions of the eighteen dynasties which the world was destined to lose during his father's reign. It was a hazardous moment in history to be a European monarch. The previous March, King Victor Emmanuel III of Italy had narrowly escaped an attempt on his life. In March 1913, when David was preparing for his German trip, Queen Alexandra's favourite brother King George I of Greece was shot dead in a street in Salonica. Just fifteen months later, another Balkan assassination would light the fuse of the First World War, placing David and his family in a supremely awkward position with regard to their European relations. The summer vacation took in more of David's German cousins, uncles and aunts. In Berlin, the high point of his trip, he visited Kaiser Wilhelm II — Onkel Willi — who greeted him seated behind his desk on a cavalry saddle set on a wooden block — apparently it helped him to think more clearly.

The Prince of Wales had originally gone to Oxford for one year, but he was persuaded to stay on for a second, which he appreciated rather more. From Oxford he took what he wanted: drinking rather too much, expanding his wardrobe, hunting and beagling four days a week and shooting for a fifth. His father's letters arrived regularly, and more often than not contained a familiar phrase: 'I must say I am disappointed . . . ' In his letters George V continually linked chastisement with endearment, just as David's nanny had mingled pleasure with pain. Sometimes the insensitivity shown was staggering. 'Eat more and rest more,' he advised his eighteen-year-old but somewhat small and still physically underdeveloped son, or 'you will remain a sort of puny, half-grown boy'. No wonder that in 1913 David found it worthwhile to record in his diary the amazed comment: 'Papa has been so nice to me since my return . . . No faults have been found . . . Such a change!!' Whatever happened, his mother, as always, stayed silent on the sidelines.

Given a measure of freedom to follow his own instincts, the Prince of Wales contrived to leave behind him the impression of an open-minded 'people's prince'. As a fellow Oxford undergraduate wrote to *The Times* in his final term, the Prince had 'had to steer a middle course between an undignified obscurity and an embarrassing prominence' and concluded that he had managed this gracefully. 'He has gone with perfect simplicity to such public acts as the welcoming of the French President or the Garter ceremonial and then returned with equal lack of ostentation to Oxford.' The President of Magdalen agreed, needless to say, writing also to *The Times*, 'Once having started on it, he pursued this narrow, nice line with increased confidence until it seemed the most easy and natural and unconscious thing in the world.'

Leaving Oxford in the summer of 1914 was a release of sorts, especially since his father was allowing him to take a commission in the Grenadier Guards the following year. But now that he was twenty, David was beginning to realise that his independence was hedged with responsibilities. Increasingly he had to put in an appearance at public functions and state occasions, and quickly concluded that the more formal and ceremonial they were, the more he disliked them. He had poor concentration and little mental self-discipline. The business of attending court and standing like a stooge next to George V he dismissed in his diary (in the American slang he affected) as 'mighty poor fun', a 'bum show'. However, given something to do which he regarded as really worthwhile and not just 'princing', he would carry it out conscientiously and with dignity, as if to confirm that he was perfectly capable of playing the royal role, but on his own terms.

While David was struggling with his first public appearances, Bertie, too, was experiencing the drawbacks of being the son of the King-Emperor. At the beginning of 1913 he joined HMS *Cumberland* for a six month cruise which would complete his training as a midshipman. At every port they visited, in the West Indies and Canada, crowds thronged to catch sight of the Prince when he went ashore. In some places, to his horror, they even caught hold of his trouser legs. Unlike David, who had already acquired the knack of handling situations like this, the shy, retiring, stammering Bertie found them a great trial and was not above asking a friend to stand in for him as a double at minor functions. In Quebec there was no escape from the round of balls and dances, though Bertie showed little inclination to dance with the girls who were all pressing to dance with him.

From the *Cumberland* Bertie transferred to the

Collingwood and received his first commission as midshipman, joining the ranks of the other snotties (junior midshipmen) under the name of Mr Johnson. Aboard ship he got on with his work thoroughly if rather silently because of his stammer. 'I can't get a word out of him,' wrote the sub-lieutenant in charge of the gunroom (the mess used by the midshipmen). 'He treated me with great respect and seems to be in an awful funk of me! Thank goodness he is treated exactly the same as all the other minor snotties.'

He had been with his new ship only a short time when she was sent on manoeuvres in the Mediterranean, and he found himself plucked from the gunroom and taken to stay with Lord Kitchener at his official residence in Cairo. While he was in Egypt, he was also taken to see the Khedive, and to visit the Pyramids. In Egypt his dislike of dancing seems to have been overcome: after the ball given for the Fleet, attended by 3,000 guests, he cheerfully recorded, 'I went to bed at 3.0 a.m. having danced nearly every dance.' He was in the spotlight once more a few weeks later when the King and Queen of Greece came on board the *Collingwood* specifically to pay him a visit. At the time of his birthday, in the middle of December, the ship had sailed westwards to be entertained by the French Navy who, he reported to his mother 'are giving us a very good time here, and have arranged all kinds of dances and theatres for us'.

There was even dancing after dinner at Sandringham when Bertie went home on leave for New Year's Day 1914, although only because the family had gone across to the big house to spend the evening with Queen Alexandra. 'We all dined with Mama,' wrote Queen Mary, sending New Year greetings to her aunt, Princess Augusta of Mecklenburg-Strelitz, '& even danced afterwards much to the enjoyment of the young people. God grant that this year may be a peaceful one & that the clouds over these dear Islands may disperse!!!' Six months later, King George recorded in his diary the assassination of Archduke Franz Ferdinand at Sarajevo. At this stage he saw the event purely as a family tragedy ('Terrible shock for the dear old Emperor') and had no inkling of its wider significance. Bertie did not mention it in his diary at all. He was more preoccupied in the ensuing days with a gaggle of fifty Roedean girls who boarded *Collingwood* as she lay off Brighton. 'We showed them over the ship and danced before tea.'

David had also been dancing away that fateful summer of 1914. His horsemanship was still not up to scratch and George V was sending him for two hours every morning to have riding lessons with the 1st Life Guards. These were over by eleven o'clock, leaving David free to enjoy the London season for the first time and revel the summer nights away. He was twenty: energetic, good-looking, with an automatic entry to all the best balls and dinner parties on offer, he enthused to his diary, 'I've had only 8 hours sleep in the last 72 hours.' For both brothers, dancing took precedence over politics and international affairs. From an Officers' Training Corps camp David wrote to a friend admitting complete ignorance 'of all happenings in the outer World, except that the Austrian Archduke and his wife have been assassinated. I expect it has caused a stir in Germany.' Five weeks later the stir it caused put a stop to the dance music and replaced it with marches and patriotic songs. On the night war was declared, David joined his parents on the balcony of Buckingham Palace to salute the cheering crowds. During the next four years, for all the cheers and adulation, the Prince of Wales would be denied all but a few distant glimpses of the action. For Bertie, on the other hand, the prospect of doing his bit looked more promising.

At the end of July the Grand Fleet had sailed north to Scapa Flow to guard the northern entrance to the North Sea and keep watch for the German High Seas Fleet which was similarly lying in readiness in its bases five hundred miles to the south. Bertie copied into his diary his father's telegram to the Fleet on the night war was declared. He looked forward to playing his part in the conflict from which he knew his brother would need to be excluded. Barely three weeks into the war, however, he was struck down — not as a result of enemy action, but by the gastric trouble which had dogged him since the cradle. On this occasion appendicitis was diagnosed and Bertie had to suffer the indignity of being transferred, first to a hospital ship and thence by cot, lifted by a crane, to a tug and the quayside at Aberdeen, where his appendix was removed in hospital. This dismal start to his war set the depressing pattern of illness and convalescence which was to be repeated over the next three years and was eventually to force him out of the Navy.

Most mortifying to Bertie were the comparisons he knew were being made between his life as a semi-invalid watching the war being fought across the Channel from the safety of his home, and the dashing figure of his older brother — not only an officer but one apparently idolised by the fighting troops. Once again, and so unfairly, David seemed to be snatching the glory while Bertie was hamstrung by a physical ailment he could do nothing about. Three months after his operation, he was given a sinecure at the Admiralty that let him wear a uniform again and spared him the accusations of cowardice levelled at young men who were not in uniform. In reality there was nothing for him to do, and his initial gratitude turned to disillusionment as the days dragged by and he chafed to get back to his ship.

In fact, David was experiencing the same frustrations. 'Oh!! That I had a job,' he complained and continued to complain right through the hostilities. 'I do hate being a prince and not allowed to fight!!' The day after war was declared he wrote to Bertie bemoaning his lot and envying 'you my dear old boy, and all naval and army officers' who were suffering hardship and risking their lives 'for the defence and honour of England'. Meanwhile, 'Here I am in this bloody gt palace, doing absolutely nothing but attend meals . . . Surely a man of 20 has higher things to hope for? But I haven't apparently . . . At such a time you will picture me here, depressed and miserable and taking no more part in this huge undertaking than Harry and George, 2 irresponsible kids who run about playing inane games in the passage. However, enough about my rotten self, for I am a most bum specimen of humanity, and so must not be considered.'

This particular bout of misery and self-hatred was short-lived. The very next day he asked for and was granted a commission in the Grenadier Guards. For the next four weeks the Prince of Wales threw himself body and soul into the role of a junior officer, naively expecting that when his battalion was ordered across the Channel he would be going with them. Uncomplainingly, he marched from Wellington Barracks out through Chelsea, Kensington and Fulham, and marched back to barracks again. At least he could feel 'that this is a stepping stone to getting out!! How we long for it.' As always, all he wanted was to be 'treated just like an ordinary officer'. Then, a week before embarkation, the King broke the news to him that he would not be going with the others to France. David was being transferred from the 1st Battalion to the 3rd Battalion with whom he would be staying behind in London.

The Prince of Wales stormed down Whitehall and into the War Office to see Lord Kitchener, Secretary of State for War. 'What does it matter if I am killed?' he is supposed to have demanded furiously. 'I have four brothers.' 'What if you were not killed, but taken prisoner?' enquired Kitchener, effectively ending the discussion. Lord Desmond Fitzgerald, a close friend of David's and a fellow officer in the Grenadiers, tried to make the Prince appreciate the splendid example he was setting of how to do one's duty — but this was not the sort of duty David envisaged for himself. Fitzgerald loyally stuck to his theme over the next two years, offering sympathy for David's lot and constant reassurance about 'the enormous amount of good you do and how much everyone loves and admires you'. But David would not be consoled by flattery.

The badgering continued and, a couple of weeks before Bertie was found something to do in the Admiralty, David was posted to the staff of Sir John French, Commander-in-Chief of the British Expeditionary Force. He would have been happy to have been employed at his rank of second lieutenant, but instead he was put to work as Prince of Wales, fulfilling a range of official duties which had little bearing, so far as he could see, on the conduct of the war. On his arrival General Lambton had written to assure the King, 'I will try to keep him well occupied and as far from shells as possible' — which meant in effect that David tagged along as a supernumerary at GHQ. Occasionally there was something useful to be done. His knowledge of German was briefly of help in interrogating prisoners. His growing ease with the troops paid dividends when he visited the wounded in hospital. With his enquiring mind the Prince could be relied upon to ask the Tommies a multitude of questions. He took everything in, and with his retentive memory found it easy to remember what he had been told and regurgitate it at the right moment. This gave him a reputation for sympathy and concern for the individual and made him much beloved by the ordinary servicemen.

The Prince was of some use in breaking the ice with suspicious French allies on the visits he made to their headquarters, but all this was small beer in his eyes, compared with the sacrifices being made by the men doing the actual fighting. As he was to find throughout the war, a single gesture sincerely made carried far beyond his immediate audience. An episode that did much to cement the affection with which he was held in the trenches occurred during a hospital visit, when David noticed one of the patients segregated behind curtains from the rest of the ward. The man had been so hideously mutilated, he was told, that the medical staff had decided it was better to keep him out of sight. The Prince of Wales, in the kind of gesture which would be repeated eighty years later by Princess Diana, asked to be allowed to see him, stood beside his bed and then leant over and kissed him.

David persisted in his requests to serve in the front line, if only for a few days. In February 1915 his father partially relented and gave permission for him to visit the front. 'You can do anything within reason except actually fighting in the trenches,' he allowed. It was the best David could expect. A month after the King's dispensation he spent two hours watching the close of a fierce battle that thrilled and horrified him in equal measure. Coming under shellfire for the first time was more than he had hoped for, but the discovery that six officers from the 1st Battalion of the Grenadier Guards had been killed in that one bombardment brought home starkly the reality of what his comrades were having to endure.

A photograph of the Prince of Wales marching at the head of his company of Grenadier Guards at the beginning of the Great War shows a childlike elfin figure, narrow-shouldered and frail-necked. He was only 5 feet 7 inches tall and dwarfed by the strapping Guardsmen following in his wake. Yet he was determined, and what he lacked in bulk, he compensated for in stamina. Oliver Lyttelton, a fellow officer on the General Staff stationed in May 1915 near Béthune, observed: 'The Prince eats little and walks much: we eat much and walk little.' In fact, the Prince, having risen early, would sometimes walk six miles before a skimpy breakfast, tramping up hill and down dale as part of an obsessive exercise and fasting regime. Still obsessed with his body and the idea of being fat, he was actually on the verge of being unhealthily scrawny. Furiously, the Prince pedalled on his regulation green army bicycle all over the British lines. He wrote up his reports with assiduous care, referred modestly in the mess to the King and Queen, as 'my people' and never shirked a task, especially if it was dangerous. 'A bad shelling will always produce the Prince of Wales,' ran the talk in the mess, something which ordinary Tommies came to recognise also. 'The Prince of Wales loved danger . . . He loved to be with the men,' said the Revd Tubby Clayton who founded the recreation club, Toc H.

Things also appeared to be looking up for Bertie: in the month that David received permission to visit the front, his younger brother returned to the *Collingwood*. But sadly Bertie's hopes were to be unfulfilled. By early summer the old trouble returned — 'the infernal indigestion has come on again' he told Hansell — and he was unable to keep food down. Harry Hamilton, the genial senior sub-lieutenant in charge of the gunroom, observed with concern that the Prince looked 'very mouldy. In fact wasting away.' He managed to hold out for his father's visit to the fleet in the middle of July, but three days later his illness forced him off the *Collingwood* for a second time. Weakening of the muscular wall of the stomach and a consequent catarrhal condition was diagnosed. At the age of nineteen, he found himself being prescribed rest, a careful diet and an enema every night. After two months of boredom and enemas on a hospital ship had failed to produce any improvement in his condition, Bertie was sent ashore at Abergeldie. Hansell and the doctor who had wrongly diagnosed his condition accompanied him, which cannot have done much to raise his spirits. Bertie was actually

74

suffering from a duodenal ulcer, which was only dealt with at the end of November 1917. For the best part of three years he remained isolated, in constant pain, humiliated and depressed as he watched the rest of his generation fight and die for their country.

He was not the only member of the family in physical pain that autumn. On 28 October 1915, George V had been thrown from a frightened horse while he was inspecting a section of the Royal Flying Corps in France. The fall fractured his pelvis and caused him a great deal of discomfort and shock. That winter he and Bertie shared a slow, painful recovery. The benefit for Bertie, apart from cementing a closer and more understanding relationship with his father than any of his brothers was ever to enjoy, was the chance to watch at first hand a King at work in wartime. Father and son talked or wrote to each other all the time, discussing the latest news of the war. Thirty years later, those long winter months Bertie spent with his father would pay dividends. In other respects his incarceration at Sandringham and Buckingham Palace was hard to bear. There was not much to eat, and there had been nothing alcoholic to drink since the King's Pledge in April 1915, when King George had led the nation in giving up alcohol until peace was restored. Bertie complained to David about the dictatorial life at Buckingham Palace where 'The parents have got funny ideas about us, thinking we are still boys at school or something of that sort, instead of what we are.' 'Awful balls the whole thing,' wrote back the Prince of Wales sympathetically.

David's attitude may have altered slightly with his twenty-first birthday in June 1915 when his father wrote to tell him that he could expect about £246,000, 'a splendid sum of money which will go on increasing until you marry and set up house'. Queen Mary made haste to assure her eldest son that they hoped that for the moment he would continue to live under his parents' roof. Although David firmly dismissed any idea of marriage — 'I trust that day is as yet afar off!!' — coming into his inheritance must have given him a comforting feeling of independence.

In September 1915 he joined the newly formed Guards Division on the staff of Lord Cavan, and soon afterwards visited the front line with him during the battle of Loos. Their party came under fire, forcing them to shelter in the trenches. When the muddy pair emerged after the bombardment had lifted, they found David's car fifty yards away riddled with shrapnel, and the driver dead. His narrow escape sent shudders through the high command but it did wonders for his reputation. Word went round the trenches. Stories circulated about him popping up unannounced behind the lines all along the front, sometimes on bicycle, sometimes on foot, always cheerful, energetic and attentive. At Loos he went to the front line immediately after a gas attack. David himself noted wryly that he was the first Prince of Wales to set foot on the battlefield of Crécy since his namesake, Edward the Black Prince, had fought there in 1346. In the eyes of King George's fighting men, here too was a warrior prince worthy of his spurs.

But David knew better. He felt he was being awarded the spurs without earning them. The King did not agree. 'It is very silly of you not doing what I told you at Easter time, which was to wear the ribbons of the French and Russian Orders that were given you,' George V scolded him, after hearing that David was not wearing the emblem of the Legion of Honour. 'So get both ribbons sewn on your khaki at once.' But such a parading of honours in the presence of fighting men who genuinely deserved them was distasteful to the Prince and deepened his sense of inferiority. In the middle of 1916 he was awarded the Military Cross which angered him even more. His promotion to the rank of captain at about the same time brought no pleasure either, 'as I have no command.'

When the Guards Division was ordered up to the line at Ypres, it was obvious that once again the Prince of Wales would be left behind. As a release for his mounting frustration, he suggested that he should be allowed to visit the allied forces in the Middle East, specifically to review the defences of the Suez Canal. The high command were no doubt pleased to get the Prince of Wales out of their hair, though they vetoed his request that Desmond Fitzgerald, his fellow Grenadier and closest confidant, should go as his equerry on the grounds that Fitzgerald held too low a rank. This minor disappointment was overtaken a week before David's departure by the devastating news that Fitzgerald had been killed by a grenade in a training accident. Like the majority of his contemporaries, David had created an emotional shield to protect him from the reality of the sickening slaughter that was taking place all around him. The death of his greatest friend was one blow he could not parry, and he left for Egypt more despondent than he had been throughout the whole war.

May 1916 brought a brief upturn in Bertie's fortunes. After months of kicking his heels at home, during which time he was asked to entertain the Crown Prince of Serbia who could not speak one word of English, he was eventually allowed to return to the *Collingwood* just in time for the one major naval action of the war, the battle of Jutland. Bertie was in the sick-bay, having unwisely treated his delicate stomach to pickled mackerel two nights earlier, when the Grand Fleet was ordered to sea on the evening of 30 May. When the *Collingwood* was called to action stations in the afternoon of the following day, Bertie ran from his sick-bed and stayed in his gun turret until the battle was over. He was on top of the turret when the fighting started, to get a better view, and watched his ship sink an enemy vessel. He was still up there when a salvo landed on either side of the *Collingwood*, sending him burrowing down into the safety of the turret like a shot rabbit.

Collingwood returned fire, the German ship disappeared, night fell and they never saw the enemy again. Two days later they were back in port. Apart from mild disappointment that *Collingwood* bore no visible signs that she had

78

been in action, Bertie was exuberant that at last he had something to boast about to David. 'When I was on top of the turret I never felt any fear of shells or anything else,' he declared. 'It seems curious,' he added, still basking in the afterglow of action, 'but all sense of danger and everything else goes except the one longing of dealing death in every possible way to the enemy.'

David was charitable in his response, envious as he must have been of Bertie's taste of real action. 'What wouldn't I give to get up to the Forth & Scapa & see them all!!' he complained. Instead he had to console himself with meeting the veterans of the abortive Gallipoli campaign — Australian and New Zealand troops who fired him with their 'marvellous imperial spirit'. This was his first exposure to the peoples of the Dominions in any numbers. The six weeks he spent in the Middle East left a profound effect both on him and on them, a legacy which would colour the next two decades. Reports reaching Britain spoke of the enthusiasm with which he was received by the battle-hardened Anzac troops, renowned for their wild drinking and indiscipline. Eye-witnesses spoke of the men being overwhelmed by the power of the Prince's personality, combining in his diffident youthful figure, charm, openness, sincerity and a deep personal interest in them. It was a tour de force and they loved him for it, as millions of those who did not know him would come to love him at home and abroad in the years ahead.

Yet David remained unsure of himself and

unconvinced by his widespread popularity. No young man could fail to be excited by such a reception, but he never lost the nagging anxiety that it was as the Prince of Wales, pumped full of royal blood, that he was being lauded by the crowds, rather than for any personal qualities of his own. But these doubts he kept private: publicly, the Middle East visit was rightly considered a great public relations success. Morale was raised, and even the Prince's slim report on the Canal Zone was favourably, if somewhat patronisingly, received. When he returned to France, his chances of being posted to the front were no stronger than before, but now he had the satisfaction of having been seen to have done something worthwhile, even if in a secondary theatre of the war.

Bertie's war, meanwhile, was limping to a close. The recovery in his health brought about by the battle of Jutland only lasted until the autumn of 1916, when sickness and acute pain drove him back to hospital where his ulcer was finally diagnosed. The following May he transferred, as acting lieutenant, to a new ship, HMS *Malaya*, on which he spent less than three months before he had to be taken ashore to hospital looking thin and ill. It was the summer of 1917 and Bertie had been bravely bearing his illness for three years. He was worn-out, dejected and deeply depressed. Eight years of training and four years as a serving officer, had rewarded him with just twenty-two months at sea. Bitter as the disappointment was, he now agreed with those doctoring him that he was no longer fit for service on board ship.

The prospect of returning to civilian life at this stage of the war was too humiliating to contemplate, and Bertie's compromise displayed the stoical pragmatism which had sustained him through the years of unhappiness and isolation brought on by his stammer and ill-health. A new branch of the Navy had come into being, the Royal Naval Air Service. Bertie suggested to his father that he might find a niche there, and was delighted when George V agreed to the idea. An added satisfaction was the decision of his close friend Louis Greig to transfer with him. Bertie had first met the Scottish doctor, fifteen years his senior, when he had gone down with whooping cough while he was at Osborne. Greig was twenty-five at the time and a sporting hero for the cadets, with rugby caps for Scotland and the Navy to his name. Their friendship grew over the following years and it was no surprise that, not long after Bertie had joined the *Malaya*, Greig too joined the wardroom as the ship's second surgeon. From then on he was to be Bertie's principal support and companion, until marriage brought Prince Albert a help-meet of equally resilient and determined Scottish blood.

To men brought up in the time-honoured traditions of the Royal Navy, the newly formed Royal Air Force, which came into being on April Fool's Day 1918, was a motley amalgamation. Part-Army, part-Navy, it had no uniform of its own and a maritime terminology that did not sit easily in the heart of Lincolnshire, where HMS *Daedalus* (later to become more familiar as Cranwell) was based. George V was known to be strongly prejudiced against flying, and Bertie must have realised that his new service was hardly what his father would have wished for one of his sons. This may account for the stern approach he took to his duties, perhaps hoping that a little naval discipline would help impart some organisation to the hybrid force.

Bertie had few friends at Cranwell among the other officers, whom he described to his mother as 'very nice, though a curious mixture of people in every walk of life'. The years of depression, and his sense of failure for himself and on behalf of his father, had taken their toll. No amount of support from Louis Greig could make up for these, and besides, Cranwell lacked the stability Bertie had enjoyed on *Collingwood* and the *Malaya*. However, it was some consolation to know that his elder brother was forbidden to fly at this time because of doubts about aircraft reliability, while as the King's second son, he was allowed to take to the skies. By the summer of 1918 he had moved to RAF Headquarters at St Leonards, and soon after that he was in France, eager to catch the tail end of the war before the fighting stopped for good. Bertie stayed with the victorious troops after the signing of the armistice on 11 November 1918 — partly, in David's words to their mother, 'to erase any of the very unfair questions some nasty people asked last year as to what he was doing'. The Great War that launched the cock pheasant into glorious flight very nearly sank the ugly duckling.

One consolation was that Bertie, who in January 1919 was billeted with the RAF at Spa in Belgium, was able to spend more time with his elder brother than at any other period of the war. Late that month, David wrote home to Mrs Dudley Ward: 'I was very sorry to leave them at Spa this afternoon, I've got to look on Advanced Hd. Qrs. R.A.F. as a sort of home on this side now & I'm very fond of my brother now that we've seen something of each other; we used to be great friends before the war but we had drifted apart & become almost strangers! We've had some great talks the last 3 days & got to know each other well again & that's a good feeling . . . he's a d — d good boy really . . . '

David was still champing at the bit as the war drew to its exhausted close. He had been forced to stand aside while friends of his in the Grenadiers were mown down by machine-guns or drowned in the mud of Passchendaele. There had been a sudden dash to northern Italy where British and French forces battled to shore up the Italian defences against a combined Austro-German onslaught, while the Prince of Wales won over the Italian nation with a speech delivered with a boyish shyness that went straight to the hearts of his audience. Now he was being sent off once again to do the rounds of the Dominion troops, laying the foundations for Britain's postwar relationship with its imperial allies and establishing the reception he would receive when he visited the Canadians and Australians at home after the war. The enthusiasm with which he was greeted gratified the Prince, but also served to remind him that the end of the war would not be bringing *him* peace and tranquillity. One positive development came from his visit to Pershing's US troops after the armistice had been signed, a meeting which initiated David's enthusiasm for all things American.

By then, the Prince of Wales had other things on his mind. Slow to mature, he had reached his twenty-first year without showing much interest in losing his virginity. Then, towards the end of 1916, his equerries Claud Hamilton and Joey Legh had taken him to a brothel in Amiens, plied him with wine and entrusted him to the expert attentions of an obliging prostitute named Paulette. From this moment, having discovered the pleasures of sex, David began to think of little else. In July 1917 he spent three days in Paris with a prostitute named Maggy, who would later attempt to blackmail him with the letters he wrote her. But for the time being, all was wonderful. 'Oh! to set eyes on one of the darlings again,' he wrote from the front line in France to a friend in the Grenadiers, 'how one does miss them, and I don't think of anything but women now, tho what's the use?' He had fallen in love with womankind — a passion which was to last for the rest of his life, and find its consummation in Wallis Simpson.

3

WALLIS AND ELIZABETH

Despite their very different wartime experiences, the relationship between Bertie and David remained close at the end of the Great War, if not as close as it had been in childhood. As yet, neither of them had close male friends of their own age outside the family. Prince Albert could at least count on the support of Louis Greig, but Greig was fifteen years Bertie's senior; besides, he was newly married and could no longer give the Prince his exclusive attention. Now grown men, both David and Bertie still lived in fear of their father's constant carping and his demoralising rebukes. Queen Mary was no more emotionally demonstrative a mother than she had been when they were in the nursery. Their epileptic youngest brother, Prince John, had died in January 1919, while they were still in France. Queen Mary was not seen to shed a tear over the loss of her youngest child. David wrote to Freda Dudley Ward, 'He's been practically shut up for the last 2 years any how so no one has ever seen him except the family & then only once or twice a year & his death is the greatest relief imaginable and what we've always silently prayed for . . . No one wld. be more cut up if any of my other 3 brothers were to die than I shld. be but this poor boy had become more of

85

an animal than anything else . . . '

If the royal family's treatment of Prince John sounds unimaginably callous today, there was nothing unusual about it by the standards of the time. Epilepsy was untreatable and, because it was considered a mental illness, carried a stigma which brought those afflicted by it, as well as their families, enduring shame. Sufferers were, quite literally, put apart. Most ended their days in institutions. Prince John, was, from the few accounts we have of him, a quickwitted, affectionate child. His aunt, Princess Alice, Countess of Athlone, thought him 'very quaint'. A prankster, he once borrowed his sister's paintbox and appeared in front of his parents and the guests they had invited to dine, with his face painted like a Red Indian. But by four he had begun to suffer the first of many epileptic fits. His parents, appalled by the idea of illness — they did not want their children near them even when they had anything as minor as a cold — naturally recoiled. Henceforth, John was rarely allowed into their presence. They did not wish to be reminded that he was, as they put it, 'not quite right'. However, his father occasionally rode with him, and he seems to have joined his siblings at Balmoral. Nor do his brothers appear to have noticed anything different about him, except that when they went climbing he was roped to an attendant. Bertie, in particular, seems to have made time for his little brother, treating him with the tenderness his mother could not or would not show.

As John's fits worsened, the overriding fear

became that he might shame the royal family in public. Little else mattered immediately, certainly not John's future, for which, although his brother Harry had recently been sent to Eton, no plans had ever been made. Then in 1917, when John was eleven, the decision was made to spirit him into hiding for ever. He was packed off with his nanny (fortunately the devoted Lalla Bill) and two burly male attendants to a remote farm on the Sandringham estate. Here he was at least close enough for his mother to visit him, but she never did. John was an awkwardness, an embarrassment to her concept of royalty, and was simply cut out of her life. His grandmother, Queen Alexandra, showed much more maternal feeling towards this forgotten 'dear and precious little boy', and would send a car to fetch him so that they could listen to music and do jigsaws together. On 18 January 1919 Prince John's short and lonely life came to an end when he died in his sleep after a severe epileptic attack. After the funeral, Queen Alexandra stayed weeping by his grave in Sandringham churchyard. Queen Mary, by all accounts, was long gone.

The Prince of Wales seems to have been similarly unaffected by his youngest brother's death to judge by his letter to Freda Dudley Ward. By January 1919 David had known Mrs Dudley Ward for nine months. The first of the two great loves of his life, Freda both mothered him and protected him from the tiresome business of looking for a wife. As with other Princes of Wales, he was plagued by the knowledge that he was duty-bound to marry and produce an heir in order to maintain the dynasty. Foreign princesses had traditionally acted as brood mares for his predecessors, but the First World War had drastically reduced the number of those eligible for the task. More to the point, the Prime Minister Lloyd George had told George V that the country would not tolerate a foreign bride for either of the two older royal princes. The King had therefore consented to let David and Bertie look for wives among the British aristocracy. Even so, David showed no inclination to follow his father's wishes. It wasn't simply that he looked for love where there was no threat of being tied down: it was that he looked for women who would provide the warmth and maternal affection his own mother had been unable to provide — and such women, almost by definition, tended to be already married.

First in the lists had been Lady Coke, daughter-in-law to their Sandringham neighbour, Lord Leicester. Marion Coke, twelve years older than her young admirer, typified the kind of lover David craved. She was small, vivacious, loved dancing and had a sense of humour that appealed to the Prince of Wales. His infatuation began in 1915 when he started writing to her from France (like his parents, he often found it easier to express himself on paper than in person). Over the next two years David's ardour grew, though the object of his passion wisely refused to compromise herself, and satisfied the eager young puppy with a maternal shoulder to cry on and a mother's soothing embrace. For all the delightful revelations between the sheets with Paulette, and the other one-night stands over which he languished in his diary for the rest of the war, David's success and probably his satisfaction in bed ran second to his desire for mothering, the mothering he found in Marion Coke and her successors. Like many other unloved children conspiring for attention, David had learned how to manipulate and seduce. The childhood succession from one nanny to the next had led him to take for granted that there would always be another woman waiting to pamper him, and he was careful never to end an affair without ensuring that there was another maternal bosom on which to lay his head. From his nannies, too, stemmed the reassurance he was to find in women of a lower class. It was thanks to the nursery years with Lalla Bill that, until he acquired transatlantic vowels in exile, he spoke with a noticeable Cockney twang.

In March 1918, when David was back in London, Cynthia Asquith was one of a gaggle of royal-watchers, noting 'the wild excitement fluttering all the girls over the Prince of Wales who, 'unbeknownst' to the king, has taken to going to all the dances. So far, he dances most with Rosemary and also motors with her in the day time. No girl is allowed to leave London during the three weeks of his leave and every mother's heart beats high.' On leave at home, David was in the habit of ducking out of evenings with his parents whenever he had the chance. His particular favourite that spring was

Lady Rosemary Leveson-Gower, daughter of the Duke of Sutherland and the only unmarried woman in his whole life in whom he showed more than a flicker of interest. They had met in France where she had been nursing wounded soldiers, and though David was prepared to admit that she was 'quite attractive and pretty' (to Lady Coke) and 'attractive tho' very cold' (to his mother), his desire for Rosemary withered in an instant when he met Mrs Freda Dudley Ward.

Nevertheless, when early in 1919 Rosemary Leveson-Gower announced her engagement to the future Lord Dudley, David could not help feeling 'a little sad'. He wrote from the Hotel Meurice in Paris to explain his feelings to Freda Dudley Ward. 'TOI knows how I used to feel about her and she was the only girl I felt I ever could marry & I knew it was 'defendu' by my family!! I really only know Eric by sight tho. I'm sure he's nice & that they'll be very happy; I only hope so for her sake as she's such a darling & I guess he's a very lucky man!!' Queen Mary had indeed been against the match. 'I agree Rosemary is attractive,' she had written to warn her eldest son, 'but pray don't think of her, there is a taint in the blood of her mother's family.' The Queen was referring, no doubt, to the gossip prevalent at the time about a strain of mental instability alleged to run through the St Clair-Erskine family. Rosemary Leveson-Gower does not seem to have been affected by this rejection, looking back upon it as a lucky escape. 'What a good thing

90

I never contemplated marrying the Prince of Wales merely for the sake of the glamour,' she wrote to her mother after her marriage had taken place. As it was, she 'had got all that as well as Eric'. Nor did David languish for long, for he had already met Freda.

In one of the accidents of fate which characterised David's lovelife, they met by chance during an air-raid when Freda took shelter at the Belgrave Square home of Mrs Maud Kerr-Smiley, the sister of Ernest Simpson and the hostess who, ten years later, would introduce into London society Ernest's second wife Wallis Simpson. It was late February in 1918: there was a party in the house which the Prince was attending; they stood side by side in the dark cellar, and not until the maroons sounded the all-clear did Freda realise to whom she had been talking.

Only ten days after recording the Prince's attentions to Rosemary Leveson-Gower, Cynthia Asquith picked up her pen again to tell her diary, 'Saw the Prince of Wales dancing round with Mrs Dudley Ward, a pretty little fluff with whom he is said to be rather in love. He is a dapper little fellow — too small — but really a pretty face. He looked as pleased as Punch and chatted away the whole time. I have never seen a man talk so fluently while dancing. He obviously means to have fun.'

Freda Dudley Ward was pretty, petite, amusing, and proved to be anything but a little fluff. Almost exactly the same age as David, she was married to the Liberal MP

William Dudley Ward, then Vice-Chamberlain of the Royal Household, by whom she had two daughters, Angela and Penelope. 'Duddie' was sixteen years older, described by a friend as 'kind, jolly and vague'. He and Freda had been married five years when David appeared on the scene, and by that time were leading amicable, but more or less separate lives. The day after the Belgrave Square party, David wrote to 'Mrs Dudley Ward' and the letter was opened in error by Freda's mother-in-law, who invited the Prince to tea. A day or two later, on 3 March, the Prince of Wales wrote to the right Mrs Dudley Ward on the pretext of returning 'your latch key which was found in the electric car after all' in order to invite himself back to see her, 'somehow, somewhere' when he returned from a trip to Scotland.

Just over three weeks later, it appears that the Prince was able to exploit the time-honoured ploy of the soldier returning to the battlefield. In place of formal communications to 'Dear Mrs Ward', his letter of 26 March is intimate and triumphant. 'My Angel!!', it begins, 'I can't tell you how much I hated having to say goodbye this morning . . . And my last night in England too.' His postscript reads, 'Please curse me if I have written a terribly stupid & indiscreet letter as I expect this is, darling; but I can't help it, sitting in my room all alone to-night thinking of you, & I'm not caring much or thinking of the consequences tho. you did say it was safe to write to you as it is to me!! Good night, my angel!!! E.'

This was the start of a feverish, anguished, passionate series of love-letters from David to Freda, which continued for years, at the rate of sometimes four or five a week, whenever he was away from her. Indeed for most of the next sixteen years Mrs Dudley Ward was never far from his thoughts. He would have affairs with other women — especially after 1923 when Freda put their relationship on a platonic basis — but always he would come back to her to pour out his woes and be petted until he was comforted. When he was in London he called on her every day at her London home, usually at five o'clock. If he had an evening engagement, he would return after it was finished. When he was abroad, he would write to Freda almost as often. For the errant prince she provided the mothering and security which got him through his spells of self-obsessed melancholy and gave him the backbone to carry out his public duties. Reluctant as David would have been in later life to acknowledge it, much of the success of his *jeunesse dorée* was inspired by his first great love. Even after she had been brutally cast aside by him, Freda continued conscientiously to carry out the public duties she had first undertaken under the aegis of royal patronage.

Freda Dudley Ward was liked by everyone, from courtiers to telephonists. Unstuffy and self-effacing, she was never tempted to use for her own advantage the significant influence she had over the Prince of Wales. The only people who were less than enthusiastic about her were David's parents. King George objected

93

to her largely on the grounds of her birth: Freda's father was a successful Nottingham lace manufacturer. Queen Mary took exception when David's passion for Freda began to divert him from his less than onerous duties at court. Had they known what lay ahead, in the form of Mrs Simpson, the King and Queen would happily have embraced Freda to their bosom. Like Mrs Keppel, the *maîtress-en-chef* of David's grandfather Edward VII, Freda maintained a dignified reticence throughout their time together and into her old age.

Apart from caring for her children, with whom she shared a relaxed and informal home life which was unconventional for its time, Freda was free to devote herself to mollycoddling David. At the start they had to be content with writing to each other while he completed his wartime service in France. David's sister, Princess Mary, acted as a clandestine postman at Buckingham Palace, forwarding his almost daily letters to Freda. For the first few months he is happy as a sandboy, just knowing that she is there for him. He sends her little presents, kisses her photographs and he dabs her Royal Briar scent on his handkerchief — 'It is too divine for words tho. of course it has a fearful effect on me & makes me temporarily insane!!!!' He chatters on about his travel plans, the news from France, his lunches with an Italian general or the Duchess of Aosta, and gossips about mutual friends in London.

The sights of Rome and Venice mean nothing to him: all his obsession is with Freda, his beloved Angel. He passes on little jokes from Paris, 'for you darling only dont be shocked, but I couldn't be shy with you & would tell you anything:-(The big gun that shoots at PARIS is called Rasputin because it comes once every 15 minutes!!!!) After that I think its nearly time I stopped sweetheart . . . ' Back on leave, in August, he can't wait to escape from the 'prison' of Windsor Castle. 'Oh!! my beloved what a dream of a night last night was only it makes me long to get back to you more & more.' Although Freda Dudley Ward's letters back to him no longer exist, it is evident that at this stage she is returning his ardour and reproaching him when he lies to her about his one-night stands, what the prince calls his 'medicine'. She accepts that 'les petits amusements ne content pas', but wants him to be honest with her and tell her if there's anybody he cares for more. David's response is self-abasement, as it would be so frequently with Wallis Simpson, fifteen years later. On 8 December he writes to Freda prophetically, 'The cutting you sent is amusing & I could do a lot worse than take on an American tho. I just can't bear to think about marriage let alone talk about it!!'

But in late 1918, as Britain prepares for peace and the Prince of Wales realises that he will have to take on real responsibilities of his own, his letters increasingly assume a note of self-pity and depression. 'I really take a very gloomy view of the future sweetheart,' he writes in early December, 'tho. as you know I'm not going to own to myself that I've got the wind up properly about everything (which I have) & am fairly going to slave for the cause, far more for the good of the Country & the Empire than for my family!!' In January 1919 he writes to her, 'Gud how thine E does loathe palace & court life . . . guess he was never intended for that sort of existence; must have been a mistake, not that he will ever treat it as anything but a huge joke, & artificial camouflage & loathing it all more and more intensely!!'

Through 1919 and into 1920 the appalling prospect of 'princing' and eventually becoming King sends him into black despair. 'It's such a sad depressed & miserable little boy thats writing to you tonight after such a dreary and pompous dinner party,' he writes to her in June 1919 — and the following month he swears he would shoot or drown himself 'to escape from this — life which has become so foul & sad & depressing & miserable for me!! I do get so terribly despondent about everything nowadays & if I hadn't got YOU to live for sweetheart I swear I couldn't face it a day longer!!'

That the Prince was spoiled and given to bouts of moodiness which he did not trouble to conceal was in no doubt. But it was also the case that he was the victim of a genuinely melancholy temperament. When depression — 'the black, black mist' as he called it to Freda Dudley Ward — suddenly descended on him, he withdrew into a brooding and taciturn silence. At such times he found his life unendurable, as he wrote on Christmas Day 1919 to Godfrey Thomas: 'A sort of hopelessly lost feeling has come over me and I think I'm going kind of mad!! . . . I'm simply not capable of even thinking, let alone make a decision or settle anything!! I've never felt like this in my life before, and I'm rather worried about it and feel incapable of pulling myself together . . . How I loathe my job now and all this press 'puffed' empty 'success'. I feel I'm through with it and long and long to die . . . ' Such an extreme bout of the black mist could be put down in part to exhaustion. The Prince was between his highly successful but indubitably demanding and stressful tours of the United States and Australia. An enforced stay at Sandringham for three weeks over the Christmas period did not help. In particular, he resented being separated, during his precious time off duty, from Freda, his 'very own darling beloved little mummie'.

As early as 1920 there are signs that Mrs Dudley Ward was gently pulling away from David, and trying to make him stand on his own two feet. David's response was to turn up the baby language and become yet more clinging and possessive. 'I dont want to live & I'm not going to live if I can't live with YOU my sweet precious beloved darling fredie my vewy vewy own lovely precious little angel,' he wrote to her in April of that year. 'I don't care a damn for the rest of the World which means absolutely nothing to me.' He nevertheless saw the impossibility of marrying her now — 'it just would not be fair on you sweetheart tho. who knows how much longer this monarchy stunt

97

is going to last or how much longer I'll be P. of W.'

While he was away on tour, David persuaded Bertie to keep an eye on his mistress and, if necessary, intercede on his behalf. His brother, as it happened, needed little persuading. He had reasons of his own for spending as much time as possible in the privacy and seclusion of Freda's London house. For his own love life, after a slow start, was at long last looking up.

As we now know from David's letters to Mrs Dudley Ward, Bertie had already lost his virginity in France during the war, as had David, thanks to the obliging Paulette. Writing on 26 October 1918 from the British Expeditionary Force's Canadian Corps HQ to his 'darling darling little sweetheart mine', the Prince tells Freda, 'I'm very amused to get a letter from my RAF brother [Bertie] this evening written from Paris where he spent a night with old Derby at the Embassy on his way to the 'Independent Force' at Nancy!! But he didn't sleep at the Embassy as in his own words 'the deed was done' tho. he gave me no details and perhaps just as well!! But you see darling *'C'etait la premier fois car il etait vierge'* which is why it amuses & interests me so much!! I'm longing to see him and hear all about it . . . '

Back in London after the war, it was David who set the pace, David to whom his younger brother looked up, and quite possibly David who suggested that the time had come for Bertie to be initiated into his first proper relationship with a woman. Phyllis Monkman was a popular dancer and leading lady of the London stage in 1919. At twenty-seven she was four years older than Bertie. Moreover, 'Looks have never been my strong suit,' she once candidly admitted, but she made up for this with an engaging sense of humour and a lively personality which won her the friendship of such celebrated contemporaries as Noël Coward and Ivor Novello. She also had very good legs — as Bertie presumably discovered after his assignation with her had been set up during her run at the Comedy Theatre in the show *Tails Up*. It appears that, as arranged, Bertie's aide Gordon Greig came to her dressing-room one evening after the show and summoned her to dine with the Prince in some rooms off Shepherd Market, a part of Mayfair which had traditionally enjoyed a red-lit reputation. More discreet than her counterparts today would be, Miss Monkman ever afterwards maintained a loyal silence about what transpired in Half Moon Street that night. Nevertheless rumour has it that Bertie used to send her presents of jewellery on her birthday. We do know that a small framed photograph of Bertie in his RAF uniform was found in Phyllis Monkman's purse after her death in 1976 at the age of eighty-four.

About this time George V's second son also admitted to a *tendresse* for Lady Maureen Vane-Tempest-Stewart, the daughter of Lord and Lady Londonderry. Bertie would regularly turn up at the Wednesday dances at Londonderry House to drink champagne and mingle shyly with the painters, writers, politicians and soldiers who frequented Lady Londonderry's salon. It is easy to understand why he was smitten. Maureen was fair-haired, blue-eyed and vivacious; moreover she was also unusually forceful — a quality Bertie associated with his mother, and which he was later to find in Elizabeth Bowes-Lyon. Bertie was always drawn towards self-confident women, at ease with themselves, who could make him feel less awkward.

But in every other respect when it came to matters of the heart, Prince Albert could not have been more different from his older brother. He was neither demonstrative nor philandering, and when the Unicorn (as the Londonderrys affectionately called Bertie) offered his gawky adoration to Maureen, it was some time before she could bring herself to inform either him or her parents that she was already unofficially engaged to the man she duly married, an up-and-coming young politician called Oliver Stanley. Later, Lady Londonderry would ruefully acknowledge to Harold Nicolson that her daughter might have been Queen.

It may be that by this time Bertie could take Maureen's news with equanimity. He had already fallen in love with a very pretty, baby-faced twenty-eight-year-old Australian girl, Sheila Chisholm, who in 1915 had married the raffish and drunken Lord Loughborough. Lady Loughborough was a close friend of Freda Dudley Ward's, and it was very possibly at her house that Bertie was introduced to her. What we know of their romance emerges in scattered fragments from David's letters to Freda — in July 1919, 'Sheila and Bertie seem to be seeing quite a lot of each other.' By October he hears from her that 'Sheila & Bertie are planning gt. things & you are being divine to them as usual angel tho. you must watch it with Loughie on the warpath.' Whatever passed between Bertie and Sheila during the next few months, it was sufficient for Prince Albert in May 1920 to write to his elder brother, then on an official visit to New Zealand, and tell him that George V was only prepared to make him Duke of York on condition that his name was no longer coupled with Sheila Loughborough's. David's private response to Freda sounds a note of brotherly exasperation. 'You & I both happen to know that they neither of them really mean anything to each other at all do they sweetheart? & never will (not that they ever have) so that personally I'm all for their really breaking apart properly & cutting out the camouflage love stunt!!'

It may be that the Prince of Wales was displaying a degree of petulance here at the thought of his younger brother enjoying the same kind of illicit trysts with a married woman as he himself was. Oddly enough, the two brothers had always been attracted to similar women. Freda Dudley Ward bore a passing resemblance to Bertie's future wife Elizabeth and, during the Great War, Portia Cadogan briefly had both princes in love with her. What David certainly knew, and Bertie apparently didn't, was that Sheila was at the same time carrying on a romance with Prince Dmitri Obolensky. Her

101

husband Lord Loughborough, meanwhile, was hot on the trail. Freda was so fond of Bertie and Sheila that although, in David's view, 'They've often been a — nuisance and vewy much in the way haven't they darling,' she had taken the risk of letting them use her house, as David wrote, 'for their — well shall we call them 'causeries'!!' But David's earnest wish was for his younger brother to give Sheila up, so that he and Freda could have her house to themselves. As he took care to remind her, 'you have'nt felt comfy having either Ob or Bertie in your house for Sheilie to play with lately & I'm not surprised so I don't feel I'm on to a new line of thought!!'

Bertie was made Duke of York on 5 June 1920. The King, still unable to express his feelings to his children in person even now that they were adults, wrote to Bertie about his new dignities. 'I feel that this splendid old title will be safe in your hands and that you will never do anything which could in any way tarnish it.' On a warmer note he told his second son, 'I know that you have behaved very well, in a difficult situation for a young man & that you have done what I asked you to do.' Within three weeks, Bertie was writing forlornly to David that George V had discovered he was still seeing Sheila and had bullied him into giving her up. This seems to mark the end of the future King's relationship with Sheila Loughborough. The following month, Lord Loughborough announced his willingness to give his wife a divorce, although she did not in fact divorce him until 1928, to marry Sir John Milbanke. It was no doubt a happy coincidence that a few weeks earlier, in May 1920, Bertie had first set eyes on his future bride, Elizabeth Bowes-Lyon.

Had her upbringing been different, Lady Elizabeth Bowes-Lyon, born in 1900, the youngest daughter of the 13th Earl of Strathmore and Kinghorne, might have been tempted to join the increasing number of gently-bred young women who were beginning to tread the boards after the end of the Great War. An enthusiastic theatre-goer, she had adored dressing up and performing since she was a little girl. Whether starring in her piano teacher's Christmas concert, or appearing as a bridesmaid at family weddings, or dancing a minuet in pink and silver brocade to entertain guests at Glamis, she had learned at a young age how to work an audience to her advantage, and never lost the skill. 'Princess Elizabeth' was the role she often chose for herself in the plays she and her siblings put on. One of her parents' guests remembered meeting her particularly for the little ritual they developed: 'I always addressed her as Princess Elizabeth, kissed her hand and made a slight bow, which she acknowledged haughtily.' Another visitor to her father was greeted by a composed and charming Elizabeth with the words: 'How do you do Mr Ralston? I have not seen you look so well for years and years.' She was four years old at the time but already developing into 'the most astonishing child for knowing the right things to say', thought a family friend.

With the war over, the season of 1919–20 saw Elizabeth effortlessly upstaging the other debs, and loving every minute of it. Unlike most of her contemporaries who were raising their skirts, bobbing their hair, downing cocktails and languidly puffing at cigarettes, she conveyed a straightforward charm and wholesomeness and paid scant regard to the modern fashions. She preferred to wear her hair in an unfashionable fringe, and dressed in what one of her admirers, Lord David Cecil, politely described as picturesque clothes. Not that there was anything dowdy about this open, smiling girl with her lovely complexion, heart-shaped face and wide, intensely blue eyes. Small and vivacious, she had a comfortingly easy manner, a sweet voice, an enormous sense of fun and a natural roguishness which men found deeply alluring. Chips Channon thought her 'mildly flirtatious in a very proper romantic old-fashioned Valentine sort of way. She makes every man feel chivalrous and gallant towards her.' And she loved dancing. She seemed, Lady Airlie noticed, 'very unlike the cocktail-drinking, chain-smoking girls who came to be regarded as typical of the 1920's'. Lord David Cecil, who knew her as a child, found her always responsive, kind and outgoing. 'The personality which I see now was there already.' Lady Longford put it simply: 'All men were at her feet.'

The last but one of a brood of nine children, her relatively lowly position in the family was marked by the fact that her father failed to register her birth in August 1900 until nearly seven weeks had passed, and even then seems to have put down the wrong address — St Paul's Walden Bury. Conflicting reports have Elizabeth born in a London hospital (very *infra dig* for the Victorian aristocracy) or even delivered at the side of the road when her mother was being raced home. It is more likely that her eccentric father, who had been away in Scotland playing cricket, simply chose their country home as the first place that came to mind. Baby Elizabeth was joined in the Bowes-Lyon nursery by her brother David, who arrived in May 1902. Lady Strathmore began calling her two youngest children 'my Benjamins'. For the next ten years brother and sister were to be as close to each other as David and Bertie once were, though for different reasons. Elizabeth's parents were kind and loving, but inclined to be aristocratically absent-minded over the upbringing of their large family. A gap of seven years isolated Elizabeth from her older brothers and sisters, so she and David spent most of their time with Clara Knight, their doting and ever-attentive but disciplinarian nanny.

When Elizabeth was four, her father succeeded to the family title of Strathmore and Kinghorne, thus ensuring that she and David would be the first Bowes-Lyon children to grow up in the comfort and security afforded by his significant increase in wealth. Like other aristocratic children, they quickly became used to being uprooted at prescribed times of the year in order to migrate between their four homes: an Adam mansion in St James's Square, St Paul's

Walden Bury, a Queen Anne house of faded red brick in Hertfordshire, Streatham Castle in County Durham — kept staffed but visited each year for only a fortnight — and Glamis Castle, the family's forbidding Scottish fastness in Forfarshire.

Elizabeth, once she had climbed out of the family pram emblazoned with the family crest, was entrusted to a French governess and a French dancing instructor to coach her in the appropriate social graces. The rest of her education seems to have been a hit and-miss affair. As with David and Bertie, riding and walking took precedence over books. But unlike the royal brothers, Elizabeth and her small brother were given considerable freedom to do as they pleased. At St Paul's Walden Bury they could escape to the Flea House, a secret den where they were safe to indulge in illicit binges of guzzling chocolates and sweets, or puffing Woodbine cigarettes. Elizabeth, who was always inclined to put on weight, found comfort in food from an early age.

At Glamis there was no need to invent secrets: the castle had plenty of its own. For a child venturing down its gloomy passages it was easy to imagine walled-up skeletons and gruesome murders and the fearful family monster reputed to be hidden within the ancient isolated fortress. An early nineteenth-century heir to the Strathmore title, the Monster of Glamis was real enough to his successors. A grotesque Humpty-Dumpty figure, covered in hair, he was supposed to have been locked away in a secret room deep in the castle walls to hide the family shame. According to the legend, the putative Earl of Strathmore lived on into hideous old age. Each succeeding earl, on coming into the title, was introduced to him — and, in the best traditions of gothic fantasies, it was said they never smiled again.

To the Bowes-Lyon children, the subject of the monster was a closed book. Their parents never allowed the subject to be raised. Although Elizabeth must have been aware of the tittle-tattle among the servants, she grew up with a clear understanding of the importance of never admitting to and certainly never divulging family secrets: a conviction she was to uphold rigidly in later life.

Glamis was still an enclosed, feudal world. A caravanserai of retainers — housemaids, nursemaids, kitchenmaids, parlourmaids, ladies' maids as well as cooks, valets and footmen — travelled there by train every August, keeping watch on a mountain of luggage, and pulling in, after the four hundred-mile journey, at the estate's private station. Glamis had its own laundry, bakery and distillery. Out of doors, Lord Strathmore employed grooms and gillies by the score. Even the shooting lunches took place in tents with the family silver on display, and liveried footmen serving. The era that Elizabeth had been born into marked the apogee of Edwardian country-house life, with its pampered comfort, its gilded, hothouse luxury, its immense privilege and abundance.

Not that Elizabeth or David need have been

conscious of any of this. While they played unselfconsciously in the glens, their every wish was catered for by a silent army, while the household itself ran smoothly to order on invisible wheels. Their comfortable, undemanding world of childhood started to show cracks only when Elizabeth was in her eleventh year. The arrival of the first Strathmore grandchild made her an aunt and simultaneously deprived her of Clara Knight, who was sent away to act as nanny to the next generation of little Bowes-Lyons. Elizabeth and David felt the parting acutely. In 1911, their brother Alex was suddenly taken ill and died at Glamis of an unspecified illness. Lady Strathmore had already suffered the loss of her eldest child, Violet, who succumbed to diphtheria at the age of eleven, and she began to suffer periods of depression. When in 1912 the dreadful day came that her youngest child David was sent off to boarding school in Broadstairs, treading the path his elder brothers had taken to Eton, Elizabeth wrote a characteristically warm and affectionate letter to cheer her mother: 'My Darling Very Precious Lovable Love: I hope you had a very good journey. Please give every kind of message to David. And do bring him up if you can. Lovie I was so sorry to have cried when you went away.'

Brave words: but Elizabeth was more devoted to David than almost anyone. He had been her ally and playmate in a childhood which, though happy, was necessarily somewhat short of parental attention. With ten children, Lady

Strathmore managed them, said a contemporary, 'much the way she managed the staff'. When depression struck, she naturally became even more remote. Now Elizabeth, deprived of her closest sibling — the next closest was seven years older — presented such a forlorn and dejected figure that Lady Strathmore felt she had to act. Despite her liking for chocolate, Elizabeth, for one of the few times in her life, was losing weight. Her mother decided that what her twelve-year-old daughter needed was the companionship of children her own age, and sent Elizabeth off to the Academy run by the blue-stockinged Misses Birtwhistle in Sloane Street, not far from the Strathmore family home in St James's Square. For a brief two terms Elizabeth distinguished herself as a scholar, gaining high marks in all subjects except arithmetic. Then, for some reason, her mother took her back home and continued her education under a succession of governesses.

These conscientious women had mixed fortunes in curbing the high-spirited Elizabeth. The first, a German governess known as Miss Fraulein, was much loved. Elizabeth corresponded with her in Germany during the war, and brought her over to England in 1937 for a reunion in Buckingham Palace. Another, a French mistress called Mademoiselle Poignard, was less popular and the butt of much teasing. One day Mademoiselle Poignard was disconcerted to receive a letter sent from 'Bedlam L.A., London'. It read in part, 'It is now 7 years since you left the Asylum; cured of your hallucinations. Your unfortunate attacks are due to return Dec. 29! We are keeping a bed for you in case you wish to return. Doctor Waring, the man you tried to murder with a carving knife is not quite recovered, and is awaiting your return with great eagerness. I think it would be advisable to return here on the 28th if possible, as we cannot vouch for your reason after that date.' The letter ended, 'Hoping we shall soon be honoured by another and more prolonged visit,' and was signed 'John Beck M.D.'

As she grew into her teens, Elizabeth increasingly often stepped into her mother's shoes in order to entertain the distinguished guests who called at their London home. Playing hostess was more fun than poring over history and geography books and besides, when in the past she had been asked to write down what she enjoyed doing best, she had written 'liking people'. Nevertheless her schooling was not over yet. Another German governess was signed up, and after eighteen months Elizabeth passed the equivalent of 'O' Levels in seven subjects — before events in Europe introduced her to a very different sort of education.

Her fourteenth birthday on 4 August 1914 coincided with the First World War, declared that very day. On the night that war broke out with Germany, Elizabeth and her parents were enjoying a birthday treat watching a variety show from a box at the London Coliseum. As they drove home afterwards, they passed through crowds waving Union Jacks and singing jingoistic songs. Nowhere was the patriotic fervour greater than outside Buckingham Palace, where King George, Queen Mary and their eldest son, David, were out on the balcony acknowledging the crowd — just as Elizabeth herself would be doing thirty-one years later at the end of World War Two.

The Great War brought Elizabeth the adulation of a smaller but no less adoring audience. From 1914 to 1918, Glamis became a nursing home for wounded officers — young men, in many cases only a few years older than Elizabeth herself who, having been exposed to the unspeakable carnage of trench warfare, found themselves miraculously spirited away to the unworldly tranquillity of the Strathmores' ancient Highland fastness. Here they were tended to and petted by the precocious fourteen-year-old, who had successfully cast herself as a cross between Florence Nightingale and Little Dorrit. Her older sister Rose had trained as a nurse for the express purpose of running Glamis as a hospital, but she was eclipsed by Elizabeth who organised whist games, wrote letters home, fetched tobacco from the village shop, and became a great favourite with the wounded soldiers who adored and depended upon the small, cheerful, bustling figure. Laid low by depression and nervous illness, Lady Strathmore increasingly withdrew into herself and opted out of family life. After her son Fergus was killed in September 1915 at the battle of Loos, three days after he had been home on leave, she sank into a lifelong melancholy decline.

Elizabeth's own grief for her brother found expression in helping the other victims in her care regain what they could of their youth and health. The role was perfect for her. She had always relished being the centre of attention; she had a kind nature and strong supportive instincts. After the loss of her brother, she naturally took pleasure in close and confiding contact with those young men who were left, whom she saw it as her duty to heal. The convalescents at Glamis were also of course a captive audience for her dramatic talents. She organised sing-songs and basked in their approving attention. Once she dressed twelve-year-old David in girl's clothes and teasingly paraded him round the ward, introducing him as her cousin to the gullible young men. Elizabeth loved pranks, always rose to the occasion given an audience, and took any opportunity for dressing up. Unlike many other girls who had found their liberation in the war, there was nothing contentious about Elizabeth as a young woman. On the contrary, four years in the close company of young men had taught her instead how to win attention by making full use of her flirtatious charm. When the armistice came, and the last of the wounded shuffled away from Glamis in the vain search for Lloyd George's country fit for heroes to live in, Elizabeth Bowes-Lyon was ready to move back to London and take it by storm. 'Elizabeth is out now and Cecilia has had a dance for her,' wrote one society matriarch. 'How many hearts Elizabeth will break.'

The Prince of Wales was also back in London. Having safely returned from a good war, he was now the heart-throb of millions of girls around the world. In an attempt to shore up the British Empire after war and revolution had swept away the pre-1914 empires of Russia, Germany, Austria-Hungary and Turkey, King George V soon decided to dispatch David on a series of gruelling tours among his imperial subjects. He was a public triumph wherever he went. When his ship docked at San Diego en route for New Zealand and Australia on 7 April 1920, the city was in a fever of expectation to catch a glimpse of 'The Most Eligible Bachelor Yet Uncaught', as the American press had already dubbed him. Among those to meet the Prince in person were the guests invited to the balls and receptions held in his honour. And one whose social aspirations made it imperative that she was one of the favoured few was the twenty-four-year-old wife of a pilot in the US Navy, Mrs Earl Winfield Spencer Jr. Lieutenant-Commander Spencer and his wife shook hands with the Prince of Wales, exchanged a few perfunctory words and then repeated the process with his cousin, Lord Louis Mountbatten, as the royal party moved down the line. The meeting was brief and was forgotten by David as soon as it was over, but for Mrs Spencer it was another significant notch in the social tally she had been building up for the best part of twenty years.

For as long as she could remember, Wallis Warfield (as Mrs Spencer had been born) had been obsessed with social status, and the money, security and power that were its adjuncts. This she saw as her birthright, and with some justification. Her parents, Teackle Warfield and Alice Montague, came from two prominent families. The Warfields were leaders of the business community in the staid and solid city of Baltimore; the Montagues were drawn from an aristocratic Virginian line, which had seen its fortunes severely depleted by the Civil War. In the opinion of the Montagues, the Warfields were parvenus. To the upright and sober Warfields, the Montagues were little better than impoverished dilettantes. From these two contrasting roots Wallis drew her inspiration. From her Montague mother she inherited her appreciation of the finer things in life, her sense of fun, her wit. From the Warfields came her steely determination, ruthless practicality and concern with money. With a pedigree like hers, Wallis could have looked forward to a life of pampered ease near the very top of the social tree, only just below the Vanderbilts and Astors, after whom as a little girl she named her dolls.

But Wallis had a disadvantage. Shamefully she had been conceived out of wedlock. Ignoring the opposition of both their families, her young parents had pursued their clandestine affair to the point where there was no turning back. Alice became pregnant. Faced with looming social disgrace and a scandal the like of which neither family had known, Teackle and Alice were exiled to a mountain resort while the crisis was hushed up. Their departure made a convincing story, for Blue Ridge Summit was a popular destination for consumptives and Teackle was in the advanced stages of tuberculosis. Wallis was born on 19 June 1895, and faced notoriety from the start. Following a ruling by elders of the Episcopalian church, of which both families were staunch members, she could not be baptised. Seventeen months later, when her parents furtively married, they were also refused a church wedding and had to make do with a makeshift ceremony in the minister's sitting-room. For Teackle and Alice this was a grim start to married life. It did not get any better. She had charm and beauty, but no money. Teackle had no money either, nor did he have long to live. When he died, at the age of twenty-seven, he left his wife penniless, reduced to living off the charity of his disapproving relatives.

At the head of the clan sat Anna Emory Warfield, as despotic and censorious in her family as George V was in his. For five years Wallis and her mother lived under the old lady's roof, barely getting by on the meagre allowance provided by Alice's rich brother-in-law. This man, a railway tycoon whom Wallis came to know as Uncle Sol, also lived at home with his mother and cast an increasingly covetous eye over his brother's widow. When the strain of the arrangement proved too much, mother and child moved out. It was an abrupt departure which Michael Bloch, author of several books about the Windsors, suspects was because of unwelcome advances, either towards Wallis's mother or Wallis herself. Certainly, Uncle

115

Sol, when mentioned in Wallis's memoirs, comes across as a powerfully dark and sexually uncomfortable figure.

For a time, mother and daughter rented a room in a cheap hotel, where Alice took in sewing. Then her widowed sister — Wallis's kind Aunt Bessie Merryman who was to guide and support Wallis through the early years of her relationship with the Prince of Wales — let them stay with her until Alice finally found lodgings of her own. To make ends meet, they gave some rooms over to paying guests. Even as a little girl Wallis proved to be an accomplished and enthusiastic hostess, helping her mother in the kitchen, waiting at table and seemingly stoically making the best of the unjust hand that fate had dealt her.

Yet already the ambition was there. Despite her poverty, Wallis's mother lavished every attention on her only daughter. Every surface was bedecked with pictures of Wallis. Even in their straitened circumstances, much attention was paid to grooming Wallis to become a young lady. Her deportment (straight-backed or there would be an ice-cold bath as a punishment), her appearance, her manners — all were of importance if her mission in life was to marry a rich, important man. All this turned Wallis into a narcissistic and demanding personality. 'Must-have, got-to-get!' were her favourite childhood expressions according to her mother, whom Wallis later quoted. Even at the kindergarten to which her mother had managed to scrape together enough money to send her, Wallis determined to get the better of adversity. As a schoolfriend famously recalled, 'Wallis was as busy as a cartload of monkeys. Oh! She was bright, brighter than all of us. She made up her mind to go to the head of the class and she did.' And when a classmate once dared to come up with an answer before her, her reaction was to smash a wooden pencil case over the culprit's head.

Life got tougher at fashionable Arundell School, where Wallis went when she was ten, and where the other girls started off by teasing her because her mother took in lodgers. Treading a tightrope between the two worlds of penny-pinching at home and conspicuous affluence at school made Wallis not only ambitious but stubborn and proud. She threw herself enthusiastically into everything the school could provide. Headstrong and wilful the teachers may have found her, but she succeeded in making herself popular with the girls from the most prominent families. From her crisply ironed uniform to her finely sharpened pencils there was no way of telling that she could not be counted as one of them.

When she was twelve, Wallis's life was thrown into turmoil much as Elizabeth Bowes-Lyon's had been at the same age. Her mother, still attractive and fun-loving, on whom she doted and whose undivided attention she had enjoyed for eleven years, suddenly remarried. Wallis found herself having to share Alice with an idle, alcoholic stepfather who read comics and drank beer in bed. It was a bitter blow to

117

such a fastidious young girl, who was already houseproud and perfectionist, and obsessed, as she always would be, with keeping everything around her ordered and flawlessly clean. In years to come, Wallis's mania for newpin neatness led to her demand that her sheets be changed and ironed twice a day. Now, she was all the more determined that she would find a prince charming to rescue her.

Wallis had no illusions about her looks. 'Nobody ever called me beautiful or even pretty,' she wrote candidly in later life. But she made an heroic effort to be well-groomed. Here her physique helped: it was lean, angular and efficient, like her sharp-planed face. Her nickname at sixteen was 'Skinny'. She also, from an early age, made it her business to know how to charm and flatter the opposite sex, cultivating a personality that was very lively, even a trifle risqué. Once she had targeted a prospective boyfriend, she made it her business to know his movements, his favourite sports and hobbies, his football scores, even what he liked to eat. It proved irresistible. Despatched with Baltimore's finest to a summer camp for gilded youth, she made off with the most promising boy there: handsome, athletic and, of course, suitably rich. There was a double triumph in this coup for, thanks to her stepfather's private income, Wallis had recently changed schools and was now a pupil at Oldfields, the most exclusive and expensive educational establishment in the state. That summer she managed to snatch her beau from under the far prettier noses of the schoolmates she had left behind. Victory and revenge rolled into a delicious romance: it was a good summer.

The dormitory at Oldfields bore the school motto, 'Gentleness and Courtesy are Expected of Girls at all Times.' During her time there Wallis made new friends, some of whom even had an international cachet, such as Renee du Pont, heiress to the du Pont chemical fortune. As she climbed inexorably up the social scale, Wallis distilled and refined the charm on which her future success would depend.

The outbreak of the Great War, though it launched Elizabeth Bowes-Lyon, scuttled Wallis's burgeoning social ambitions. Her step-father died, leaving Alice and Wallis without the benefit of his private income. Then, with Europe at war, Uncle Sol decided it was inappropriate to give a large coming-out ball for his niece. With no ball of her own at which to shine, Wallis found herself just one of forty-six debutantes selected to attend the exclusive Bachelors Cotillion which opened the Baltimore season. Wallis knew what she wanted: Uncle Sol succumbed to her charms and coughed up the not inconsiderable sum of twenty dollars for her ballgown. Wallis spent it on an exact copy — white satin and chiffon, embroidered with pearls — of the dress in which the dancer Irene Castle was appearing to packed houses on Broadway. If her Montague heart drew her to it, her Warfield head sanctioned the outlay. Uncle Sol's dress turned his niece into the belle of the ball.

Like Elizabeth, Wallis too was on her way — or so her mother must have thought. After the years of scrimping and saving, and living with the stigma of being a poor relation, Alice Warfield was bound to hope that her only daughter would repay the sacrifices by making an advantageous match. When she did not, and indeed, it looked as if she was set to repeat the mistake of Alice's own youth, it came as a cruel disappointment. The man who swept Wallis off her feet was Earl Winfield Spencer, a dashing naval pilot several years older than her and the son of a Chicago family of no great riches or significance. It was an odd marriage for someone of Wallis's social ambition, though flying, still an exceptionally dangerous pastime, had a corresponding glamour. If Wallis hoped to find in Spencer a substitute father figure, she was rapidly disillusioned. Win soon showed the darker side of his nature, lapsing into aggressive alcoholic binges and sometimes locking up his young wife or tying her to the bed while he went out alone for the evening.

The entry of the United States into the war in April 1917 brought a brief respite. Win was promoted, and he and Wallis were posted to San Diego where he knuckled down to training new pilots. It kept him away from the house and it kept him sober. Wallis was now the wife of a commanding officer and used her new status to begin her career as a consummate hostess. Whether or not it brought her happiness, it brought her recognition and admiration from men. The end of the war signalled the virtual end of the Spencer marriage. Win started to go downhill fast, and Wallis must have looked back ruefully at all her careful scheming, the years of adolescent planning and dreaming that seemed to have been squandered. Shaking hands with the world's matinée idol, the Prince of Wales, may have momentarily raised her spirits, but it must have thrown into stark relief the life with which she had saddled herself.

On 20 May 1920, six weeks after that brief encounter in southern California, Derby Night was celebrated in London. Bertie dutifully accompanied his mother to a ball at Lady Farquhar's house while King George entertained the Jockey Club at Buckingham Palace. Bertie was coming to the end of a lonely and fairly pointless sojourn at the University of Cambridge where his father had decided it would be a good idea for him to spend a year. When David had gone to Oxford, he had been allowed the relative freedom of living in college. No doubt disapproving of the use David had made of this freedom, George V ensured that Bertie — and Harry, who joined him from Sandhurst — were immured far from the centre of university life in a house specially chosen by the King for its seclusion. His third son Harry had a few friends from Eton with whom he could continue to behave like a schoolboy, shrieking with laughter at all and sundry as a courtier noted. But the only friend Bertie made at Cambridge — at least the only one of whom his father approved — was his cousin Louis Mountbatten. But he too, like others before him, soon fell under David's spell

121

and switched his allegiance from Bertie to his elder brother when he went as aide-de-camp to the Prince of Wales on the tour that took them to San Diego. Although five years Bertie's junior, Mountbatten was strikingly handsome and had the self-assurance Bertie lacked. Being taken up by him only to be dropped in favour of David did nothing to help Bertie's self-esteem.

Derby Night of 1920 was to mark the beginning of the long upward curve in Bertie's fortunes. As soon as he saw Elizabeth Bowes-Lyon, at Lady Farquhar's ball, dancing with his newly appointed equerry, Jamie Stuart, Bertie was entranced, and asked Jamie to introduce him. It would not be an easy courtship, did he but know it: Elizabeth would make sure of that. But some intuition in him must have sensed that this was the woman he needed beside him.

The Hon. James Gray Stuart, whose father was shortly to become the seventeenth Earl of Moray, would have been in the eyes of many women a more attractive proposition than stammering, diffident Prince Albert. Tall, good-looking, dashing and high-spirited, he had distinguished himself in the war, winning a Military Cross and Bar. A third son, he had little money and fewer expectations, though in the event he would go on to become Secretary of State for Scotland, and be made a Viscount in recognition of his distinguished career in public service. All that lay ahead. For the moment he was chiefly interested in women — and one in particular, Elizabeth Bowes-Lyon. The Strathmores and Morays were both Scottish neighbours and friends but that is not why Jamie Stuart hit it off with Elizabeth. Three years her senior (and just over a year younger than Bertie) he shared her waggish sense of humour and fondness for teasing. In September 1919 he had been to stay at Glamis. From then on, for the rest of the year and through 1920 and 1921, he and Elizabeth talked and danced and flirted, and danced some more, over dinners and walks, at balls and at country house weekends. Most of their contemporaries were convinced that they were serious about each other. According to Elizabeth's dresser, Mabel Monty, 'It was obvious when you saw them together that they were madly in love.'

This was the man who in May 1920 was appointed Bertie's equerry. From the start it was not a close relationship. James Stuart found Bertie rather stuffy and, like many people in the Prince's circle, he gravitated to the livelier quarters of the Prince of Wales, where he could be with old friends like Godfrey Thomas and Bruce Ogilvy. Meanwhile he spent as much time as possible with Elizabeth Bowes-Lyon, exchanging billets doux and at least once, it is believed, managing to have lunch *à deux* with her. It seemed that the announcement of their engagement could only be a matter of time.

Dancing in the arms of such a dashing war hero, Lady Elizabeth might have been forgiven for finding Bertie somewhat unimpressive. Shy and stammering, he was now starting to show signs of addictive smoking and drinking. His royal lineage would not have pressed his cause with her either: the Strathmores, an old Scots family who had never been courtiers or in the social whirl, were markedly unimpressed. 'Some people, dear, have to be fed royalty like sea-lions with fish,' Elizabeth's mother had been heard to say. Lord Strathmore, who had been appalled by the behaviour of Bertie's grandfather as Prince of Wales, agreed with her: 'If there is one thing I have determined for my children, it is that they shall never have any post about the Court.' On the other hand, Elizabeth had a soft spot for wounded, dependent and uncritically devoted young men. Maybe all was not lost.

In the summer of 1920 there was the usual round of Scottish house-parties. Bertie, kicking his heels at Balmoral, was rescued by James Stuart who took him over to Glamis. There was dancing and Lady Elizabeth took the floor dressed, we are told, in 'a rose brocade van Dyck dress with pearls in her hair'. She sparkled — but for whom? The fairytale setting of Glamis certainly worked its magic on the already susceptible Prince. Lord Gorell, another of Elizabeth's conquests, tried to explain its very special atmosphere when he talked to Elizabeth's biographer Lady Longford. 'Everything at Glamis was beautiful, perfect. Being there was like living in a van Dyck picture. Time and the gossiping, junketing world, stood still. Nothing happened . . . but the magic gripped us all. I fell madly in love. They all did.' When Bertie went south, James Stuart stayed on in Scotland. There is a photograph of him taken in the autumn at a Glamis shoot, looking contented, at ease, proprietorial even. Elizabeth is there. For the moment one can imagine a future for them.

Things seemed to be going better for Bertie with the King that summer. A few weeks after setting eyes on Elizabeth, he had been made Duke of York. Bertie was deeply grateful, as he always was when his father showed him the slightest sign of favour. The Prince of Wales, however, wrote dismissively to Freda, 'personally I think he's an ass to accept the title as he's universally known as Prince Albert which is what he was in the war & who cares a — about 'the D. of Y.'?' By this stage in Bertie's life, the similarities between him and the King were becoming more apparent. Both were second sons of domineering fathers. Both had become used to playing second fiddle to their elder brothers who would one day be crowned King-Emperor. Both, possibly as a result of all this, had developed notorious tempers. They shared a love of country life, particularly when it came to exorcising their ill-humour by gunning down birds. Both had blighted naval careers to look back on with some cause for bitterness. And both had an unquestioning faith in the power and authority of ritual and tradition: Bertie was as devout a freemason as he was an Anglican, and later Defender of the Faith.

When they had so many things in common, it was hard for Bertie to understand why his father found fault in so much that he tried to do. George V continued to hound and criticise all his sons, particularly about their social lives.

He was fed regular reports on their supposed misdemeanours, the most slanted of which came from the King's sharp-tongued spinster sister, Victoria. In fact, of course, while Bertie was still living at home, the chance he had of cutting loose in the way that his father seemed to fear was virtually nil. While the rest of Bright Young London was partying to excess, the royal children were forced to endure evening after evening with their parents. These evenings followed an unbending routine which frequently included an interrogation by the King, and invariably ended in morgue-like silence by 10.30. For formal dining, the King favoured George III's Windsor uniform, namely white tie and waistcoat, breeches and a dark blue tailcoat, red collar and cuffs. For dinner the women had to remove their armpit-length white gloves. Dinner, during which a string orchestra played, lasted one hour precisely and then, following a lead from Queen Mary, the female guests once more donned their gloves. The playing of the national anthem ended an evening of stiff ceremonial. George V's hate-list included cocktails, jazz, card games, going away for weekends — indeed all that was modern about the postwar age.

It was worse still at Balmoral, where the princes contrived to spend as little time as possible. The unbroken rule of tradition meant that the head butler served at table dressed incongruously in shepherd's plaid, simply because one of his predecessors once, long ago, had donned this costume to stand in for the Prince Consort while he was having his portrait painted by Landseer. Nor was Windsor free from archaic rituals. In the Waterloo Chamber the forks for banquets were laid face down, a hangover from the days, a century earlier, when the prongs might have caught in lace ruffles. 'Traditionalism is all very well,' a restless Bertie confided during a conversation with Lady Airlie, 'but too much of it leads to dry rot . . . ' 'No new blood is ever introduced,' he complained, 'there's no spring in it, and no originality in the talk — nothing but a dreary acquiescence in the order of the day.'

Set alongside the King's veneration for the past and his undisguised loathing of the present, was his anxiety about bad women, harpies who might prey upon his sons. Ceaselessly he harried them to find good wives and settle down. Queen Mary was more concerned about Bertie than about David. At this stage she knew very little about Elizabeth Bowes-Lyon. Together with the Duchess of Devonshire, her Mistress of the Robes, she was considering marrying Bertie off to the Duchess's fourth daughter Rachel Cavendish, a sweet, pretty girl. The Queen brought Rachel to stay at Windsor, during Ascot — but by then, for Bertie, there was only one woman in the world.

'I like him so much and he is a man who will be made or marred by his wife,' Elizabeth's mother wrote to Lady Airlie. No doubt Mabell Airlie passed this on to Queen Mary who during the Scottish sojourn of 1921 had gathered up Bertie, still doggedly pursuing his courtship, and borne him over to Glamis Castle so that she herself could have a closer look at the quarry. Lady Strathmore was unwell, and Elizabeth understudied her mother as hostess with such grace and engaging ease of manner that Queen Mary left Glamis (according to Lady Airlie) convinced that this was the girl who could make Bertie happy — and the King too. She invited Elizabeth to be one of Princess Mary's eight bridesmaids for her wedding in February 1922 to the elderly Lord Lascelles.

Now the only one who needed convincing was Elizabeth herself. She had already turned down Bertie's first proposal. Helen Hardinge, who as Helen Cecil had watched the new Duke of York's laboured courtship at first hand, told biographer Michael Thornton that, 'Lady Elizabeth initially found the Duke an extremely disconcerting figure. He was totally smitten by her — but she didn't know what to say to him. There were long awkward silences, then he would take her hand and she would firmly tug it away.' Marriage was Elizabeth's destiny, but she knew well enough from her parents and from her own instinct that marrying into the royal family was much less certain to end happily than marrying the royal prince in the fairytale. With the Duke of York would come all the cumbersome, ornate baggage of royal duty, protocol and public scrutiny. Whoever married the Prince of Wales could at least look forward to taking top-billing as Queen-Empress; Bertie would always be second best, as would his wife.

Elizabeth was not good at coming second. She had started life as an extra and had spent twenty-two years working her way to centre-stage. Was it worth sacrificing all the adulation, the flirting, the excitement of the pursuit, to give this unglamorous suitor the right to imprison her in the strait-laced world of the royal family? It was a hard decision, made no easier by the suitor himself who was moody, temperamental and deeply insecure — definitely second best compared with most of the other rich and eligible young men queuing up to marry her. However, the trouble with many of these others was that Elizabeth was not the sole object of their admiration. Other girls had come before, and might come after. The losses and bereavements of Elizabeth's childhood had made her question the enduring quality of love. Disliking competition and used to getting her own way, she demanded the right to be prized exclusively and above all others. Jamie Stuart loved her and wanted to marry her, and Elizabeth, from all accounts, loved him: but she was chary of committing herself. The special devotion she expected took time to become established and recognised, and Jamie Stuart had yet to pass the test. Although he had broken it off, he had after all very recently been engaged to another Scottish neighbour, the pretty heiress daughter of a millionaire Glasgow industrialist.

Time was not on Elizabeth's side. Queen Mary was not in the habit of waiting upon the whims of other people. Her son was miserably

129

unhappy. Together with Lady Strathmore and James's mother Lady Moray, she hit upon a cunning plan. James would be despatched to the oilfields of Oklahoma, to work as a rigger. It would be good experience for him. Dutifully James Stuart sailed off to the New World, returning a year later to pick up his consolation prize in the shape of Lady Rachel Cavendish. What Elizabeth thought of his departure we don't know: but the photograph of the wedding, shortly afterwards, of Princess Mary and Lord Lascelles, shows Elizabeth stuck at the back without a trace of her habitual smile — indeed looking so glum and unlike herself that the official artist elected to leave her out of his painting.

All through 1922 Elizabeth was subject to gentle pressure. Her country, it was implied, needed a favourable decision. At the start of 1923, the evening papers declared that the Prince of Wales was about to announce his engagement to a young Scottish woman of noble birth. This was the first David knew about it, and an official denial was quickly published. Elizabeth was rattled. Bertie, conditioned to believe that his brother would always take the prize from him, was mortified. Although he reasoned that there was no truth in the story, it stung him into a final bid to gain her hand. A week later, walking with her in the grounds of St Paul's Walden Bury, he once again proposed. It was his third time of asking. Elizabeth, at last, said yes.

Sarah Bradford, a recent biographer of

George VI, believes that it was Bertie's vulnerability more than anything else which finally won Elizabeth over. Friends she trusted claimed to discern a sweetness about the Duke of York. Beneath the shyness and stammer, there beat steadfastness, honour and a capacity for true loyalty and affection. Like Elizabeth, Bertie was sincerely religious and, unlike David, he also shared with her a sense of noblesse oblige. Bertie at once gratefully acknowledged his luck. His intuition told him that with Elizabeth's unwavering support, his life would be transformed. Chips Channon was one contemporary who quickly saw how things stood. 'He had few friends,' was his verdict on the Duke of York, 'and was almost entirely dependent on her, whom he worshipped. She was his willpower, his all.' Not that Elizabeth appreciated people saying this. James Lees-Milne tells us that when John Wheeler-Bennett finally finished his weighty official biography of King George VI, he 'sensed that the Queen Mother was not pleased with the dominant role he had assigned to her.' Edwardian that she was, she preferred to make her influence felt in a less obvious manner. She preferred to pull strings subtly — though no less forcefully — from behind the throne. But Bertie knew where the truth lay. As he wrote to his daughter, the present Queen, on her wedding day, he was quite certain he was marrying the most wonderful woman in the world.

The Prince of Wales had not yet met his own most wonderful woman in the world — or rather he had met several of them, all unsuitable — and his parents were beginning to confront the possibility that he never would. In love, as in life, David was driven by restless energy and haunting self-doubts that made him a demanding and at times tedious lover. On the other hand, given his experience of family life within the royal family, he was profoundly wary of the demands that lifelong attachments would make on him. Casual affairs which required no effort or obligation on his part suited him fine: he was too far self-absorbed to want the responsibility of looking after a wife, unless she was the sort of woman who would look after *him*. Much as he might have despised the aura that surrounded the title of Prince of Wales, many of his conquests were undoubtedly due to its mesmerising effect on the succession of women (frequently married) who allowed themselves to be seduced. Had he been judged on equal terms with other eligible bachelors of his day, the consensus was that David would not have measured up well, physically or emotionally.

Meanwhile, with Freda Dudley Ward, and her lively daughters Angela and Penelope, David had found a substitute nursery where he could escape from being Prince of Wales to take part in children's games and indulge his playful sense of humour. 'You see, you are so much loved you are spoilt,' he once remonstrated with one of the girls. 'You have no idea of the lives of many children.' He brought them presents for their birthdays; the girls called him Little Prince

132

and adored him. His devotion to Freda, who was now more a mother than a lover to him ('From now onwards I'll twy to teach myself to look on you only as Fredie Mummie,' he'd written to her in June 1920, 'tho, it's going to be the hardest task of my life'), further strained his relationship with George V.

The difference in character between the two men, made greater by the generation gulf caused by the Great War, led to distrust on both sides. This was rarely diffused, because father and son had such difficulty in expressing their feelings face to face. As the tension increased between the king and the Prince of Wales, Bertie remained David's staunchest ally. 'His great complaint against you, of course, is due to jealousy,' he wrote to David with uncharacteristic perception. 'He knows too well what a success you have been . . . and I must tell you that at times his jealousy is quite apparent.'

It was evident to his courtiers as well as to the princes that George V was jealous of his sons, and would continue to be jealous of them until they married. He took out on them this unconscious resentment by railing at them whenever they behaved with more latitude and freedom than he allowed himself. He was anxious that David should follow his example and tour the Empire; he was pleased and proud when his eldest son proved so popular overseas, greeted by cheering crowds wherever he went; but at the same time he lost no opportunity to scold the Prince of Wales for not behaving on tour with the proper dignity. 'From various photographs of you which have appeared in the papers I see that you wear turned-down collars in white uniform, with a collar and black tie. I wonder whose idea that was, as anything more unsmart I never saw; I have worn tunics for 20 years in white, which was very smart.' When the pictures reached him of David and Louis Mountbatten wearing swimming trunks, as they cooled off in the tropics, George V wrote caustically, 'you might as well be photographed naked, no doubt it would please the public.'

David found his father contradictory. After having it drilled into him since childhood that he should not set himself above other people, the Prince of Wales was now being reprimanded for bringing the monarchy nearer its subjects and continually reminded by the King that he could not behave like other people. He had other, legitimate complaints. George V expected his sons to have a grasp of world events, but refused to let them see the Cabinet minutes and other instruments of government which would have kept them well informed. Instead, here was another area in which he could set traps and then humiliate them for their inadequacy. One of Bertie's most poignant anxieties on the first night of his reign was that he had never properly tackled a state paper. David, too, instead of being shown the ropes of government and encouraged to take an interest in the role he would one day inherit, was sent out as his father's stooge — 'princing' as he called it — or, worse, made to accompany him, 'trotting round like a wee doggie'. Looking back from exile many years later, David was to comment that as some men were chained to their desks, 'I was chained to the banqueting table.'

George V remained obsessed all his life with punctuality and dress. 'Late as usual, Harry,' was his greeting once to Prince Henry when his son, after spending several months abroad, appeared in the Palace dining-room moments after his father had sat down to dine. The King was even more nit-picking about his sons' appearance. His disapproval was not restricted to uniforms or the correct wardrobe for an imperial tour. At home there were explosions over hunting boots with pink tops, trousers with turn-ups and dancing without gloves. Mabell Airlie watched from the wings and later commented sadly, 'As the heir to the throne grew older the stream of paternal criticism increased, but the Prince's behaviour when his father hauled him over the coals for being 'the worst dressed man in London', and laid traps for him with orders and decorations, showed the utmost forbearance.'

Bertie took after his father in the belief that presentation was all-important, and throughout his life displayed an almost obsessive punctiliousness about the proper wearing of uniforms and decorations. David's reaction was to rebel. In George V's eyes his eldest son's unwillingness to conform to the prescribed dress code looked very like an unwillingness to take on the royal duties he would be inheriting. And it was true that for David his interest in clothes ran far deeper than just a young man's passing

135

enthusiasm for fashion. The informality he favoured — soft collars, dinner jackets, in effect, dressing down — was a clear signal of the Prince's dissatisfaction with royal life. His colourful casual clothes — loud checks, plus-fours and Argyll socks — cried out his need to be approved and admired. Throughout his life the cock pheasant would always pay close attention to his plumage.

In the Prince of Wales's dress George V detected a symptom of the raffish lifestyle into which his son was being drawn by unsuitable company. Chief among the culprits was Captain Edward Metcalfe, a close chum of the Prince's known to everyone as Fruity. He was a wild Irish cavalry officer who had joined David's staff during his tour of India and had travelled home with him. David proved 'very obstinate' when the King tried to get rid of Fruity Metcalfe, and even after Fruity had been returned to India, he found his way back into David's service within two years. Fruity was an accomplished horseman and encouraged David to ride in steeplechases, a natural progression for an energetic young man from the hunting his father had urged him to take up at Oxford. Riding in point-to-points was exciting and took guts. It was also the only activity in which David could compete on equal terms with all comers. No wonder David dug his heels in when the disapproving King tried to get Fruity Metcalfe posted to India indefinitely. His father was challenging his right to have a life of his own.

Along with Freda Dudley Ward, there was

always Bertie he could count on. 'I am not going to let you fight your battles alone with the family,' Bertie wrote in fraternal support, and, true to his word, behind the scenes tried to build bridges between David and his parents. 'We must all help him to get back to our way of thinking,' was how Bertie put it to Queen Mary. Two years later he was telling David, 'There is a dreadful blank in my life directly you leave on one of your tours.' But just as David drifted further from his father, the tide was slowly carrying Bertie closer to the King. On the day he married Elizabeth, George V wrote to him, 'You have always been so sensible and easy to work with and you have always been ready to listen to any advice and to agree with my opinions about people and things, that I feel that we have always got on very well together (very different to dear David).'

By marrying Elizabeth Bertie immediately rose in the King's estimation. 'You'll be a lucky fellow if she accepts you,' was the characteristically grudging response when Bertie sought his father's consent to propose. But there was no question about George V's approval of Bertie's bride. Even the King's obsession with time moderated when confronted with his delightful new daughter-in-law's unpunctuality. When she arrived two minutes late at table on one occasion, apologising sweetly, the King remarked that he must have sat down two minutes too early. When Elizabeth gave a newspaper interview after the news of her engagement (the only one she has ever given), it was only the mildest of rebukes from the palace that informed her that the royal family did not give interviews.

David was equally enthusiastic. 'Splendid news about Bertie and Elizabeth . . . She is a very sweet girl . . . and I am delighted,' he wrote to Queen Mary. As he got to know his new sister-in-law, the bond strengthened. He told Diana Cooper that Elizabeth was 'the one bright spot' at Buckingham Palace. 'They all love her,' he continued, 'and the King is in a good temper whenever she is there.' This last detail was important for David. It took the heat off him and may subconsciously have helped to establish in George V's mind the idea which may well have been germinating in David's — that Elizabeth could make a serviceable Queen, with the strength of will to carry Bertie along with her. The Prince of Wales gave the newly-married couple a sports car as a wedding present, but hoped deep down that they would not be going too far away in it.

Everybody was charmed and delighted by the Smiling Duchess. The people of Yugoslavia, to whom Bertie was becoming a familiar figure after being sent to the Ruritanian backwater as his father's representative twice in the previous two years, were enchanted by Elizabeth. In October 1923 the Duke of York grudgingly took his new wife on yet another visit to Belgrade, this time for a double-bill put on by the royal house of Karageorgevitch: the christening of Bertie's godson, Crown Prince Peter, and the wedding of Prince Paul to Princess Olga. In spite of the funny names, and the rickety palace into which the assembled crowned heads were crowded, it was very much a family gathering. The groom was an Oxford friend of David's and the bride was the granddaughter of Uncle Willy, Queen Alexandra's brother who had been assassinated in 1913. She was also the sister of Princess Marina, who would enter Bertie's life in a few years time as the decorative and tolerant wife of his youngest surviving brother George, Duke of Kent.

Elizabeth's sparkle radiated beyond the palaces of Europe. The first state ball to be held under Britain's first-ever Labour government was a tense affair at which the guests stood around unsure what to do. Elizabeth and David broke the ice and led off the dancing. Later that year, 1924, David was dancing in New York. He was off-duty, in holiday mood and, for George V, was hitting the headlines for all the wrong reasons. Elizabeth understood his ordeal. A year later she wrote to him from her own holiday in Africa, sympathising with his frustration at the 'petty little annoyances and restrictions that drive one crazy' at home, and admitting tellingly, 'I hate being always under the eye of a narrow-minded autocrat'. By this stage she was very fond of him. 'Dear David,' she wrote in another note full of fellow-feeling, 'of course you are very, very naughty, but delicious!'

Elizabeth found another chink in her auto-cratic father-in-law's armour when she became the mother of the world's most popular baby — Princess Elizabeth, later to be crowned Queen Elizabeth II — in the spring of 1926. David was delighted by the news — Bertie now had an heir, and the succession was ensured one way or another. The King was especially pleased because his second grandchild's arrival briefly helped switch attention from the grim economic conditions. The General Strike was to start a fortnight after Princess Elizabeth's birth.

Now that she had done her duty in helping secure the House of Windsor, the new Duchess of York turned her attention to putting some steel into her husband. This she did by focusing on the outward sign of his inward insecurity — his stammer. Elizabeth knew the debilitating effect this had on Bertie in private, and by now she had witnessed enough of his humiliating, stuttering public appearances to realise that in the eyes of the world at large the Duke of York was an embarrassment to himself, to his family and to the nation. David, needless to say, was a skilled and effective public speaker, thanks in part to the coaching of his mentor, Winston Churchill. The contrast between the two brothers was starkly displayed at the end of October 1925, when Bertie closed the Empire Exhibition at Wembley. David was out of the country touring southern Africa, although his presence was there in one of the most popular exhibits in the exhibition — a life-size statue carved out of butter. The King had opened the exhibition with the first of his speeches ever to be broadcast. Bertie had taken over from David as President of the exhibition and now it was his turn to take to the airwaves, addressing listeners around the Empire who were familiar with his brother's clear, confident and compelling tones.

The Duke of York was frankly terrified. 'I do hope I shall do it well,' he had written apprehensively to his father. 'But I shall be very frightened as you have never heard me speak & the loud speakers are apt to put one off as well. So I hope you will understand that I am bound to be more nervous than I usually am.' If the King did understand he kept it to himself, sitting grim-faced as his son stumbled through the agonising public ordeal. Elizabeth was there, smiling as always and willing him on, but to no avail. 'Bertie got through his speech all right,' his father wrote to Prince George, 'but there were some rather long pauses.'

In a little over a year's time the Yorks were due to make a world tour, the highlight of which would be a visit to Australia. Stanley Bruce, the Australian Premier had grave misgivings about letting the Duke of York loose at the microphone, especially after the Prince of Wales had been such a spectacular success during his visit to the Dominion a few years earlier. Very fortunately another Australian, a speech therapist conveniently living in London, had greater confidence. His name was Lionel Logue and, next to Elizabeth's, his was probably the most supportive role in the life of the future King. Bertie had been to speech therapists before and had come away disillusioned, showing little sign of improvement. Logue caught him just in time to stop his speech defect becoming ingrained, and saved him from losing his confidence

141

irretrievably. Almost a year after his Wembley débâcle, Bertie went to Harley Street to meet him. 'He entered my consulting-room at three o'clock in the afternoon,' Logue noted, 'a slim, quiet man with tired eyes and all the outward symptoms of the man upon whom the habitual speech defect had begun to set the sign. When he left at five o'clock, you could see that there was hope once more in his heart.'

In simple terms, Logue taught Bertie to breathe properly. Along with breathing exercises, he also devised tongue-twisters to help Bertie master the consonants that caused him greatest difficulty, and in addition helped him loosen up and laugh at his affliction. For a man whose modest successes to date had been largely physical rather than intellectual, who showed an aptitude for practical solutions and who was prepared to stick at a given task, provided he could see the sense in it, this was an ideal course of treatment. Logue taught him, too, that speech was as much a presentation of himself as the clothes he wore, and took him back to his childhood to uncover the root cause of his impediment. Elizabeth, determined to keep her husband at it, frequently sat in on his sessions with Lionel Logue, and a slow improvement resulted. By the time they set sail to Australia at the beginning of January 1927, Bertie was 'full of confidence'. Elizabeth was at his side, as she would be on all of his imperial tours. Having made Bertie presentable, she was not going to deny herself the esteem of a wider public audience. Lilibet may only have been eight and a half months old, but in the best traditions of royal wives, duty came first.

Some of David's success rubbed off on the Yorks who took Australia by storm. Bertie's big speech at the opening of the new Parliament at Canberra passed without a hitch, which encouraged him so much that he threw in a short impromptu address as an encore. Glowering at his newspaper in Buckingham Palace, the King might have forgotten which son he had sent to Australia: the cantankerous tone of his letters was depressingly familiar. 'It was an unfortunate moment for the photograph to be taken,' Bertie explained patiently in reply to a broadside from the King whose eagle eye had lighted on a picture of him 'inspecting a Gd of Honour (I dont think much of their dressing) with yr Equerry walking on yr right side next to the Gd & you ignoring the officer entirely. Yr Equerry should be outside and behind, it certainly doesn't look well.'

David would ruefully have recognised his father's welcome when Bertie and Elizabeth returned in the triumphal glow that he had come to expect. 'Frock-coat & epaulettes, without medals & riband, only stars,' ran the King's advance greeting. 'We will not embrace at the station before so many people. When you kiss Mama take yr. hat off.' After six months away, it was good to be home.

It had to be said that home life in Richmond Park for the Duke and Duchess of York — even when enlivened by Lilibet and by Margaret Rose, who followed her in 1930 — was dull and

143

uneventful, with only a smattering of public duties to brighten an otherwise mundane routine. As the family face of the royal family's next generation, the Yorks spawned a whole industry of sentimental memorabilia and appeared on many magazine covers, but their cosy image was a far cry from the life of London's Bright Young Things. They were not part of the smart set, preferring the staider world of old society. Elizabeth still carried about her a sweetly old-fashioned aura. Virginia Woolf recognised her at the theatre in 1929 and saw 'a simple, chattering sweet-hearted, little round-faced young woman in pink . . . her wrists twinkling with diamonds, her dress held on the shoulder with diamonds'. Harold Nicolson, no less critical, was a good deal less dismissive after he met her while serving as chargé-d'affaires in Berlin. 'She and Cyril Connolly,' he wrote back to his wife Vita Sackville-West, 'are the only two people who have spoken intelligently about the 'landscape' element in *Some People*,' his recent book. Elizabeth was still young enough to love going out and parties. If she missed the fun, her Bowes-Lyon reticence would not let her show it. When it all got too much for her, she would retire to her bedroom with a minor ailment which managed to right itself as soon as the problem had passed. For the most part, she put her shoulder to the wheel and smiled, smiled, smiled.

Unlike David, the Yorks were not glamorous. Nobody wrote a song about dancing with a man who danced with a girl who danced with the Duke of York. They did not go dancing to Ambrose's Band at the Embassy Club, or skiing in St Moritz, or gambling in Deauville. Instead, Bertie rented houses in Northamptonshire to hunt with the Pytchley. 'Elizabeth could make a home anywhere,' he boasted proudly. Together the Yorks projected a comforting image for a nation exhausted by war and newly disillusioned with peace. David, though still Prince Charming to millions, was viewed by a significant minority as the standard-bearer of out-moded or distasteful values. His close association with the Royal British Legion identified him with the jingoistic, all-pull-together sentiments which were rapidly losing favour with bitter ex-servicemen who wanted work not words, housing not hurrahs. At the other end of the social spectrum, he was viewed as the playboy cheerleader of a privileged band of youthful socialites whom ordinary people resented.

By the late 1920s, members of the Prince of Wales's own staff, confronted by his mounting self-indulgence, were beginning to voice their concern about his suitability as a future monarch. Like a spoilt child David constantly complained about his lot — 'its just the chronic state of being the P of W — of which I'm so heartily and genuinely fed up' — and, when he felt like it, could be childishly provocative and wilful. Freda Dudley Ward was well aware of his capacity for bad behaviour, and so were dozens of other women with whom he had enjoyed brief flings. In 1920 when his contemporary, Alan 'Tommy'

Lascelles, joined David as his assistant private secretary, he thought at first, 'He is one of the most attractive men I've ever met.' Eight years later he had turned into one of the Prince of Wales's sternest critics, believing, as he was later to say, that, 'For some hereditary or physiological reason his mental and spiritual growth stopped dead in his adolescence thereby affecting his whole consequent behaviour.'

Prime Minister Stanley Baldwin was also forming the reluctant conclusion that the Prince was too immature to shoulder the great duties which lay ahead of him. Like Lascelles he had witnessed David's antics on a recent tour of Canada, during which the Prince of Wales and Prince George, his soulmate in self-destruction, had behaved appallingly. The two men met after Baldwin returned from Canada. Captain Lascelles had asked for the interview and, finding common ground with the Prime Minister, admitted that at times when the Heir Apparent was riding in a point-to-point, he 'couldn't help thinking that the best thing that could happen to him, and to the country, would be for him to break his neck.'

'God forgive me,' Baldwin replied, 'I have often thought the same.'

The final straw for Tommy Lascelles came when he accompanied David and his brother Prince Henry on a safari in Kenya in October 1928. Towards the end of the tour, coded telegrams began arriving from the Prime Minister announcing that the King was seriously ill and urging the Prince of Wales to cut short his holiday and hurry home. David was not impressed. He scoffed, 'It's just some election dodge of old Baldwin's. It doesn't mean anything.' Lascelles was forced to rejoin that it meant a great deal to the Prince's staff, even if it meant nothing to him. David responded to this by storming out and later told Lascelles that he had spent the remainder of the evening in the successful seduction of a Mrs Barnes, wife of the local Commissioner. Nevertheless he did hurry home. The King took one look at him, offered a customary greeting — 'Damn you, what the devil are you doing here?' — and immediately began to get better. Tommy Lascelles resigned his post.

Bertie tried to jolly his elder brother along. He had just been made a member of the Council of State and was feeling in a constitutional mood. For David's benefit he recounted 'a lovely story going about which emanated from the East End, that the reason of your rushing home is that in the event of anything happening to Papa I am going to bag the Throne in your absence!!! Just like the Middle Ages . . . ' But David was not in a humour to be amused. At the age of thirty-four he had been confronted by the appalling prospect of his destiny. The King might be recovering, but clearly it was only a matter of time before David's fate caught up with him. That winter, at the King's behest, he gave up steeple-chasing and sold his hunters. Tommy Lascelles and Stanley Baldwin may have been indifferent to the prospect of him breaking his neck; his father was not.

Bertie and Elizabeth offered him a welcome at their new home, 145 Piccadilly, an imposing Crown property which boasted twenty-five bedrooms, a ballroom and an electric lift. Now that Elizabeth had turned this dilapidated house into a home with a peach-coloured drawing-room and a nursery floor, it might have been almost as welcoming an address for David as Freda Dudley Ward's. The two brothers were getting along well together, and Bertie was showing signs of a new-found confidence which must have pleased his elder brother. Bertie now felt happy and fulfilled, after the ordeals of his earlier years. If his life were now to follow a tranquil and unglamorous path, so much the better. He could still beat his older brother at golf, easily. And there was the reassurance that their brotherly bond would hold David close to him, come what may, just as it had always done.

But David had no desire for the satisfaction of married domesticity, even at second-hand. By now he himself had taken up with someone else — a voluptuous American beauty called Thelma Furness, the loosely attached wife of the elderly shipping magnate, Viscount Furness, and the twin sister of Gloria Vanderbilt. David first laid eyes on her at a livestock show in Leicester in 1929. Six months later, he whisked her off to Kenya, to complete the safari that had been interrupted a year earlier. It was quite a holiday, if Viscountess Furness's description can be trusted — 'This was our Eden, and we were alone in it. His arms about me were the only reality; his words of love my only bridge to life. Borne along on the mounting tide of his ardour, I felt myself being inexorably swept from the accustomed moorings of caution. Each night I felt even more completely possessed by our love.' Thelma's breathless account continues, 'carried ever more swiftly into uncharted seas of feeling, content to let the prince chart the course, heedless of where the voyage would end.'

The sustained metaphor might have come straight out of a cheap novel but it was not misplaced. Thelma Furness encouraged the self-indulgence in David that Freda Dudley Ward had tried to curb. In her company the Prince, too, was 'swept from his moorings'. Thelma represented an escape, not just from his family and the oppressive restrictions of his royal duties, but from the whole stuffy, deferential British establishment in which he had a predetermined place. Whether or not Thelma Furness realised this, her successor in the Prince's affections certainly did. It was through Thelma that David came to know one of her newest American friends, a recent arrival in London. Wallis Spencer, née Warfield, had changed her name again. When, early in 1931, she first met the Prince of Wales, Thelma Furness introduced her, quite properly, as Mrs Simpson.

4

THE FEUD BEGINS

Wallis's second meeting with the Prince of
Wales, at Burrough Court, the Furness's hunting
lodge near Melton Mowbray, was almost as
fleeting as the one in San Diego a decade
earlier. She and her husband, Ernest Simpson,
had been invited at the last minute when other
friends of Thelma's had had to drop out of the
house-party. They travelled up through snow
and freezing fog and Wallis had a streaming cold
by the time they arrived. Alongside her hostess,
whose opulent good looks had been compared
by Cecil Beaton to the flower of a hothouse
magnolia, Wallis made little impact. When
in November 1936 Bernard Tussaud began
modelling her figure for the famous waxworks
museum, his notes read, 'High forehead, firm
jaw-line, Skin smooth, opaque. Hair is long,
dressed in plainest possible style, parted in
middle and fastened in a bun at nape of the
neck.' Cecil Beaton's first recollections of her
were of a somewhat brawny woman, raw-boned.
Her voice had a high nasal twang. She and
Ernest, ill at ease among people whose chief
interest was horses, struggled to remain part of
the conversation. During dinner, Wallis, in a bid
to attract the Prince's attention, reputedly leaned
forward in her seat opposite him and asked: 'Sir,

do you think me very like Rita Kruger?' (Rita Kruger was a woman the Prince had romanced in New York). 'Good God! no!' was the royal reply, whereupon the Prince turned back to his neighbour.

Twenty years later, David was to recall a spirited conversation he had with Wallis about the gulf between Britons and Americans some time over the course of that weekend. But for the most part he does not seem to have paid much attention to the Simpsons — and indeed, after Melton Mowbray, Wallis wondered if she would ever be introduced again. It was to be five months before this happened, and six months more (according to Wallis herself) before a third meeting. Nevertheless, it was in high excitement that she wrote swankily to Aunt Bessie. 'You can imagine what a treat it was to meet the Prince in such an informal way. It was quite an experience and as I've made up my mind to meet him ever since I've been here, I feel relieved.' For the moment, Wallis had her hands full trying to reconcile a circle of smart new acquaintances with her somewhat modest household and unexceptional middle-class existence. Along with Thelma's twin sister, Gloria Vanderbilt, she had now met their friend Nada, Marchioness of Milford Haven. 'It is nice for us to meet all these swell people,' she wrote again to Aunt Bessie, 'even if we can't keep up their pace!'

However, as Dorothea Simpson, Ernest's first wife, knew to her cost, the second Mrs Simpson was not easily defeated. Dorothea, herself a

151

divorcee, had married Ernest Simpson in 1923. Three years later he met Wallis and fell under her spell. As Dorothea wryly recalled, 'Wallis moved in and helped herself to my house and my clothes and, finally, to everything.' The final blow came when Ernest Simpson walked out on her while she was lying ill in hospital in Paris. The couple had a young daughter and Ernest a well-starched background, but by the beginning of 1928 he had divorced his first wife, left her and little Audrey in America and moved to London, where he married Wallis that July.

Wallis had also left her old life behind to start afresh in London. There had been fruitless attempts to patch things up with Win Spencer, including a couple of years in China which lent a certain exotic mystery to her past. Alone and back in Washington, she had enjoyed a few love affairs, but, as she wrote to her mother, 'I can't go on wandering the rest of my life and I really feel so tired of fighting the world all alone and with no money.' It was thus in a deliberate quest for security, and some much-needed respectability after ten mildly scandalous years, that she settled on Ernest Simpson and prised him away from his family. Wallis's reference to having no money was significant. In a deathbed display of disapproval at her pending divorce from Win, the previously pliable Uncle Sol had left his niece a mere $15,000 out of his railroad fortune. The balance had gone to the founding of a home for the distressed gentlewomen of Baltimore, where Uncle Sol had guaranteed Wallis a room should she ever need it.

In these circumstances, Ernest Simpson looked like a safe bet. Harold Nicolson in his memoirs called him 'a good-looking barber's block'. Wallis in *her* memoirs described him carefully as 'an unusually well-balanced man'. With antecedents on both sides of the Atlantic, Simpson was every American's idea of an English gentleman, pink-cheeked, square-jawed, dependable and punctilious, with a rectitude which could starch a collar at ten paces. Raised in New York and Harvard-educated, he was a passionate Anglophile who opted for a commission in the Coldstream Guards at the end of the First World War in preference to American citizenship. His father was head of a firm of ship brokers with offices in London and New York, and Ernest had every prospect of doing well under his patronage. Whatever cracks people might make during the abdication about the Unimportance of Being Ernest, he was a man to be reckoned with.

By all accounts, including Wallis's own, it seems that the new Mr and Mrs Simpson were quietly content with their early married life in London. Having bought a flat at 5 Bryanston Court off the Edgware Road, they frequented the smaller antique shops of Chelsea and Kensington in order to furnish it, bearing off a William and Mary walnut chest, a painted Italian table and several Queen Anne pieces. Ernest Simpson liked the theatre and the opera and, before they got to know many people, took Wallis on sightseeing weekends to stay in country hotels all over England. When they did begin to form a circle — mostly of Americans — they gave small punctiliously elegant dinner parties at Bryanston Court. Wallis Simpson's pursuit of excellence in all things led to her terrorising the local tradesmen in order to secure the best cuts for her guests. 'I cannot say,' she wrote in *The Heart Has Its Reasons*, 'that my fishmonger was . . . visibly elated by my habit of pressing the breastbone of a fowl to see whether it was tender, nor was the greengrocer other than disapproving at my punching and squeezing the fruits and vegetables to determine their quality. I knew all the cuts of beef; and, when the butcher failed to cut me the T-bone steak I wanted, I produced for him my *Fannie Farmer Cookbook*, with a diagram showing how to cut a steak the way I liked.'

Wallis's tales of extravagance belied the fact that by now the Simpsons were ground down by money worries. The shock waves from the Wall Street crash had hit international trade. Ernest's shipping business was foundering, and Wallis's father-in-law was failing to deliver the regular top-ups of cash she had been led to expect. 'Everything everywhere seems to get worse and worse and you can't help but be depressed by it all,' she wrote to complain to Aunt Bessie. 'We have nothing but a series of unpleasant business or family news . . . Mr Simpson [father] in a panic and so disagreeable. He would not give a penny as I wrote you. He chopped $3000 off the loan he had agreed to make E and as

154

you remember last year he did not give us an Xmas cheque.' Luckily for Wallis, Aunt Bessie had a soft heart. Her niece's moaning regularly had the desired effect and brought a cheque in time to keep the household afloat.

As part of her campaign for social acceptance, Wallis spent as much time as possible with Ernest's sister, Maud Kerr-Smiley, in whose house the Prince of Wales had first set eyes on Freda Dudley Ward. Through Mrs Kerr-Smiley she was introduced to Thelma Furness, with a warm recommendation from Thelma's glamorous and well-connected sister Consuelo Thaw — 'Mrs Simpson is fun. You will like her.' Her credentials were accepted, which is how it was that Wallis found herself rattling through the Midlands to Melton Mowbray on a foggy winter afternoon in 1931, powdering her reddened nose and practising how to curtsey in a railway carriage.

Six months later, when Wallis was presented at court, she strove to make up for that unpromising first meeting with the Prince. The Lord Chamberlain's office had only admitted her after it had first checked through her hastily cobbled-together divorce papers to confirm that she was the innocent party. Consuelo Thaw lent her a dress, and Thelma Furness the obligatory Prince of Wales feathers and fan. With the money she saved, Wallis splashed out on a striking aquamarine cross to go with the band of aquamarines that held her plumes in place. She was now ready to join nine other American women and a host of British debutantes when

155

they paraded before her next husband and his parents at the final court of the 1931 season.

As she glided forwards towards the thrones to do her 'bobbing' to the King and Queen, Wallis's sharp ears picked up an observation from the watching Prince of Wales to the effect that 'Something ought to be done about the lights: they make all the women look ghastly.' That evening Thelma Furness held a cocktail party to which the Simpsons were invited. Wallis saw another chance to make her mark with the Prince. This time she was more successful. As the heir to the throne politely complimented her on her gown, she countered pertly, 'But, sir, I understood that you thought we all looked ghastly.' This was perhaps the first time that David paid direct attention to Mrs Simpson, and evidently he liked what he saw. When Thelma's party broke up at 3 a.m. he offered the Simpsons a lift back to Bryanston Court. Wallis invited the Prince and his equerry, G. Trotter, in for a night-cap, which David declined with the apology, 'I'd very much like to see your flat one day; I'm told it's charming. But I have to be up so early. Still, if you would be kind enough to invite me again, I'd like to do so.'

However, it was the Prince who sent the first invitation. Seven months later, Ernest and Wallis were asked to spend the last weekend of January 1932 at Fort Belvedere, his private bolt-hole at Sunningdale, on the fringe of Windsor Great Park. 'What could you possibly want that queer old place for? Those damned weekends I suppose,' George V had grumbled when David

156

had asked in 1929 if he could have the use of it. Certainly, with Bertie settling so happily into family life, the Prince of Wales had felt the need for somewhere of his own — a retreat from the court, from his parents, and from the London social whirl. With the help of faithful Freda Dudley Ward, he had set about creating his very own place in the country.

Of the many mansions David was to live in, Fort Belvedere was his favourite. He had refused point blank to move, as his parents had wanted, into the regal grandeur of Marlborough House. Fort Belvedere, decorated simply for intimacy and comfort, represented a telling alternative to royal formality. More than any of his other houses, it bore his stamp. Lady Diana Cooper, a frequent visitor who knew the house and its master well, described it as 'a child's idea of a fort . . . it had battlements and cannon and cannon-balls and furnishings of war. It stood high on a hill, and the sentries, one thought, must be of tin . . . The house is an enchanting folly and only needs fifty red soldiers stood between the battlements to make it a Walt Disney coloured symphony toy.' In other words it was the perfect plaything for a spoilt little boy. To complete the atmosphere of an overgrown nursery, the drawing-room contained a long table built specially to hold the Prince's jigsaws, 'the largest and most intricate to be obtained', according to one breathless American commentator at the time.

The sight of this table would have warmed Wallis's heart: completing jigsaw puzzles was the closest she and David were ever to stray towards an intellectual pursuit. In other respects the domestic life of the world's most eligible bachelor must have come as a surprise to her; it was 'a model of sedateness', she later recalled. The Prince did needlepoint in the evenings, a comforting reminder of his mother's boudoir where, as he sat at her feet, Queen Mary had taught him to sew and knit. Like his brother Bertie he had a passion for gardening, although whereas Bertie enjoyed cultivating plants, David enjoyed nothing so much as hacking away at the laurel bushes and dense undergrowth to create space for himself. In this task he expected all his male guests — even Ernest Simpson, who disliked hearty exercise — to lend a hand. Fort Belvedere was his, and he could do what he liked in it with whomsoever he liked, far away from his father's critical gaze. He could dress the way he wanted, for instance. Every Saturday evening, his weekend guests would be treated to the sight of their host in Highland dress, sporting one of the many kilts he was entitled to wear, topped with a dark blue tunic fastened with silver buttons over an inside collar of fine white lawn. He loved to make a lot of noise, marching around the house and grounds in his kilt playing tunes on the bagpipes, while his guests patiently waited for him to finish. He also strummed on the ukelele.

The Simpsons were not alone in feeling the pinch in the early 1930s. The royal family were themselves having to tighten their belts. Both the King and the Prince of Wales put £50,000 apiece into the national exchequer. Bertie did his bit by giving up hunting with the Pytchley and selling his half-dozen hunters for less than a thousand guineas. Perhaps as a compensation his father gave him a country house as well — Royal Lodge, which was also in Windsor Great Park, not far from David at the Fort. In these cash-conscious times, the Yorks reined in their spending on their new home and limited their improvements to restoring the great saloon, and in due course adding a few bathrooms and a new wing.

In the spring of 1932 their household was joined by Marion Crawford, a governess whom they came to know — and after her later indiscretions despise — as Crawfie. The anodyne picture of the Yorks' home life that she gave in her 1950 book *The Little Princesses* appears so sweetly innocuous by modern standards that her treatment by the royal family, who cut her out of their lives immediately and for ever, seems callously disproportionate. But Crawfie made the mistake of underestimating the Bowes-Lyon taste for privacy, especially when it came to the children. 'No one ever had employers who interfered so little,' she wrote tellingly of her early days with the Yorks. 'I had the feeling that the Duke and Duchess, most happy in their own married life, were not over concerned with the higher education of their daughters.' On this subject their grandparents could not resist putting their oar in. George V insisted that Margaret and Lilibet should be taught 'to write a decent hand'. 'I like a hand with

159

some character in it.' Queen Mary suggested that her granddaughters might benefit from the study of genealogies and the geography of the Empire. To that end, on her fourth birthday, Lilibet was given a set of building blocks made from fifty different timbers grown in various parts of her grandfather's vast realm. Normally her parents preferred less sophisticated games like Snap and, naturally, Happy Families. The children's education took place in a leisurely manner following an undemanding curriculum based upon handwriting, and stories taken from the Bible, fairy tales and 'anything we can find about horses and dogs'.

Dogs were important to the princesses, if not to the staff in whose memories 1933 was grimly registered, in Lady Longford's words, as 'the year of the corgi'. In a family where everyone was known by several different names, Rozavel Golden Eagle became Dookie and soon started drawing blood from the royal household who, unlike the dogs, were muzzled from complaining. Bertie had his yellow labradors to keep the corgi dynasty company, and there were ponies and horses to complete the image of open-air informality of which the nation never tired. It even touched David who told his sister-in-law one evening as he left, 'You make family life look such fun.' As close neighbours, the brothers paid frequent visits to each other's homes. Elizabeth liked mixing with David's smart friends at the Fort; it rekindled memories from a decade earlier when she had been a leading light of the social firmament. By the early 1930s, motherhood and a healthy appetite had contributed to her putting on a considerable amount of weight. The eyes still sparkled, the smile was still radiant, but the gamine face had filled out. Elizabeth was showing signs of becoming matronly.

Thelma Furness was no emaciated waif herself, which may have helped foster Elizabeth's liking of her. At Fort Belvedere they could all let their hair down and frequently did. Their father's taste in music tended to the ceremonial and sententious. After dinners at Windsor or Buckingham Palace, King George would commonly make his children and guests listen to marches and military airs, played by a small orchestra crammed behind a grille. David and Bertie especially loathed the King's particular favourite, called 'The Departure of the Troopship'. At the Fort, music was for fun and dancing. On one visit Bertie noticed a stack of 78 rpm records sent to David from the States. 'Come on, David, let's see if they really are unbreakable as the label says,' Bertie is supposed to have urged his older brother. Out on the terrace they hurled the records skywards and watched them crash, but not smash, on the flagstones. Bertie then demanded some target practice and, as Thelma Furness recalled, 'While the brothers roared with laughter, the Duke had us ducking and dodging like rabbits.'

One freezing day at the end of January 1933, Virginia Water, the lake near the Fort, froze over for the first time in living memory, forming an irresistible skating rink. Of the three women in the party, neither Thelma nor Elizabeth had ever skated, so when skates were found for them, Bertie brought out a couple of kitchen chairs for them to hold on to. Together they slithered and slid across the icy surface. Recalling the gales of laughter that afternoon, Thelma wrote warmly about Elizabeth, 'I remember thinking at the time that if I ever had to live in a bungalow in a small town, this is the woman I would most like to have as a next-door neighbour to gossip with while hanging out the washing in our backyards.'

Mrs Simpson, the third woman that afternoon, was never to express such enthusiasm for the 'Dowdy Duchess', or 'Cookie', as she came to call Elizabeth derisively. But then, she also made sure she did not have to skate alongside her, holding on to an old chair. In her youth Wallis had learned to roller-skate: she took off with the boys.

At the time of the Simpsons' first visit early in 1932, Thelma Furness was very obviously the lady of the moment — 'the Princess of Wales', Wallis described her in a letter to Aunt Bessie — and hostess of the Fort. Wallis was content with the arrangement: after all it had been through Thelma's introductions and Thelma's patronage that she, Wallis, had been able to soar to such dizzy social heights. But the sharp-witted, irreverent Mrs Simpson had obviously begun to amuse and intrigue the Prince. By now, with Ernest happily in tow, she had spent several weekends at Fort Belvedere. What was more, the signs of a deeper compatibility with the Prince were already visible. At Christmas,

162

David had given her a table for the drawing-room at Bryanston Court and discovered that, just as his mother used to do, Wallis made sure of the acceptability of the present by choosing it herself.

Wallis's direct pursuit of anything she wanted did not surprise those who knew her well. Somebody who did not know her at all was the German handwriting expert Gusti Osterreicher who was shown a sample of Wallis's handwriting by someone close to events during the abdication crisis. This is her verdict on the unknown writer: 'A woman with a strong male inclination in the sense of activity, vitality and initiative, she *must* dominate, she *must* have authority, and without sufficient scope for her powers can become disagreeable . . . In the pursuit of her aim she can be most inconsiderate, and can hurt, but on the whole she is not without some instincts of nobility and generosity . . . She is ambitious and demands above all that her undertakings should be noticed and valued. In the physical sense of the word sadistic, cold, overbearing, vain.'

This devastating character assessment was to be echoed by one of Wallis's closest intimates, the American businessman Herman Rogers who had known her since she stayed with the Rogers family in Peking. He famously described Wallis as the most selfish woman he had ever met. She was witty, and had a steely charm: but she was also assertive, demanding, brusque when she felt like it, and what we would today describe as refreshingly un-English in that she was wholly unfazed by rank, and totally undeferential even

163

in the presence of royalty.

No English subject in those days could have felt the freedom to behave as Mrs Simpson did. Sir Samuel Hoare, then Secretary of State for India, described Wallis as attractive and intelligent, when he first met her, but also 'very American with little or no knowledge of English life'. Had it not been for her predecessor, Lady Furness, she might never have captured the interest of the Prince of Wales, even if she had eventually been introduced to him. Thelma Furness, declared Chips Channon, was the mistress who first 'modernized him and Americanized him, making him over-democratic, casual and a little common'. To accuse poor Thelma, as Chips Channon did in his diary as the abdication loomed, of bearing 'the true blame for this drama' was manifestly unfair to a warm-hearted woman who throughout her life was more sinned against than sinning. But it is true that she paved the way for Mrs Simpson.

There were other more complex reasons for how Mrs Simpson's personality came to captivate the Prince. To find them, we must look at what he had become as the excitement of the war years faded, and what seemed like monotonous years of 'princing' lay ahead. The Prime Minister Stanley Baldwin had come to the conclusion that the Prince 'is an abnormal being, half child, half genius'. The Prince did indeed have all the best attributes of a child — directness, inquisitiveness and zest for life — but with them went a childish lack of self-control, an inability to concentrate, and a

164

tendency to give way to tantrums if his whims were not indulged. The black dog of depression hounded him: his familiar name for it as we have seen from his letters to Freda Dudley Ward was 'the black, black mist'. Not mature enough to handle these mood swings he often allowed them to affect his public role, cancelling long-established arrangements at short notice, or keeping people waiting for hours and then sulking when he did appear.

He had confessed to Tommy Lascelles on the day he resigned from his service, 'I suppose the fact of the matter is that I'm quite the wrong sort of person to be Prince of Wales.' Lascelles, who had not minced words about what he thought of the Prince's self-indulgent way of life — 'I always feel as if I were working, not for the next King of England, but for the son of the latest American millionaire' — was touched, despite himself, because it 'was so pathetically true'.

The Prince had no sense of history or of his place in it, according to another courtier, Godfrey Thomas, a diplomat who was David's private secretary for seventeen years until the abdication. This accounted for his belief that, 'provided he carries out his public duties to the satisfaction of the Press and the man in the street, his private life is entirely his own concern'. Even in the early 1920s Thomas foresaw disaster ahead. Privately, the Prince had few interests apart from women, nightclubs and golf. Publicly, his disaffection with his royal role was evident enough for him to show boredom at the very suggestion of official engagements.

Increasingly, too, David was becoming isolated. His household had lost respect for him. His ill-concealed resentment of his position, the 'silly stunting' as he had been known to refer to it, 'all that silly artificial nonsense', diminished their own sense of worth. Nor did he see his parents on any intimate or regular basis. Once he had established his own household at York House in St James's Palace, he had given up his habitual pre-dinner visits to his mother. Freda Dudley Ward was the recipient of many of his more whingeing confidences, couched in that curious mixture of arrogance and diffidence which is the hallmark of people of low self-esteem. 'If only the British public really knew what a weak, powerless misery their press-made national hero was, they would have a nasty shock and be not only disappointed but d — d angry too.' The British public were not to know, until it was too late, and their unstinted adulation further spoiled his character. Fortunately, he had an ally still in the family, his faithful brother, the Duke of York. As always, Bertie loyally tried to bridge the gap between the Prince of Wales and his family. 'We must all help him to get back to our way of thinking.'

The Duke and Duchess of York had naturally been overjoyed when a suitable potential consort appeared on the horizon, and they were the first to meet her. As was often the case with David, they received an impetuous telephone call inviting them and the friend who was dining with them to come round immediately to York House. When they arrived, they found

166

the Prince of Wales dancing with the proud and beautiful Princess Marina of Greece, with whom he continued to dance for the rest of the evening, 'an hour or two or three'. After Rosemary Leveson-Gower, Princess Marina was the only single woman to whom David was attracted with any spark of enthusiasm, but Freda Dudley Ward came back to London the following day, and that was the end of that. Nevertheless David did appreciate her beauty and when in 1934 she married his brother George, the Duke of Kent, they became his allies within the family, displacing Bertie and Elizabeth who enjoyed a staider lifestyle. As for Freda, and the mistress who followed her, the message was clear: never leave the Prince alone for long. Like nature, the Prince of Wales abhorred a vacuum and looked around for someone with whom to fill it.

Thelma Furness knew him well enough to understand this, and as part of her planning for a trip to America in the first three months of 1934, she asked Wallis to help her out. Both women give an account of this in their memoirs. Not surprisingly, the accounts differ. Hearing that her friend was going to be away until Easter, Wallis is supposed to have commented, 'Oh, Thelma, the little man is going to be so lonely.'

'Well, dear,' Lady Furness recalls having answered. 'You look after him for me while I'm away. See that he does not get into any mischief.'

Whether out of a misplaced sense of her own control over the Prince, or a disregard for

167

Wallis's potential as a rival, Thelma misjudged the situation disastrously — the more so because of an extreme public shipboard romance she indulged in on the way home with the celebrated roué, Prince Aly Khan, news of which came to David's ears.

Thelma left for America shortly after Christmas. At the end of January 1934 Wallis disingenuously reported to Aunt Bessie that she was 'feeling lost' without her friend. Meanwhile, she went on, she and Ernest had been spending time at the Fort, where she had 'tried my best to cheer [the Prince] up'. Ten days after Thelma had sailed for New York, the Simpsons were invited to dine with David at the Dorchester. No doubt thinking selflessly of the Prince's loneliness, Wallis made haste to accept. Now, with Thelma safely out of the way, she saw her chance to move in and took it. The Duke of Windsor's memoirs detail the exact moment he finally began to see Wallis in a romantic light. It was that evening at the Dorchester, in the course of which, according to Wallis's memoirs, the Prince began talking about his work. Then, checking himself, he apologised for boring her. 'On the contrary,' she replied, 'I couldn't be more interested. Please, please go on.'

Wallis probably recognised the look that came into his eyes. She had been working to achieve it for long enough through her teenage years, when she had studied the boys she was attracted to in detail, learning how best to flatter them and pander to their interests. The stakes were higher this time, but the game was the same.

168

When David evidently answered, 'Wallis, you're the only woman who's ever been interested in my job,' she knew that at last her strategy was working. Thelma Furness, scatty, good-natured, unpossessive and (most telling of all) absent, was no match for Mrs Simpson. Now that she finally had awakened the Prince's interest, Wallis used the remaining time Thelma was away ruthlessly to shed her rivals.

Already, David had betrayed Freda Dudley Ward whose relationship with him, comforting and undemanding as it now was, meandered on. His flattering words to Wallis had been a gross injustice to Mrs Dudley Ward who had not only taken a close and detailed interest in every part of his public work, but had joined him only a few months earlier in helping to start the Feathers Club Association to give aid to the unemployed — a commitment that she continued to fulfil well into old age. All this was forgotten, as David threw himself into his new affair, the start of an obsession which would last until the end of his days.

The day after the dinner at the Dorchester, the Prince of Wales had cocktails at Bryanston Court and stayed so late he had to be offered supper. Weekends at the Fort multiplied; so did visits to nightclubs, and dinners alone with Mrs Simpson. Wallis wrote to Aunt Bessie of night after night with the Prince going on till 4 a.m., then, winsomely, 'I am sure the gossip will now be that I am his latest.' She asked through Aunt Bessie for Thelma to bring her back a dress, adding soothingly, 'It's all gossip about the Prince. I'm not in the habit of taking my girlfriends' beaux.' But she obviously still felt obliged to offer Aunt Bessie some kind of explanation: 'I think I amuse him,' she wrote of the Prince, 'and we like to dance together — but I always have Ernest hanging round my neck so all is safe.' Such an obviously disdainful reference to her husband said it all: in Wallis's eyes, Ernest was already disposable.

Thelma was quick to realise the sea-change in her relationship with the Prince. After a strained reunion with him at her London home, she drove the Simpsons to the Fort on Good Friday. At dinner the following evening she saw that 'the Prince and Wallis seemed to have little private jokes'. Once he picked up a piece of salad with his fingers: Wallis playfully slapped his hand. Thelma gave a look to warn Wallis that she was daring too much in her familiarity, but the look she got back showed that her friend needed no advice from her. 'I knew then that she had looked after him exceedingly well,' Thelma wrote in her memoirs. 'That one cold, defiant glance had told me the entire story.'

The following morning, Easter Day, Thelma Furness left the Fort. She would never see or hear from David again. Nor, when as Duke of Windsor he came to write his memoirs, did he see fit to mention the woman who had introduced him to his future wife. Bertie showed greater loyalty. Twelve years later, as King George VI, he spoke warmly to Lady Furness when she came with one of her sons to receive the Victoria Cross awarded posthumously to his brother.

Less than a couple of months after Wallis had seen off Thelma Furness, it was the turn of Freda Dudley Ward. Freda's oldest daughter, Penelope, to whom as a child the Little Prince had shown such affection, had been seriously ill and for some weeks had occupied all her mother's thoughts. When she was on the road to recovery, Freda telephoned York House, as she had done regularly for so long, and asked to speak to the Prince of Wales. The switchboard operator, who knew and liked her well, found it hard to reply, so great was her distress.

'I have something so terrible to tell you that I don't know how to say it,' she blurted out. 'I have orders not to put you through.' Sixteen years of love, discretion and devoted friendship were snuffed out in a casual order to a switchboard operator. Prince George showed some loyalty to her, as did Louis Mountbatten, but the Prince of Wales expunged Freda Dudley Ward completely from his mind, refusing even to acknowledge a charming letter from one of her daughters. Like Lady Furness, Freda did not merit so much as a mention in his memoirs.

Her two greatest rivals disposed of, Wallis began to tighten her grip on the Prince's life. She began with the Fort. 'She ploughed it up,' in the words of one member of staff, dismissing servants, meddling in the kitchen and generally creating an atmosphere of tension and paranoia. Apparently happy to abase himself before such a forceful dominatrix, the Prince of Wales saw

171

no reason not to give her equally free rein over the household servants. Nor was Ernest Simpson yet prepared to have it out with his wife. Whether or not he was also under her thumb, the snob in him basked in reflected glory, as people of consequence came to know of the heir to the throne's infatuation with his wife. To Mrs Merryman (Aunt Bessie) in New York he declared, 'I'm a British subject, and it's an honour for me to have the Prince sit at my table and accept us as his friends. Wallis isn't alarmed; neither am I.' But Aunt Bessie was. When she questioned her niece's new relationship, Wallis wrote in reply that, 'If Ernest raises any objections to the situation I shall give the prince up at once. So far things are going along beautifully and the 3 of us are always together in the little spare time PW has at this time of year.' In an earlier letter she had openly gloated, 'Thelma is in Paris. I'm afraid her rule is over . . . since I've produced PW several places, we are filled with invitations from many sources who have been quiet up to now. Wouldn't mother have loved it all?'

In the summer of 1934, Wallis with Aunt Bessie as chaperone (Ernest was in America on business) spent a month with the Prince's party in a rented house in Biarritz. Here Wallis revealed the peevish side of her character, complaining that she was not being introduced to all the influential British people she felt sure were also holidaying there. Things improved in September. Aunt Bessie departed for Italy, and the royal party sailed for the Mediterranean on the yacht *Rosaura* which had been chartered from Lord Moyne. The Prince's equerry, John Aird, noted that 'the Prince has lost all confidence in himself and follows W around like a dog'. For Wallis it was, as she less than tactfully told Ernest Simpson, like being 'Wallis in Wonderland'. Henceforward, Ernest would refer to the Prince of Wales as 'Peter Pan'.

As the American press began for the first time to speculate on the Prince's new friendship, the Court Circular in London carried the news of the engagement of the King's youngest son, Prince George, to David's dancing partner from the year before, Princess Marina of Greece. For Bertie and Elizabeth, the news was a mixed blessing. Had David married Marina, not only would it have scotched what they had already come to see as the pernicious influence of Wallis Simpson, it would also have ensured for the Prince an orthodox position at the very pinnacle of established society, from which the succession could be assured and the monarchy kept safe for another generation.

On the other hand, through her marriage to the Duke of Kent, Princess Marina might provide the solution to an even more unsavoury family problem — her new husband. To all outward appearances, the King's youngest surviving son was the most gifted of them all. He was taller and, if anything, better looking than his eldest brother. Seven years younger than Bertie, he had escaped the stifling tutorial influence of Henry Hansell, adopting a carefree independence which enabled him to shrug off his

173

father's stubborn, angry interference with more insouciance than his older brothers. Queen Mary was closer to George than any of her children, sharing with him her love of *objets d'art* and finery. He was quick-witted, a good pianist and an asset to any party. No wonder David found him such congenial company. As young blades about town, the brothers lived together at York House and George had a room set aside for him at the Fort.

George V did not entirely lose control of his youngest boy. George was bundled into the Navy, as unhappily as David had been. In 1929, aged twenty-seven, he made his escape and quickly set off after the Prince of Wales to make up for lost time. Following David's lead, George had a string of affairs with upper-class girls and showed enough interest in at least two of them, Poppy Baring and Lois Sturt, for his father to issue an embargo on both as future royal brides, much as he had ordered an end to Bertie's relationship with Sheila Loughborough some years earlier.

The King's anxieties about 'fast' women were soon overtaken by worse fears. Prince George revelled not just in experimenting with novel sensations but in taking them as far as he could go. Bisexual, he was taken up by the raunchier element of the 1920s showbusiness mafia. His name was linked to several notable homosexuals, among them Noël Coward. He enjoyed wearing scent and make-up, frequented transvestite clubs in London, and on one occasion was picked up by the police wearing women's clothes. Rumours circulated of incriminating letters he had written to a young male prostitute in Paris, and of the high blackmail price that had had to be paid by the Prince of Wales to retrieve them. Certainly, George had been heavily involved with drugs, having been introduced to them by a lively American girl, Kiki Preston, in 1928.

In the late 1920s and 1930s cocaine was the smart society drug, freely available in the louche circles in which Prince George moved. His indulgence in this, and in morphine, must have been more recreational than addictive, since a brief spell of cold turkey in the country under the supervision of David, helped by Freda Dudley Ward, cured him with no lasting ill-effects. Here, the Prince of Wales could be seen at his best, shutting himself away with his brother, playing the role, in his words, of 'doctor, gaoler and detective combined', giving up his holiday to sit by Prince George's sickbed, and meanwhile poking away at his needlepoint to soothe his nerves. He continued to worry about his brother for several years afterwards, telling his mother with no apparent self-irony, 'He seems to lack all sense of knowing what is so obviously the wrong thing to do.' For once, David had the admiration of his family. 'Looking after [George] all those months must have been a great strain on you,' the King wrote with warm approval, 'and I think it was wonderful all you did for him.'

After five years as David's sidekick, however, George needed bringing to heel and it was his good fortune that one of the most beautiful and aristocratic women in Europe was prepared to take on the task. Freda Dudley Ward, who knew more than most about the affection of princes, was in no doubt that George was very much in love with Princess Marina. The newly engaged couple were ideally matched, as the crowds greeting her arrival at Victoria Station recognised. 'Don't change — don't let them change you!' they shouted to the royal fiancée. Marina, a royal princess in her own right and very conscious of her lineage, did not.

At the ball held to celebrate Princess Marina's wedding to the newly created Duke of Kent in November 1934, the royal bride-to-be dressed understatedly in a simply-cut white evening dress. Wallis, on the other hand, who was being presented to the King and Queen that evening by the Prince for the first and only time, had taken care to appear anything but understated. All eyes followed her in her strikingly outré violet lamé dress, slashed by a vivid green sash and set off by a tiara borrowed from Cartier. (The Prince of Wales had not as yet thought of giving Wallis her own tiara, although she was wearing the diamond and emerald charm he had given her that summer.) Already disturbed by her presence — George V had already scratched her name from the guest list once — the King and Queen were horrified by her appearance, her 'metallic elegance', as Ronald Tree was to describe it. Until now Wallis had only been an unpleasant rumour: now she was a distasteful reality, even though as yet they had no idea of the extent of her hold over their eldest son. Queen Mary told Lady Airlie later that she 'had shaken hands with her without thinking much about it'. For the moment, Ernest was still in evidence, a bystander allowed along to maintain some semblance of decorum.

All evening the Prince of Wales brought friends and relations to be introduced to Wallis, making it clear how important she was to him. As Prince Christopher of Greece was being taken over to be introduced, he asked the Prince, 'Mrs Simpson, who is she?'

'An American,' the Prince replied, then smiled. 'She's wonderful.'

'The two words told me everything,' Prince Christopher later recalled. 'It was as though he had said: 'She is the only woman in the world.' '

Prince Paul of Yugoslavia, brother-in-law of the bride-to-be, could hardly contain his enthusiasm. 'Mrs Simpson, there is no question about it,' he exclaimed, 'you are wearing the most striking gown in the room.'

Mrs Simpson, brash, skinny and triumphant in her shimmering violet sheath, also curtsied to the Duchess of York, a soft, well-rounded figure in old-fashioned orchid pink. It was a meeting neither of minds nor of temperaments. As Wallis curtsied, she looked up to meet what she later remembered as 'the almost startling blueness' of the Duchess of York's eyes regarding her coolly. Lady Hardinge of Penshurst, the Duchess's friend who was also present, was to recall the evening to the historian Michael Thornton. 'I am afraid Mrs Simpson went down badly with the Duchess from the word go. It may have been the rather ostentatious dress, or the fact that she allowed the Prince of Wales to push her forward in what seemed an inappropriate manner. The Duchess was never discourteous in my experience, but those of us who knew her very well could always tell when she did not care for something or someone, and it was very apparent to me that she did not care for Mrs Simpson at all.' Wallis would never experience in the company of the Duchess the naturalness, warmth and moments of shared high spirits which Thelma Furness so appreciated. As yet there was no feud, but the battle lines were being drawn.

The Yorks' spirits must have sunk further at the Duke of Kent's wedding, where Wallis and Ernest occupied two of the best seats. That Christmas of 1934 David delegated the present-buying for his 250 staff to Wallis, and further offended them by inviting her own staff from Bryanston Court to gather round the servants' Christmas tree at York House. Meanwhile, he showered presents on Wallis at every opportunity: two jewelled bracelets, a diamond hair clip, and a cairn puppy called Mr Loo, known to the Prince as Slipper. In photographs Wallis's face always looks softer when she is holding a small dog.

Following family tradition, the Duke of York took his wife and daughters to Sandringham for Christmas, where he saw at first-hand the effect that anxiety about David's obsession with Mrs Simpson was having on their ailing father. No longer able to bully his eldest son, as he had done in childhood, George V had no other means of communication to fall back on. He grumbled to others, telling his old friend Count Mensdorff, 'He has not a single friend who is a gentleman.' When Mensdorff argued that the Prince had many qualities, the King replied, 'Yes, certainly. That is the pity. If he were a fool we would not mind.' Yet George V refused to have it out with his son directly, perhaps conscious that he had no effectual sanctions should David simply defy him. He said nothing when David whisked Wallis away for a skiing holiday in Kitzbühel, followed by visits to Vienna and Budapest. The American press pursued the couple and plastered the story across the United States and, more damagingly for the royal family, across the border into royalist Canada. 'Suggestive stories', in the words of the King's private secretary Sir Clive Wigram, were beginning to circulate in well-informed circles at home, but British newspapers maintained their complicit silence about the antics of the heir apparent and his married mistress.

Wallis's self-confidence was growing. Almost a year had passed since Thelma Furness and Freda Dudley Ward had been removed from the stage, a year in which she had held the Prince of Wales's full attention. In February, when she returned with him from a skiing holiday *à deux* in Kitzbühel, she found herself the quarry of society hostesses like Sibyl Colefax and her arch-rival, Emerald Cunard. She could feel, she was to write later, 'a rising curiosity concerning me'. She was aware of 'new doors opening, and a heightened interest even in my casual remarks'. She was, she admitted, 'stimulated; I was excited; I felt as if I were borne upon a rising wave that seemed to be carrying me ever more rapidly and even higher. Now I began to savour the true brilliance and sophistication of the life of London.' By the spring of 1935 she felt ready to assert her ascendancy over David in the eyes of his family. Knowing that Elizabeth strongly, if silently, disapproved of her, Wallis developed a party piece that mimicked the voice and mannerisms of the Dowdy Duchess. Early in 1935 Elizabeth caught her at it when she entered the drawing-room at Fort Belvedere. This was a defining moment in the relationship between two proud and implacable women. Elizabeth was an accomplished mimic herself, but to find herself being lampooned in front of guests by her brother-in-law's mistress made her Bowes-Lyon blood boil. According to one of those guests present, it was at this point that the Duchess of York's dislike of Wallis hardened into real hostility.

As the weeks passed and the flightier elements of society vied to curry favour with the mistress of Bryanston Court, the politician and socialite Chips Channon, who like Ernest Simpson was all the more snobbish for being an American by birth, wrote of Wallis in his diary: 'she has already the air of a personage who walks into a room as though she almost expected to be curtsied to. At least, she wouldn't be too surprised. She has complete power over the Prince of Wales.' Evidence of that power was

180

there for all to see at the time of George V's Silver Jubilee on 6 May 1935. Wallis wanted a prime spot from which to watch the procession. The Prince of Wales, caught between his father's refusal to allow Mrs Simpson inside the palace and Wallis's insistence on a ring-side seat, asked the King's assistant private secretary, Alec Hardinge, to provide a suitable vantage point in his own home overlooking the route for a couple of 'scullery maids' in David's household. The scullery maids who took their places at the Hardinges' bedroom window were Wallis and a friend. The Little Prince's mantra to the Dudley Ward girls, 'Anything to please!', was now being chanted to a woman who would test that mantra to the full.

Up at Alec Hardinge's window Wallis would not have heard the greeting that met the Duke of York and his Smiling Duchess as they drove out of Buckingham Palace in a state landau, together with Lilibet and Margaret Rose. 'There goes the hope of England!' one man shouted from the crowd as the landau passed, Bertie waving shyly. In private King George was forming the same opinion. The court ball, which opened the season one week later, was the final nail in the coffin of David's relationship with his father. Having refused to admit Wallis to any of the events of the Jubilee season, the old King relented only after David swore to him solemnly that Mrs Simpson was not his mistress. Sir Clive Wigram's subsequent assertion to George V that his son had lied was based on the positive assurance of all the Prince's staff that he slept with Wallis, although none of them was in a position to know whether she was his mistress in the full sense of the word. However, the King had no reason to disbelieve his private secretary, and watched stone-faced as David danced Wallis past him at the ball.

At the end of the evening, George V said not a word as David escorted him to the door of his private chambers, not even to wish his son goodnight. But to a close friend, Lady Algernon Gordon-Lennox, he later confided, 'I pray to God that my eldest son will never marry and have children, and that nothing will come between Bertie and Lilibet and the throne.' And to his Prime Minister, Stanley Baldwin, he predicted with chilling accuracy, 'After I am dead the boy will ruin himself within twelve months.'

The tension that night would have been felt by Bertie and Elizabeth. Eleven years earlier Elizabeth had been David's chosen partner to start the dancing at the court ball — now she was being upstaged. There would be uncomfortable reminders of this throughout the 1935 season. George V baled out of Ascot that summer and buried himself away at Sandringham, leaving the Duke and Duchess of York to keep up the legitimate royal presence, while David strolled through the Royal Enclosure with Wallis on his arm. Although their own visits to the Fort had dropped off since Wallis had taken control, Bertie and Elizabeth were kept informed by gossiping courtiers about the state of the affair. Stories would have got back to them

182

Queen Victoria ('Gangan') at Osborne, surrounded by her York great-grandchildren.

May, Duchess of York, proudly shows off her firstborn, the future Edward VIII, to her mother the Duchess of Teck, herself a granddaughter of George III and wife to an emotional weakling.

The royal children. Prince John, the youngest, an epileptic, is in front of Prince Albert on the left.

The Prince of Wales with his father, King George V.

The Prince of Wales talking to French and Italian officers during the First World War. 'It was a real eye-opener,' he said, after a night spent in the trenches.

The Prince of Wales and his cousin
Lord Louis Mountbatten fooling for the camera
during a fishing trip in New Zealand in 1920.

The Duke of York playing doubles in the 1926
Wimbledon Tennis Championships.

Freda Dudley Ward, wife of a Liberal MP and the Prince of Wales's 'darling, darling beloved Fredie Wedie'. (*DailyMail*)

The Duke of York with Elizabeth Bowes-Lyon in January 1923, after she finally consented to marry him. 'Bertie is supremely happy,' wrote his mother.

The Duchess of York encourages her apprehensive husband at the opening of the Australian Parliament in Canberra at which he had to speak.

Wallis photographed on 3 December 1936 – the day the news broke of her affair with the King, and a few hours before she fled to the south of France.

The Duke of Windsor
with his unsavoury
Nazi host, during his
ill-advised 1937 visit to
the Third Reich.

Back in England in September 1939, after three years
away, the Windsors were confronted, in Wallis's words,
'with a barrier of turned backs'.

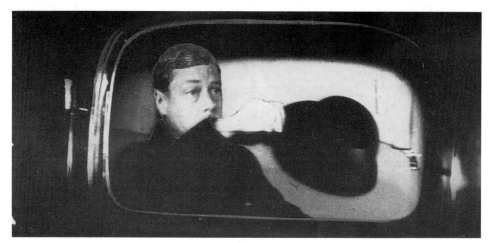

The King leaving Marlborough House after discussing the abdication crisis with his mother. (*Daily Mirror*)

The strain shows as the Duke of Windsor meets his mother, Queen Mary, in October 1945.

about David's humiliating subservience to Mrs Simpson. They would have heard about the country house-party, when the Prince of Wales asked for a light and Wallis, in full view of other guests, made him squat down and beg for it like a dog. Bertie would have got wind of David's indiscretion during the Naval Review in July when, unable to see Wallis for two days, he used the wireless on board HMS *Faulknor* to send two telegrams via public telegraph operators direct to Bryanston Court. Elizabeth almost certainly knew, what she would anyway have guessed, that Wallis was getting money from David. A sum of £6000 a year was bruited, and there were rumours that Wallis and Ernest together were out to soak the Prince of Wales for all they could get. This under-estimation of Wallis Simpson extended to the Prince's own immediate staff. In Cannes that summer his equerry, John Aird, wrote in his diary, 'I feel she is getting tired of the pace and having secured the cash will chuck her hand in.'

At the close of the London season, the Duke and Duchess of York did their duty at Cowes and then headed north with the little princesses to shoot and stalk in Scotland, as everyone expected the royal family to do. David meanwhile, the epitome of a modern prince, was holidaying on the Riviera surrounded by cosmopolitan socialites, though once again spared the company of Ernest Simpson, who coincidentally was making a long-planned visit to the States. As at Fort Belvedere, Wallis took charge of the Prince's domestic arrangements, planning menus, seating arrangements and guest lists. 'Have the table moved back as far as possible and if the Vs are coming there would be far more room for 10 if the Finn could produce chairs without arms,' began one of her notes to the Prince of Wales. 'Here is a suggestion for seating,' it continued. 'I would also have two sorts of cocktails and white wine offered as well as vin rosé, the servants to serve the wine. Also I didn't see a green vegetable on the menu. Sorry to bother you but I like everyone to think you do things well.' The little girl who waited at table on her mother's boarders in Baltimore had come a long way. David, who had been waited on hand and foot all his life, now did as he was told.

The presence of the Vs — Sir Robert Vansittart and his wife — was in part a token of the growing concern among officials about the Prince and Mrs Simpson. Sir Robert was Permanent Under-Secretary at the Foreign Office. Along with the security services, the FO was beginning to wonder about Wallis's influence on the political views of the heir to the throne, especially in the light of the interest now being taken in Mrs Simpson by the German Embassy in London, which had invited her to dinner in July. The Prince of Wales in fact needed little encouragement from Wallis. He was strongly pro-German, at a time when Hitler's treatment of German Jews was scarcely known abroad, and when appeasers in the Cabinet were actually pushing through an Anglo-German Naval Accord which would allow Berlin to build up her naval power.

184

The Vansittarts in fact sat at Wallis's table as friends of the Prince of Wales — indeed, Sir Robert was there to give advice on their Mediterranean itinerary during this period of international tension — but Wallis could not fail to be aware of the security interest in her and in several of her friends.

While the secret service kept an eye on Mrs Simpson, the royal family went out of their way to avoid her. Elizabeth announced that she would not speak to her, and then suffered the embarrassment of running into her by chance on more than one occasion. Marina took an even loftier attitude and frequently refused to join George on the now rare occasions when he and David got together. Even young Harry (recently created Duke of Gloucester) had misgivings about his eldest brother's fancy woman. Harry got married that winter, and spent his honeymoon hunting in England and shooting in Northern Ireland — one of his reasons being that he didn't want to run into Wallis and David, who were again skiing in Austria.

'Now all the children are married but David,' George V wrote in his diary on the night of the Gloucesters' wedding. That was true, yet his eldest son certainly had marriage on his mind. In spite of the overwhelming difficulties he would face, the Prince of Wales had now convinced himself that he could not live without Mrs Simpson. His letters to her show a man agonisingly, even slavishly in love. 'Oh! a boy does miss and want a girl so terribly tonight,' he wrote to her at three o'clock one morning not long after their holiday. 'I love you more and more every minute and *no* difficulties or complications can possibly prevent our ultimate happiness.' He celebrated the arrival of 1936 by writing to her on New Year's Day with more than a hint that they would finally be united as man and wife, 'Oh! my Wallis I know we'll have Viel Glück to make us *one* this year. God bless WE.'

In her forty-first year Wallis had clawed her way to the top of the tree, far outstripping any of her Montague or Warfield predecessors. It had taken her two years but now the little man was indisputably hers. Through winning the world's most eligible bachelor she had acquired the influence and admiration that she felt she deserved. David, too, had found something he had been searching for since his nursery days at York Cottage. With Wallis he was able to act out, and thereby neutralise, the pain, frustration and humiliation of his childhood. Her complete domination over him made onlookers squirm, as did her rudeness and scolding which could reduce the Prince publicly to tears. But for David this rejection and denial of love, followed in due course by tender cosseting, seems to have represented a pattern of consolation. It replayed his mother's rejection of his love for her, but as a game, which would now end each time with consoling embraces.

The strong sado-masochistic element in David's relationship with Wallis can be seen as part of the same pattern. His first nanny, as we have observed, had the brutal habit of hurting him to make him cry, and then comforting him with loving kisses. Like other such victims of abuse in infancy, David had come to find a perverted pleasure in persecution. Sex may have played only a minor role in the relationship, as it may have done with Freda Dudley Ward whom he once begged to 'chase me into bed with a big big stick'. Like the language of his love letters, the gratification of the nursery, in all its forms, may well have been enough to satisfy his long-repressed desires. In Wallis, the Prince at last discovered in one woman the dominant maternal influences of his childhood: and it bound him to her until the day he died.

George V may have considered Mrs Simpson 'unsuitable as a friend, disreputable as a mistress, unthinkable as Queen of England', but there were powerful psychological forces binding her to his eldest son. It was no accident that two dysfunctional personalities should be so strongly drawn to each other. David's masochism found its answer in Wallis's compelling need to control. Whether it was her weight (she starved herself on grapefruit juice and black tea in order to remain her desired size 6), her household (even during meals she made notes — 'Salt in soup?' 'Try truffles with this dish'), or organising the private life of her royal lover — in everything she undertook, Wallis's drive for perfection was paramount. Everyone, including the weak and only too willing Prince, was subject to it.

It had been a stupendous year for Wallis, the most exciting of her life — but now, three weeks into 1936 the fairytale began to unravel. The King's health had been failing for some months. Early in the New Year he began rapidly to decline. Dutiful to the very end, he held a Privy Council meeting on his deathbed, and several times signed in the air, before having his hand guided by his doctor Lord Dawson, to authorise a Council of State. That evening, Monday 20 January, his doctor gave George V a lethal injection to ease him into the next world, so that news of his death could be carried in *The Times* the following morning rather than making headlines in the less respectable evening papers.

Bertie, David and the rest of the family had been summoned to Sandringham for the last rites. Elizabeth had retired to her bed in London with pneumonia, leaving Bertie to face the ordeal of his father's death and his brother's accession alone. Wallis was at a charity gala in a West End cinema when the celebrated bulletin was read out to the audience — 'The King's life is now moving peacefully to its close.' While David was at Sandringham, she remained in London. The absence of the two dominant women in their lives meant that David and Bertie saw more of each other during those grim January days than they had for months. Together they went up to London to prepare Stanley Baldwin for the handover. Together they hurried back to Sandringham to wait for their father to die and stop the Archbishop of Canterbury, Cosmo Lang, from stealing the limelight — although that most egocentric of prelates still managed to slip on his cassock and deliver the King into the arms of his Maker while George V's sons were downstairs.

Rigid as ever in her observance of protocol, Queen Mary's first action was to go over to her eldest son, take his hand and kiss it. The reign of King Edward VIII had begun. According to Wigram, the new King 'became hysterical, cried loudly, and kept on embracing the Queen'. Helen Hardinge, from whose bedroom Wallis had watched the Silver Jubilee procession, described his emotion as 'frantic and unreasonable', adding, 'In its outward manifestation, it far exceeded that of his mother and his three brothers.'

In retrospect it is clear that David's hysterical grief was not directly on his father's account — he expressed no sorrow in his autobiography *A King's Story* — but stemmed from panic at his own predicament. The event he had dreaded since childhood had arrived. His life of privilege without responsibility, a life he felt entitled to and bitterly resented losing, was at an end. Moreover, his letters to Wallis seem to suggest — what some of those close to him certainly believed — that the Prince of Wales had been planning to elope with her before his father died, probably in just a few weeks' time. Now he was King he couldn't do a bunk: he had left it too late. It was some time before David could pull himself together and declare, as he stood by his father's bedside, 'I hope I will make good as he has made good.'

Nobody more devoutly wished that this pious

hope would come true than Bertie. He had noted David's decision to call himself King Edward after his grandfather Edward VII ('Wasn't my grandfather very popular with everyone?' David used wistfully to ask his uncle, the Earl of Athlone). He had stood by, as had Queen Mary, as the new King rose from his father's deathbed and almost immediately gave the order for the Sandringham clocks (which, as one of George V's idiosyncrasies, had traditionally run half-an-hour ahead of GMT) to be put back to normal time — an impulsive act carried out with a suddenness which seemed to many who knew him to symbolise a rejection of everything his father stood for. Now all that Bertie could do was pray.

The morning after George V died, Bertie flew down to London with David, who was already making history as the first reigning British monarch to take to the air. After the Accession Privy Council, as Bertie returned to 145 Piccadilly to check on his ailing wife, David sped to the Ritz to meet Wallis. She was late and the new King was spotted stamping up and down the long hotel corridor with increasing impatience until she joined him. The first day of Edward VIII's reign ended with David and Wallis dining alone, while Bertie and Elizabeth went to bed mourning the old King and fearing for the new one. Matters did not improve on the Wednesday, when David broke with precedent and raised eyebrows by appearing with Wallis to watch the proclamation of his accession from a convenient window. The day after that, the royal family gathered once again at Sandringham to hear the reading of George V's will.

It was a brief affair. The new King's sister and three brothers each received a sum in excess of £750,000. 'Where do I come in?' complained David more than once. 'My brothers and sister have got large sums, but I have been left out.' It was explained to him that he had been given a lifetime share in Sandringham and Balmoral, and it was assumed that as Prince of Wales he had been able to establish a considerable fortune from the Duchy of Cornwall; in fact, David had squirrelled away about a million pounds. In addition, he could look forward to substantial savings culled from the Civil List and Privy Purse. None of this appeased the new King. When the reading was over, he stormed out of the room, 'striding down the passage,' said Tommy Lascelles, 'with a face blacker than any thunderstorm', and went straight to telephone Wallis and break the news that the additional fortune he had led her to expect would not be forthcoming.

As far as the public was concerned, Prince Charming had become King Charming and all was well with the world. In the eyes of millions of his subjects, the new King was a symbol of youth and a fresh start. Much as they had loved, and now mourned, his gruff old father, David possessed a popular touch which seemed in keeping with the modern, fast-paced, democratic age. Queen Mary was prepared to put her doubts behind her. When, on the night of 27 January 1936, David led his three brothers into Westminster Hall to join the Guards standing watch over their father's coffin, dressed in uniform and resting on their swords, she was so taken with the gesture that she commissioned a painting of the scene, 'The Vigil of the Princes'. She gave it to David, as the architect of the scheme, on his birthday that year — although it was actually Bertie who had suggested the idea to his elder brother.

David was nevertheless scrupulous in his public dealings with Bertie, who was now heir presumptive to the imperial throne. The names of the Duke and Duchess of York were added to Church of England prayers for the royal family. Bertie was placed on the committee planning the coronation. Certain government telegrams and state papers were made available to him. In every outward respect David was showing due deference to his trusted and loyal younger brother. He may also, consciously or not, have been setting up Bertie to step into his shoes, should the need ever arise.

One of Bertie's less agreeable tasks was to comb Sandringham, the house and the estate, in order to draw up a list of savings that could be made there. Goaded by Wallis to make economies in every area of royal expenditure, the King had been stung into penny-pinching by his father's will. Bertie suggested axing one hundred of the four hundred staff, a fairly drastic reduction which was not nearly drastic enough for his brother. Ignoring most of Bertie's carefully considered plan for Sandringham, David instituted his own savage staff cuts and the sale of several estate farms. Bertie was distressed, and Elizabeth furious. All George V's old homes suffered from the new King's sudden parsimony but Sandringham came off worst. Early childhood memories of York Cottage and dismal walks on the estate with Hansell may have turned him against what he called 'the voracious white elephant'. There was a further cause for resentment. Not long before George V died, David had written off a loan of £90,000 made by the Duchy of Cornwall to pay for the purchase of additional land at Sandringham.

There were more important things David wished to spend money on. As Prince of Wales he had been used to drawing £10,000 at a time from the Duchy of Cornwall to buy jewels for Wallis. Cartier and Van Cleef & Arpels could have done brisk business with the £90,000 his father had borrowed to spend on his Norfolk 'hobby'. Not that Wallis felt the loss. At Christmas David had spent £50,000 on jewels for her (approximately £1,350,000 at today's prices), and he added to these at New Year with a further £60,000 worth. This might have been easier for people to accept if he had not, a few months later, sacked, without a qualm, many of the longest-serving and most faithful members of his father's household. David's natural generosity of spirit could still be seen in his professions of sympathy for the poor and unemployed, but it no longer had any practical expression now that Mrs Simpson had taken control of the royal purse-strings.

In public, she was seen to be in better spirits than the King. There was open house at Bryanston Court. The King dropped in frequently for cocktails; in February one evening during the official mourning, Wallis had the assembled guests crowing with laughter as she explained how she had not worn black stockings since giving up the Can-Can. There were numerous smart dinner parties. The writer and diplomat Harold Nicolson was present at one of them and decided that the whole atmosphere and setting 'was slightly second rate'. Mrs Simpson's taste was over-theatrical: the flat was suffocating, with white arum lilies and orchids giving off a heady scent in every room.

The Duchess of York's life was rather more muted that spring of 1936. She and Bertie were now living in a vacuum, alienated from the new court, and missing the sense of continuity that George V had personified. When Bertie returned from Sandringham, and Elizabeth got out of her sickbed, they quit London to gather their strength in the bracing air of Bournemouth. 'He was so kind, and so dependable,' she wrote of her late father-in-law to his doctor. 'I am . . . suffering from the effects of a family break-up — which always happens when the head of a family goes. Though outwardly one's life goes on the same, yet everything is different — especially spiritually and mentally.'

In some respects David, though, was still clinging to his father's reign. In his St David's Day speech on 1 March he departed from the government-prepared script to remind his listeners that as far as he was concerned nothing really had changed. 'I am better known to you as Prince of Wales . . . And although I now speak to you as King, I am still that same man.' Asked to approve the name *King Edward VIII* for a new battleship, he erased it and substituted *Prince of Wales*. At Easter he presented the sovereign's Maundy money, by tradition given to one man and one woman for every year of the sovereign's age. On this, the only occasion on which Edward VIII presented Maundy money, he specified that there should be seventy-one recipients of both sexes, as many as there would have been if his father had still been alive. Wallis was present, watching him perform the task. Those attending the service noticed that as he walked down the aisle to take his place beside the Archbishop, his eyes never left her face.

Since news of Mrs Simpson's absolute authority over the King inevitably filtered back to the Yorks, they would no doubt have heard how she had ticked off the King in public for not paying proper attention to his state papers. In this she had a point. Edward VIII's staff despaired of his feckless attitude towards the red boxes containing the government papers he had to read. Some were returned bearing unmistakable rings from cocktail glasses. Others were sent back weeks late, not initialled and obviously unread. The King's boredom with his official duties was becoming increasingly plain. After Stanley Baldwin discovered that sensitive Cabinet documents had been left scattered about the Fort in full view of Wallis and some of her questionable friends the red boxes sent to the monarch were censored, to weed out diplomatically sensitive material. David paid such little attention to the workings of his government, and was so preoccupied with his private life, that he probably did not notice.

Almost the only area of official business in which he did take a close interest was the new Civil List. Although he had already settled a considerable fortune on Wallis, he was adamant that suitable provision be made within it for a Queen Consort. When it was published in April 1936, the Civil List made available £40,000 a year, rising to a sum of £70,000 if the Queen, whoever she was, outlived the King. If Wallis was told of this by her adoring lover, she no doubt gave a tolerant smile. Much as she enjoyed running the King's life, there is no indication, either from her letters or her reported conversation in the early months of 1936, that she entertained the idea of becoming his Queen. In early May she wrote to Aunt Bessie that if the King were to take another lover, 'I should be comfortably off and have had a most interesting experience, one that does not fall to everyone's lot and the times are exciting now and countries and politics madly thrilling. I have always had the courage for the new things life sometimes offers.'

Relations with the Yorks continued to deteriorate. In April the King bought an American station wagon, in keeping with his delight in all things American. Soon afterwards, he and Wallis took it for a spin, dropping in at Royal Lodge so that Bertie (who had a lifelong fascination with the way things worked) could look it over. It was probably fortunate that three other guests from the Fort went along for the ride, because the two brothers immediately jumped into the car and disappeared down the circular drive, leaving Wallis and Elizabeth face to face. 'Her justly famous charm was highly evident,' Wallis was to write scathingly in her memoirs when she recalled her meeting with the Duchess that afternoon, but David had put her in an impossible situation. Princess Elizabeth was sufficiently struck by the atmosphere at tea that when she and her sister were led out to go, at their mother's suggestion, 'into the woods for a while', she asked her governess, 'Crawfie, who is she?'

In the presence of the others, both women pursued neutral topics of conversation. Gardening should have been one subject guaranteed not to be contentious, but between the Duchess of York and Mrs Simpson by now every exchange came laden with the presumption of slights and innuendos. On this occasion, with the two brothers back in the drawing-room of Royal Lodge, Wallis led the King over to the window and in the presence of her host and hostess lectured him as to how certain trees could be cut down, and part of a hill removed to improve the view. The proprietorial arrogance of this may not have registered at the time with Bertie, even though he was as deeply involved in laying out the garden and grounds at Royal

Lodge as David was at the Fort. But it rendered Elizabeth speechless with indignation.

The Duke of York's natural concern was that his brother's relationship with Mrs Simpson might erupt in open scandal. For the time being the British press by tacit agreement continued to observe a mutual silence. The great majority of the British people — unlike those abroad — remained completely unaware of the King's infatuation with a married American divorcee. But David was becoming increasingly reckless, especially when at the end of May he had the names of Mr and Mrs Simpson published in the Court Circular, the morning after they had been among his guests at his first official dinner at York House. It was the first appearance of her name in the better newspapers, and the last occasion the Simpsons were seen together in public. As Wallis recounts in her autobiography, the King said, 'It's got to be done. Sooner or later my Prime Minister must meet my future wife.'

' 'David,' I exclaimed, 'you mustn't talk that way. The idea is impossible. They'd never let you!' '

' 'I'm well aware of all that,' he said almost gaily, 'but rest assured, I will manage it somehow.' '

Wallis later revealed that she found the Baldwins 'pleasant but distant', acting as if they considered she had 'stolen the Fairy Prince'.

Six weeks later Mrs Simpson acted as hostess at the King's second official dinner, this time without the encumbering irrelevance of Ernest.

The Duke and Duchess of York were the guests of honour. Elizabeth's old friend Helen Hardinge, wife of Edward VIII's new private secretary Alec Hardinge, surveyed the dinner table with pursed lips. In her memoirs she records that, 'Winston Churchill was one of the few people . . . who found Mrs Simpson acceptable . . . he believed that, in the ultimate analysis of the Monarchy, she simply did not count one way or the other.' Whatever the cause, Churchill had the devil in him that night. After dinner he made a beeline for the Duchess of York, settled himself beside her on the sofa, and began a rambling monologue about the affair of George IV (as Prince of Wales) with Maria Fitzherbert, the Roman Catholic widow he married in secret, and in defiance of the law or royal marriages.

Elizabeth was in no mood for history lessons, least of all about the mistresses of kings and remarked dismissively, 'Well, that was a *long* time ago.' Undeterred, Churchill launched into another monologue about the Wars of the Roses between the royal houses of York and Lancaster. The point needed no labouring: Mrs Simpson was driving a wedge between Bertie, the Duke of York, and his older brother, David, the Duke of Lancaster. Elizabeth with unaccustomed sharpness closed the conversation: 'That was a very, *very* long time ago.' Her exasperation was understandable. There was now a real gulf between the fashionable society represented by the circle of celebrated hostesses who gave parties for the King and Mrs Simpson, and the staider old-aristocratic society in which the Yorks moved. Yet she knew that the publication of the guest list in the Court Circular the following morning would make it appear to the world at large as if the Yorks saw no objection to Wallis 'enthusiastically moving into the regal role into which she had cast herself', in the words of Helen Hardinge.

If anything the 1936 season was even unhappier for the Yorks than the previous year's. For Bertie it was compounded by the sad fate of *Britannia*, his father's much-loved but now unseaworthy racing yacht, which on the day after David's dinner, was scuttled in deep water south of the Isle of Wight. Edward VIII had been prevented from going to Ascot by the period of official mourning for his father, but Wallis went instead, riding in his car. Later in the month, when a cloudburst drenched the Buckingham Palace garden party held for six hundred debutantes and their parents, the King seized the opportunity to duck out of the entire proceedings. With a casualness which deeply wounded many of those present, he left instructions that 'those ladies who were unable to pass the King's presence will be considered as having been officially presented at Court.' It was very different from the stately manner in which Wallis herself had been presented at court five years earlier.

'The Simpson scandal is growing,' Chips Channon confided to his diary, 'and she, poor Wallis, looks unhappy. The world is closing around her, the flatterers, the sycophants, and the malice.' Nevertheless for Wallis it was still a heady cocktail. And soon, she and David, lightly disguised as 'the Duke of Lancaster' were able to leave censorious English shores and sail away on their long-awaited summer holiday. The yacht *Nahlin*, 'furnished rather like a Calais whore-shop', according to David's equerry John Aird who checked it over for him, was chartered to convey the monarch and a changing party of guests down the Dalmatian coast of Yugoslavia and through the Aegean to Istanbul. The library shelves were stripped of books, and crates of golf balls were brought on board, so that the King and his lord-in-waiting the Earl of Sefton (both of them living with other men's wives) could practise their drives into the green of the Mediterranean. Wallis and David, wearing identical gold crosses, as the Duff Coopers observed, occupied the state cabins in the forward part of the boat, away from everyone else who squeezed into the minor cabins. Apart from the fact that there were other people with them, it could have been a honeymoon, complete with post-marital tensions and tantrums. European and American newspapers tailed the yacht through the Adriatic, snapping photographs of the King and Mrs Simpson, sometimes hand in hand. Neither of them attempted to keep a low profile. Frequently, the English King and his American mistress came ashore to go sightseeing, or pay calls on royal relatives. Crowds appeared by the thousands to greet and serenade them. 'It's all for you,' Wallis records David telling her, 'because these simple people believe a king is in love with you.' In Dubrovnik they were mobbed by enthusiastic crowds shouting, 'Long live love.'

In private, or semi-private, matters sometimes went less smoothly. After dinner with King George II of Greece and his very attractive English mistress (who had just been divorced by her soldier husband), there was an unpleasant scene between David and Wallis when they got back on board the *Nahlin*. Noticing that the hem of his beloved's dress was trapped under the foot of her chair, the King got down on all fours to release it. Lady Diana Cooper, who witnessed this scene, describes Wallis glaring down at him. ' 'Well, that's the *maust* extraordinary performance I've ever seen,' she snarled, and then started to criticize him. She berated him for his manner, for the way he had talked to the King of Greece's mistress Mrs Jones, even for his attitude to his fellow-monarch. David looked completely crestfallen, as he always did when she found fault with him.' Nevertheless, to Alan 'Tommy' Lascelles, who had known David for more or less seventeen years, the King had never seemed more contented than 'in those days in the *Nahlin* when there was nothing to remind him that he was a king'.

Diana Cooper's conclusion was that: 'Wallis is wearing very badly.' Furthermore, 'Her commonness and Becky Sharpishness irritate.' In Lady Diana's opinion, Wallis was getting bored with the King. Certainly she was becoming

202

frustrated by the anomalies of her situation. Here she was, the King's consort in all but name, all-powerful within the confines of their relationship, yet with no standing of any kind outside it. Nor could she envisage any change in the indignity and insecurity of her position. For all her ignorance of royal protocol, Wallis could see that marriage to David was probably out of the question — yet she had no intention of spending the rest of her days in a deckchair while the King adoringly painted her toenails and courtiers sniggered.

After the Mediterranean cruise Edward VIII went on ahead alone to Balmoral, leaving Wallis in Paris to shop for the autumn season. It was mid-September. Wallis caught a cold and took to her bed in the Hotel Meurice, where she had ample opportunity to catch up on all the mail that had been forwarded to her. It made alarming reading. Friends in the States, led by a worried Aunt Bessie, had sent cuttings of the sensational press coverage the *Nahlin* cruise had attracted. In her memoirs Wallis recorded her realisation that her relationship with King Edward was now 'a topic of dinner-table conversation for every newspaper reader in the United States, Europe and the Dominions'. Worse, Wallis was being painted as a scarlet woman and not as the Cinderella of her fantasies. Alone and feeling decidedly ill, she came to a decision. Lying in bed, she penned a letter to the King, her lover. She had made up her mind, she told him, that it was time to call a halt, and that it was better for all concerned she should return to Ernest, her loyal, dependable, indisputably normal husband.

'I know Ernest,' she wrote, 'and I feel I am better with him than with you. I am sure you and I would only create disaster together . . . I want you to be happy. I feel sure that I can't make you so, and I honestly don't think you can me . . . I am sure dear David, that in a few months your life will run again as it did before and without my nagging. Also you have been independent of affection all your life. We have had lovely beautiful times together and I thank God for them and know that you will go on with your job doing it better and in a more dignified manner each year.'

Today, as in the 1930s, public opinion is divided as to whether the King or Mrs Simpson was the villain of the piece. Those who regard Wallis as the evil genie who precipitated the abdication, ascribe to her a Machiavellian cunning in which this letter features as a ploy to bind David more tightly than ever to her side. But to read it in full is to perceive a woman who had genuinely lost her bearings, and was frightened about what the future might bring. Even so, she must have known, as soon as she sent the letter, what David's reaction would be. That same evening, as she lay paralysed with self-pity in the Hotel Meurice, David was writing to her. 'Mr Loo and I are up here in our blue room and missing you like the dickens,' he began. And, masochistically, 'its hell but its lovely in a way too.'

There was no turning back, for either of

them. When Edward VIII in Balmoral received her letter, his reaction was nothing short of hysterical. According to Tommy Lascelles, back on the King's staff, he rushed in a frenzy of distress to the nearest telephone, rang Wallis and threatened that if she did not come over to be with him in Scotland, he would take a knife and cut his throat. Within a week, the Court Circular announced that Mrs Ernest Simpson, accompanied by Mr and Mrs Herman Rogers, had arrived at Balmoral.

5

THE ABDICATION

The high drama of the interchanges between Balmoral and the Hotel Meurice would have profoundly shocked the other royal party in Scotland that summer of 1936. While the *Nahlin* party had been sunning themselves in swimsuits and dining on Mediterranean seafood, the Duke and Duchess of York were staying on the Balmoral estate, some six miles distant, in their pretty Georgian house, Birkhall. There, Bertie and Elizabeth followed the tradition of royal holidays established by Queen Victoria. They battled with midges; they dug for vegetables; they strode across the heather. Except when they made bonfires so that the two little princesses could cook sausages, they caught or shot their supper before tucking into it. Joining them in the Highlands was the Archbishop of Canterbury. Having not been invited to Balmoral for the first time in twenty-five years, it was left to 'the kind Yorks' to extend to Cosmo Lang the hand of royal hospitality — and pointedly to invite him to return to Birkhall the following year, 'so that the links with Balmoral may not be wholly broken'. As it was, the sybaritic delights of the *Nahlin* cruise were not entirely lost upon the good Presbyterian folk in Crathie, the local village. The vicar chose, on the Sunday morning

206

before the King arrived at Balmoral, to preach on the subject of the dissolute Roman Emperor Nero.

'GREAT ENTHUSIASM MARKS ARRIVAL OF THE KING' was the frontpage headline of the Aberdeen evening paper the next day, expressing the general pleasure which greeted the new monarch's arrival among his Scottish subjects. At Birkhall, Bertie and Elizabeth received the news coolly. They would have read in the British press about David's enthusiastic reception whenever he stepped off the *Nahlin* to go ashore that summer: but they would also have known that David's affair with Mrs Simpson was the subject of gossip in diplomatic circles throughout Europe, and covered in every foreign newspaper. In virtually every picture, the King Emperor was seen walking beside Mrs Simpson, eating or dancing with Mrs Simpson, or just gazing adoringly at her. And now Mrs Simpson herself was trespassing on Elizabeth's home ground — effectually stepping into Queen Mary's shoes as hostess at Balmoral.

Wallis was due to arrive in Scotland on Wednesday 23 September. It was a day of ill omen. The King had been asked to open the new Royal Infirmary in Aberdeen. It was a major engagement, which he had casually turned down on the grounds that he would still be in court mourning for his father, although mourning officially ended in June. Bertie, embarrassed by this feeble excuse (which, had it been true, would have applied to him as well) nevertheless had agreed to stand in for his brother, and

207

endure, as so often in the past, the polite disappointment of hundreds of local people who had worked hard and long to prepare for the new King's visit. In the event, Aberdeen and the Aberdonians gave the Yorks a tremendous welcome. But while Bertie and Elizabeth were at the hospital performing their royal duties, the King suddenly put in an appearance in Aberdeen after all. Although supposedly back at Balmoral in mourning, his anxiety that Wallis might not have heeded his pleas was so great that he could not resist coming into Aberdeen to meet her off the train. Wearing Highland dress and motoring goggles, he was hoping to pass unnoticed, but about the only person who failed to recognise the King, as he drove to the station and hung about waiting, was the policeman who ticked him off for parking in the wrong place. A few days after its fulsome words of welcome, the Aberdeen *Evening Express* carried the bald headline: 'HIS MAJESTY IN ABERDEEN — SURPRISE VISIT IN CAR TO MEET GUESTS'. Alongside was a picture of the Duke and Duchess of York opening the new hospital buildings. The contrast between the values of the old court and the new could not have been more pointedly displayed: there was no question about which members of the family were upholding the standards of the monarchy that September.

For the loyal Bertie, the fact that his brother should make so crass a public relations gaffe was further proof of the terrible strain that David was under. His brotherly feelings of concern, disappointment and hurt, went far deeper than his wife's spirited disdain for the American 'adventuress'. In the words of his official biographer Sir John Wheeler-Bennett, the future George VI found himself 'shut off from his brother, neglected, ignored, unwanted . . . He felt that he had lost a friend and was rapidly losing a brother.'

Had David confided in Bertie after the *Nahlin* cruise, and told his brother of the anguish that Wallis's letter from the Hotel Meurice had caused him, he would undoubtedly have found some sympathy, if not understanding. Indeed, had he at any point enlisted Bertie as a confidant, it would at the minimum have reduced his isolation in the weeks and months leading up to his renunciation of the throne, and bolstered his confidence in his dealings with the Prime Minister, Stanley Baldwin. But, engulfed in the turmoil of his passion for Wallis, Edward VIII could not and would not look beyond her pervading presence in his life. The sum of his desire was to be putty in her hands. All other links — of love, affection, friendship, loyalty — fell away from him, save only a fearful respect for his mother, Queen Mary. As for Bertie, the new King chose to forget the brotherly affection that had sustained them both through the traumas of their father's dictatorial regime, and sidelined him.

The gossip of courtiers, in any age, tends to be self-interested and melodramatic, and it is impossible to know how much credence Elizabeth or Bertie generally placed in it. According to the reports that would have reached their ears, when Wallis arrived at Balmoral she was installed in the suite of rooms that for twenty-five years had been Queen Mary's exclusive preserve. In fact, she was put into the best spare bedroom, and it was the King who started tongues wagging when he shunned his father's old room and moved into the poky little dressing-room that adjoined Wallis's suite. The King and Mrs Simpson were commonly supposed to have been seen strolling around the grounds and even through the village of Crathie, dressed in shorts. More reliable accounts suggest that far from being under-dressed, Wallis was, true to form, rather overdressed for the Highlands.

The staff at Balmoral were certainly on edge, primed by rumours of sackings and changes at royal residences south of the border. And it all seemed to emanate from Mrs Simpson, whose control over the King was evident to everybody who saw them together. Edward VIII would hover over her while she was playing bridge, except when he went off meekly to fetch her more champagne. He listened avidly to all her suggestions for changes, whether it was the royal plate or the placing of furniture (both of which were probably long overdue). Her introduction of the American three-decker toasted club sandwich seems to have been greeted in the Balmoral kitchens with as little enthusiasm as a flask of brandy in an Arab mosque. In less fractious circumstances, Mrs Simpson's quips about the preponderance of tartan might have been treated as evidence of her amusing wit. But clever conversation had never made a significant contribution to life at Balmoral. Those who wanted to find fault with Mrs Simpson had plenty of ammunition.

George, Duke of Kent, came to stay, and Wallis flirted with him over dinner, so that the guests could observe the palpable distress of the King, 'beaten into a frenzy of jealousy and desire', as the Prime Minister's private secretary reported Prince George saying to him. Whatever George's feelings about this may have been — and there is no evidence that any of David's brothers were remotely attracted to Wallis — he certainly went on record as saying that he couldn't believe the atmosphere at Balmoral could have changed so radically. 'It was all so comfortable and everyone seemed so happy — it was really fun.'

On the Saturday evening, three days after the disagreeable events in Aberdeen, the Yorks went to Balmoral for dinner. Elizabeth was all for calling it off; but Bertie, dutiful as ever, felt that David might need his support. In fact it was an occasion which would expose and publicise the rift between the two women. Almost twenty people were gathered in the drawing-room when Elizabeth, preceding Bertie, walked in. Instead of the King it was Wallis, deliberately or unthinkingly, who detached herself from the throng and came forward to greet them. This was a flagrant breach of court protocol, giving the clear impression that Wallis was claiming for herself the status of official hostess and, according to one account, Elizabeth, Duchess of York, responded by showing her resentment as pointedly. Ignoring Wallis completely, she brushed past her and marched on into the room announcing in a clear voice, 'I came to dine with the King.'

Bertie, behind her, looked nervous. Edward VIII, appearing surprised, broke off his conversation and came forward to greet his sister-in-law. At dinner Elizabeth took precedence, sitting on the King's right hand. As soon as the pudding course was finished, it was the Duchess, not Mrs Simpson, who promptly rose to lead the women from the table. After dinner, the King had laid on a screening of the latest Fred Astaire-Ginger Rogers musical *Swing Time*. Songs such as 'A Fine Romance' and 'Pick Yourself Up' were not sentiments calculated to appeal to Elizabeth that evening. She was still smarting the next morning: so much so that on one of the very rare occasions in her life she failed to go to church, sending Bertie and the little princesses to Crathie without her. It was a Pyrrhic victory, from which both these formidable women retired hurt. Wallis would have been reminded — as if she could forget — that without official recognition of her status as the King's consort, her life with him would be a series of such petty humiliations.

Three days later the King and Mrs Simpson left Balmoral, never to return. They were not missed by the staff, whose worst fears had been confirmed by the sacking of more old and loyal retainers. Unlike the cost-cutting measures he had undertaken earlier in the year at Sandringham, the King this time wielded the axe without a word to his brother. 'David only told me what he had done after it was over,' Bertie wrote glumly to his mother from Glamis in the middle of October, 'which I might say made me rather sad. He had arranged it all with the official people up there. I never saw him for an instant . . . ' Elizabeth wrote to Queen Mary in similar terms: 'It will never be quite the same for us . . . David does not seem to possess the faculty of making others feel *wanted*. It is very sad, and I feel that the whole difficulty is a certain person. I do not feel that I *can* make advances to her and ask her to our house, as I imagine would be liked, and this fact is bound to make relations a little difficult . . . The whole situation is so complicated and *horrible*, and I feel so unhappy about it sometimes, so you must forgive me, darling Mama, for letting myself go so indiscreetly.'

As the tone of these letters makes clear, Bertie and Elizabeth felt a real sense of loss at their estrangement from David. He was weak and foolish: but he could also be lovable and fun to be with, possessing qualities of humour, seriousness, tenacity and personal courage which his fateful relationship with Wallis have tended to eclipse. On the way back from the ceremony of Trooping the Colour on Horse Guards' Parade in July, as the King rode with Bertie up Constitution Hill, an Irishman with a grievance threw something metallic under the feet of his horse. David thought it was a bomb — in fact it was an unloaded revolver — but he rode on without spurring his horse. 'Bloody fool,' was the only comment to Bertie.

Queen Mary felt a similar sense of loss, but was unable to express it — more's the pity, since his mother was the only member of the family David might have listened to. 'I am so pleased to hear that you and David can talk over everything together,' Queen Maud of Norway had written to her sister-in-law, but the truth was that Queen Mary did not dare talk to David about anything except trivialities. When he dined with his mother after the *Nahlin* cruise, he wondered how much she had read and heard about Mrs Simpson, but 'her conversation told me nothing', he wrote in his memoirs. Instead, they had a farcical conversation about the weather. Hadn't he found it terribly warm in the Adriatic? He was looking well and had put on a few pounds (which was good). How was dear George (the King of Greece)? George had lost weight and was missing his happy exile in London. 'Poor George,' murmured the Queen. 'I don't envy the rulers of those Balkan countries.' It reminded Edward VIII about 'how she used to talk to us when we returned from school'.

On 1 October, just after David returned from Scotland, his mother packed the last of her bags into three luggage brakes, gathered up a cairn terrier which had belonged to George V, and moved out of Buckingham Palace — her home for a quarter of a century — to settle in Marlborough House down the road. The new incumbent Edward VIII would have been delighted for her to stay: he hated Buckingham Palace and everything it represented. But the old Queen knew it was time to leave the limelight. She was receiving an increasing number of letters and press cuttings from British residents abroad — the same sort of letters which were now pouring into Downing Street, Lambeth Palace and the offices of *The Times* — urging her to act before it was too late. She responded to them in the way she reacted to anything unpleasant, by withdrawing into her private world and busying herself with arranging her furniture, pictures and beloved *objects d'art* in Marlborough House. But soon it would no longer be possible for her to avert her eyes. American and European newspapers were now openly predicting that Mrs Simpson would in due course marry the King and join him on the British throne. And in mid-October it became known that Mrs Simpson's petition for divorce from her second husband would shortly be heard at the county court in Ipswich, in Suffolk.

Wallis, too, had moved house that October, furtively slipping into a rented villa in the Suffolk seaside town of Felixstowe. It was somewhat beneath her dignity after queening it at Balmoral, but it was a necessary and, she hoped, temporary move. Eight months earlier, her endlessly accommodating husband had finally run out of patience and requested a private meeting with the King at York House. According to the friend who accompanied him, Ernest Simpson did some straight talking. Things could no longer go on as they were:

Wallis would have to choose between the two of them. What were His Majesty's intentions towards her? Reportedly, the King rose from his chair, more in astonishment than in indignation. 'Do you really think that I would be crowned without Wallis at my side?' he exclaimed. It was the first time that he had openly declared his hand. Agreement was reached that Ernest Simpson would engineer an end to his marriage, and the King, for his part, would stick by Wallis and look after her. Wallis was about to burn her boats — or rather, David was burning them for her.

Tommy Lascelles very soon got wind of the scheme, nothing tartly that 'plans were already afoot to liquidate Simpson (matrimonially speaking) and to set the crown upon the leopardess's head.' The Prime Minister and Lord Wigram, both brought up in an age when this kind of thing simply wasn't done, at first refused to take the news seriously. It was blackmail on Simpson's part, Wigram assured Stanley Baldwin. What a pity the blaggard was a British subject, so it wouldn't be possible to deport him. They missed their opportunity to scotch the King's plan. In July 1936, Ernest Simpson left Bryanston Court and moved into the Guards Club. Later that month, he booked into the Hotel de Paris in the polite little Berkshire town of Bray, where he was joined by Wallis's old schoolfriend Mary Raffray, with whom Ernest was now intimate. Their presence was carefully noted in the hotel register. Later, two waiters were separately to declare on oath

216

that on consecutive mornings they had arrived with the breakfast tray and seen the aforesaid lady and gentleman in bed together. All the ritual evidence required to validate divorce proceedings on the grounds of adultery was now in place.

At this point, Walter Monckton, David's legal adviser and Attorney General to the Duchy of Cornwall, began to take a hand. A highly respected barrister, with a forensic eye for detail, Monckton had become a friend of the King in their Oxford days when he had been President of the Union. A charming, witty and agreeable man, he was to play the vital role of intermediary between the two royal brothers in the stormy negotiations which lay ahead. Later in his distinguished political career, before being created first Viscount Monckton of Brenchley in 1957, he would, as Minister of Labour, initiate the policy of conciliation which ruled British industrial relations for two decades, but in none of his future dealings with the trade unions would Walter Monckton be called upon to exercise such delicate skills of conciliation as were required of him over the abdication and its aftermath.

He put Mrs Simpson in touch with Theodore Goddard, the solicitor who would handle her divorce petition. En route from the Hotel Meurice to Balmoral in September, David's hysterical pleas still ringing in her ears, she had stopped off to see Mr Goddard, who set the legal wheels in motion. Ipswich happened to be the first convenient Assizes at which divorces were being heard that season, which was why Mrs Simpson was being obliged to take up residence in Suffolk in order to meet the requirements for a divorce in the country.

All of this had been set in train long before word got out. When the news did break, in the middle of October, Wallis was already in purdah on the windswept Suffolk coast. David, obliged to stay well away from Wallis until after the hearing, was fretting alone in Buckingham Palace. Bertie and Elizabeth were winding up their holiday at Glamis. Alec Hardinge first got wind of it on 15 October, when the Press Association telephoned to say that the Simpson divorce petition had been scheduled at Ipswich Assizes twelve days later, on 27 October. After doing some quick mental arithmetic, Hardinge realised that if a decree nisi was granted, the decree absolute would follow a statutory six months later on 27 April 1937, leaving the King time to marry Mrs Simpson before his coronation on 12 May. The murmured possibility of Queen Wallis sitting on the Consort's throne suddenly began to look like a well-planned strategy. Hardinge was appalled. He dashed off a letter to Baldwin, urging him to persuade Edward VIII to put a stop to the proceedings forthwith.

The Prime Minister was dubious about his chances of success, but eventually agreed to buttonhole the King. The two men had the first of their celebrated meetings that autumn at Fort Belvedere on 20 October. It was an unedifying overture to what the American journalist H. L. Mencken was later

218

to describe waspishly as 'the greatest story since the Resurrection'. Baldwin was deeply uncomfortable: physically because his arthritis was playing up, and emotionally because he had no stomach for tackling the monarch about his love life. He had little hope that Edward VIII could be persuaded to talk Mrs Simpson out of her divorce proceedings — and so it proved. The King refused to conduct the affair more discreetly. 'The lady is my friend and I do not wish to let her in by the back door.' As for the divorce proceedings, they were Wallis's private business. When Baldwin ventured to ask if Mrs Simpson might be able to leave the country for six months, he did not even get a response except indirectly in David's declaration that Mrs Simpson was 'the only woman in the world, and I cannot live without her'. His Prime Minister did not ask him to elaborate. Cautious and prudent in this as in all things, Baldwin did not care at this juncture to confront the King with the full consequences of his infatuation.

Towards the end of their meeting, Stanley Baldwin felt the need for a whisky and soda, and proceeded to toast his sovereign with lumbering gallantry: 'Well, sir, whatever happens, my Missus and I wish you every happiness from the depths of our souls.' Edward VIII responded by bursting into tears, which made the Prime Minister lachrymose as well. 'What a strange conversation-piece, those two blubbering together on a sofa,' concluded the diarist Harold Nicolson, to whom the scene was later described. Baldwin himself, motoring back to London in his little black Hillman, felt that he had handled things rather well. He had pointed out to the King that respect for the monarchy could disappear overnight if the general public — who could tolerate this kind of thing in private but not in the life of a public personage — were to get wind of what was going on. Hardinge, who knew David better, thought the PM had blown it. By not taking this first opportunity to spell out the truth, he had allowed Edward VIII to hope that there might be some constitutional latitude by which he could keep the throne and Wallis too.

It was therefore with a renewed sense of urgency that Major Hardinge hurried round to the Duke and Duchess of York at 145 Piccadilly. They had just returned from their summer holiday, but whatever sense of tranquillity they had found in Scotland must have evaporated as they listened to the King's private secretary catalogue the ominous events of the last few days. Hardinge concluded by turning to the Duke and warning him that it might end with his brother's abdication. According to Helen Hardinge, Bertie was 'appalled and tried not to believe what he had been told'.

What most distressed and frustrated Bertie was that all the information he received about his brother's intentions came to him at second-hand, at first through Hardinge, later, as the crisis deepened, from Stanley Baldwin in Downing Street. Over the next two months David contrived to keep his younger brother and heir to his throne at arm's length. On the rare occasions when he did tell him anything, it was in the form of announcing *faits accomplis*. Even in these harrowing weeks when the King's plans for the future should have hinged on the Duke of York's willingness to cooperate with them, David kept Bertie in the dark. That this does not appear to have been deliberate is a mark of how little concern the King paid to the future security of the British Crown. The brother in whom he had confided his fledgling romance with Freda Dudley Ward, with whom he had light-heartedly enjoyed the company of Thelma Furness, now had to watch helplessly as he went further and further down the road towards self-destruction.

Bertie agreed with Hardinge that the British people would not condone the marriage of their King with a twice-divorced American woman. Like his father, a stickler for the proprieties, he could see that if David ignored popular sentiment and pursued his marriage plans, it would set him at odds with his ministers and provoke an appalling constitutional crisis. His anxiety was wholly justified. At stake was not only the royal family's reputation, but that of the monarchy itself, whose national standing had been the chief and lifelong concern of Queen Victoria, then of her son when eventually he came to the throne, and then of his son George V. Beyond this, Bertie had personal fears. Hardinge had voiced the frightful prospect that as Duke of York, he might have to take over from David as King, at a time when public opinion was likely to be hostile, and the stature of the monarchy markedly diminished. However remote a prospect it seemed, it weighed heavily on him.

For a week both brothers nervously awaited the Ipswich Assizes hearing of the case of Simpson vs Simpson. David, as the days passed, appeared increasingly embattled. Through his friendship with Max Beaverbrook, proprietor of the *Daily Express*, and Lord Rothermere who owned the *Daily Mail*, he had persuaded the British newspapers to limit their coverage of the case to the bare facts. Astonishingly, in the light of present-day royal relations with the press, they complied. The American papers, however, were in full cry. Two days before the Ipswich hearing, Geoffrey Dawson, editor of *The Times*, brought a letter to the Palace, which showed starkly what was being said and written about the King and Mrs Simpson on the other side of the Atlantic. The letter had been sent by an anonymous British resident who had lived in the United States for some time, but clearly still had the traits of the bulldog in him. Signing his letter 'Brittanicus in Partibus Infidelium', the message he conveyed was that while 'George V was an invaluable asset to British prestige abroad; Edward has proved himself an incalculable liability.' There was not much new in this, but the letter ended with a more startling comment: 'nothing would please me more than to hear that Edward VIII had abdicated his rights in favour of the Heir Presumptive, who I am confident would be prepared to carry on in the sterling tradition established by his father.'

On the day of the Ipswich hearing, Alec

Hardinge wrote to thank Dawson, confident that the Brittanicus letter would 'make the desired impression' on Edward VIII. In this he completely misjudged the King. Far from being chastened by the views of the disaffected letter-writer, David took it as a sign of a growing establishment conspiracy against him. He even went so far as to claim the letter was a concoction, forged by 'a traitorous member of his own staff' (privately, he had fixed on Tommy Lascelles). In fact Dawson's action, which Hardinge had backed to the hilt, backfired on both men. The idea of abdication had been simmering in the back of David's mind; it was now presented to him in black and white. As he saw it, abdication solved everything. It would offer him not only the chance to spend the rest of his life with the woman he loved, but also the opportunity to escape his role and responsibilities as King — a role which he had never wanted, and which his father's constant denigration had made him feel unworthy to fulfil.

The day after Dawson gave Hardinge the 'Brittanicus' letter, the *New York Daily Mail*'s headline was confidently predicting 'KING TO MARRY 'WALLY'. WEDDING NEXT JUNE'. Twenty-four hours later, when cables reached the United States that Mrs Simpson had been awarded her decree nisi (with costs, which she later reimbursed to Ernest as agreed) the news knocked the Spanish Civil War and the US presidential election campaign right off the front pages. One paper excelled itself with the celebrated headline: 'KING'S MOLL RENO'D IN WOLSEY'S HOME TOWN'. The British reporters who had thronged Ipswich dismally filed their copy for the hell of it, knowing that their stories would be reduced to a brief announcement no bigger than a classified ad.

For Wallis, the rewards of the successful divorce case far outweighed the inconvenience of her brief stay in Felixstowe. From Ipswich, the King's chauffeur sped her back to London, to the frustration of pressmen barricaded inside the court-room. That evening, David bestowed upon her a gift extravagant even by his standards: a ring bearing one of the world's finest emeralds, which had once been a prized possession of the Great Mogul. In today's money it had cost him over a quarter of a million pounds (though rumour had it that he had baulked at paying the full price, whereupon the jewellers, Cartier, had cut the emerald in half). It was in all but name an engagement ring, as its inscription, 'WE are ours now 27 × 36', indicated. In the King's love letters, and inscribed in his gifts, WE always stood for Wallis/Edward. The two of them were one — and Wallis came first.

Bryanston Court was now a distant recollection of small-scale middle-income living. The King installed Mrs Simpson, and her Cairn terrier Slipper, in an elegant Nash mansion at 16 Cumberland Terrace, in Regent's Park. Here, three or four times a week, she held court for the cream of fashionable London society: 'friends of the King' who after the abdication were to be reviled by Osbert Sitwell as the Rat Pack. At

224

five o'clock in the afternoon, her guests would arrive — the Duff Coopers, Lady Oxford, Nancy Cunard, Sibyl Colefax, and the sharp-eyed diarists Chips Channon and Harold Nicolson MP — to be greeted with tea by their hostess and served canapés out of a shelved silver box by the maid. Meanwhile beyond Britain's media black-out, the furore was intensifying. Some reports spoke of Wallis referring to herself as the future Queen of England. Others suggested that she had attempted to have the royal cypher embroidered on her underwear. For those in the know, it made for the juiciest possible gossip. When King Edward VIII undertook his first and only State Opening of Parliament, on 3 November, Mrs Simpson, though absent in person (she was shopping in Harrods) was very much present in spirit. Some blamed her influence, unfairly, for the King's Americanised vowel sounds. Others freely speculated as to whether, at the next State Opening, Wallis in all her finery would occupy the Consort's throne beside the King.

Just as David had convinced himself that the 'Brittanicus' letter was false, the rest of the royal family suspected the Simpson divorce to be a put-up job, manufactured to smooth the path to matrimony for the two lovers. History was to prove them right, though at the time Wallis took care to spread it abroad that the divorce had been at Ernest's instigation, and at no wish of hers. This was a line she would stick to. Indeed, she had to stick to it, for if any evidence of collusion between the parties were to be produced before the granting of the decree absolute, her divorce would be null and void.

Ever since Hardinge's visit, the Duke of York had been hoping against hope that David would see sense. Throughout the first week of November he made efforts to talk the matter through with his brother, but was not accorded the opportunity. Three days after the State Opening of Parliament, he wrote plaintively to Queen Mary: 'I have been meaning to come & see you but I wanted to see David first. He is very difficult to see & when one does he wants to talk about other matters.' Bertie's restraint, given his older brother's extraordinary self-absorption, was indeed admirable.

Four days later the debate about the King's private life finally reached the floor of the House of Commons. On 10 November, an innocuous question about the coronation, scheduled for the following May, provoked an outburst by an Independent Labour member from Glasgow, John McGovern. In his diary Chips Channon recorded him as having jumped up and shouted, 'Why bother, in view of the gambling at Lloyd's that there will not be one?' To roars of 'Shame! Shame!' Mr McGovern then defiantly shouted, 'Yes . . . Mrs Simpson.' It was the first time there had been a public reference to the affair, yet the country did not get to know about it, for next day no newspaper reported it. The shields of loyal silence surrounding the King still held firm. In the middle of November, David left behind him a capital buzzing with rumour, and went to Portland for two days to visit the Home

Fleet. In spite of the huge personal strain he was under, it was a public relations triumph, proving that in the right circumstances — when he put his mind to it — he could still be an unsurpassable Prince Charming. He returned to Fort Belvedere well pleased with himself, quite unprepared to be confronted by what he later described as 'the most serious crisis of my life'.

In his absence, Alec Hardinge had been taking soundings in various quarters, most of them hostile to Edward VIII. He set down what seemed to him their inescapable conclusions in a characteristically pompous letter to his employer. ('The King Receives a Disturbing Letter' was how David headed the chapter describing it in his memoirs). In it, Hardinge warned the King that Baldwin's government was now so concerned about his relationship with Mrs Simpson that there was a risk that it might resign unless the King agreed to approaches it would shortly make to him. He also had information, he wrote darkly, that the silence of the British press could no longer be maintained, and indeed was likely to be broken any day. Hardinge concluded with the suggestion that 'the one step which holds out any prospect of avoiding this dangerous situation' was 'for Mrs Simpson to go abroad *without further delay*'.

According to Hardinge, his letter was 'a last bid to enable the King to remain on the throne'. Whether or not he expected it to have any sobering influence on Edward VIII, the effect his letter actually had could hardly have been more counter-productive. There rose before David the forbidding spectres of his old tutor, Hansell, and his father George V, lecturing the unhappy child. Worse, the recommendation that Wallis be sent abroad — significantly, the only paragraph that he thought important enough to quote in his memoirs — reminded David of the similar recommendations which had been made in the past when his brother George was consorting with one of his floozies. He was enraged. There was plainly a conspiracy afoot: Hardinge was a traitor siding with Stanley Baldwin. Many years later, according to Charles Murphy who helped him write his memoirs, David confided to a friend, 'Hardinge was a tool, a catspaw. I doubt if he ever knew how the family got rid of my younger brother's girls. Scotland Yard could be quick, silent and invisible in these little jobs. No strong-arm measures, mind you — only a firm suggestion. Then a bank address in a foreign land, or a packet of £5 notes. A stateroom reservation and a departure in the dead of night, with an unobtrusive stranger a step or two behind to make sure that the lady was on her way. I was having none of that.'

All his private secretary's warnings about the constitutional implications appear to have fallen on deaf ears. In the grip of his blinkered obsession, David could focus only on the insult to Wallis, and set out to protect her with the stubborn chivalry of an Arthurian knight. 'They had struck at the very roots of my pride. Only the most faint-hearted would have remained unaroused by such a challenge,' he wrote in his memoirs. 'This was not the crisis of a Prince; it was the crisis of a King. And because it was not my nature to watch and wait, I resolved to come to grips at once with Mr Baldwin and the nebulous figures around him.' As ever, David saw himself as an individual, Wallis, by his side, tilting against the establishment. There was no thought of the country or empire, none of his royal lineage or office, no consideration for the verdict history might pass upon him. At the very least, his was a most unstatesmanlike position.

Edward VIII refused to have anything more to do with Major Hardinge. From then on, Walter Monckton acted as David's go-between. The two men met that weekend at Windsor Castle. Hardinge's letter was discussed, and was later shown to Wallis back at Fort Belvedere. She was, by her own account 'stunned', and was of a mind to pack her bags and run, as Hardinge had suggested. But David would hear none of it. 'On the Throne or off,' he told her, 'I'm going to marry you' — and on this one issue his resolution never faltered. The following evening, 16 November, he summoned the Prime Minister to Buckingham Palace and told him that he intended marrying Mrs Simpson as soon as she was free, and that he was prepared to renounce the throne in order to do so. Baldwin tried to explain the seriousness of what he was proposing. He appealed to Edward VIII both as King and as Emperor, pointing out that the throne was the one link uniting the British Empire and that a shock such as this might lead to it breaking up. But, as he told his family afterwards, the King 'simply could not understand and he [Baldwin] could not make him'.

Later that same evening, the King went to dinner with his mother at Marlborough House. As well as Queen Mary, he had asked his sister, the Princess Royal to join them. Unfortunately his new sister-in-law, Alice, Duchess of Gloucester, had also arrived for dinner, which meant that conversation had to be restricted to small-talk about the Newmarket sales and the exterior redecoration of Buckingham Palace until after the meal was over, when Alice could decently leave them. Only then, when they were sitting alone in Queen Mary's boudoir, did David summon up the courage to tell them what he had come to say. At first, they were sympathetic as he explained the depth of his feelings for Mrs Simpson, but when he went on to tell his mother and sister that he was prepared to give up the throne to marry her, the two women responded with shock and consternation. As Queen Mary would later say to members of her family, no single event in the whole of her life caused her so much distress, or left her feeling so deeply humiliated, as hearing of her son's resolution to give up the throne. Her daughter-in-law Elizabeth is quoted as having confided much later to Victor Cazalet that the events of the Abdication 'very nearly killed poor Queen Mary. There is indeed such a thing as a broken heart.'

The Duke of Windsor's description of this conversation illustrates, more plainly than any

230

other passage in his memoirs, how far he had distanced himself from the rest of the royal family. As he put it, 'The word 'duty' fell between us.' For Queen Mary, there was no question where her son's duty lay. 'To my Mother,' David wrote, as if it came as a surprise, 'the Monarchy was something sacred and the Sovereign a personage apart.' To *her* mind, it was inevitable that he must surrender Wallis Simpson because the alternative, to give up the throne, was unthinkable. The Crown was his destiny, and his only true happiness should be to serve it. But David's conception of duty was altogether more modern. His happiness, indeed his destiny, was to marry Wallis. Who knows, it might even make him a better King — after all, was not his father George V a better king for being happily married? If he could not marry Wallis, then he could not fulfil his proper functions as King, and it therefore became his duty to abdicate the throne.

He may have been right. As Michael Bloch has pointed out, when Edward VIII was sure of Wallis, 'when she was standing by him, he was a good king' for the eleven months of his reign. 'Otherwise, he was hopeless.' At any rate, 'There could be no question,' David wrote in his memoirs, 'of my shirking my duty' in this respect. Yet he was still convinced that all would be well, if only he could bring his mother to meet Wallis Simpson and talk to her, and see that she was the most wonderful woman in the world. Walter Monckton would later argue, rather unconvincingly, that if Queen

231

Mary that evening had agreed to meet Wallis Simpson, she could have won her round to a true understanding of the position, and the crisis would have been avoided. It was not to be. David's mother and sister both categorically refused ever to receive Mrs Simpson. When her son asked why, Queen Mary is reported to have replied, 'Because she is an adventuress!' — a remark which David never forgot and which, he would say years later, 'lay like a coiled malevolence' between him and his mother.

Eighteen months passed before Queen Mary felt able fully to express her feelings to her son, by which time he was in exile. Inevitably, she had to resort to writing them down. After recalling how miserable she was when David had told her of his plans, and 'how I implored you not to do so for our sake and for the sake of the country', she got to the heart of the matter: David's utter self-interest. 'You did not seem able to take in any point of view but your own . . . I do not think you have ever realised the shock, which the attitude you took caused your family and the whole Nation. It seemed to us inconceivable to those who had made such sacrifices during the war that you, as their King, refused a lesser sacrifice . . . After all, all my life I have put my Country before anything else.' She ended her letter, 'My feelings for you as your Mother remain the same' — and David would have felt the chill benevolence of those closing words, reminding him of his strained and loveless childhood. He had found in his relationship with Wallis a substitute for his mother's neglect and cold reserve, and it was his refusal to let go of something so precious to him which precipitated his abdication and exile.

The unsettling effect which David's announcement had had on his mother clearly registered with Stanley Baldwin, who called on her the next day and was astonished to be greeted by the icily formal royal matriarch striding purposefully towards him, with her hand outstretched, exclaiming uncharacteristically, 'Well, Prime Minister — here's a pretty kettle of fish!'

The following day, Bertie heard confirmation from David in person of the news he had been dreading ever since Hardinge's warning three weeks earlier. Looking back on their meeting in his memoirs, the Duke of Windsor commented blandly, 'Bertie was so taken aback by my news that in his shy way he could not bring himself to express his innermost feelings at the time.' Not until 1962, writing in the *Sunday Express*, did he bring himself to admit the shock that Bertie experienced when he realised that the succession was indeed going to pass to him.

' 'Oh,' he said, 'that's a dreadful thing to hear. None of us wants that, I least of all.'

' 'I'm afraid there's no other way,' I said. 'My mind is made up.' ' The Duke then added, 'The ties between us had always been close. His feelings towards me then were very warm. Whatever the outcome, [Bertie] said, he and I must stay in touch; we were brothers, before anything else.'

Prince Harry, predictably enough, 'appeared little moved', when the King called on him with his news. His chief worry was that if David gave up the throne, he would become Regent Designate and would have to resign from the Army, which would be damned annoying. Prince George heard the news from David two days later. According to Chips Channon, at whose house the two brothers were due to dine later that evening, 'The Duke of Kent gasped' when the King told him of his plan to marry Wallis, and asked what she was going to call herself.

' 'Call herself?' the King echoed. 'What do you think — Queen of England of course.'

' 'She is going to be Queen?' '

' 'Yes and Empress of India, the whole bag of tricks!' '

According to David's later recollection of the encounter, his brother 'was reconciled to my decision'. This was decidedly not how Prime Minister Stanley Baldwin saw it. He told his sister that Prince George had been furious, and was to be heard repeating angrily that the King was 'besotted on the woman'.

'Something must be done' was Edward VIII's widely-quoted criticism of his government's laisser-faire attitude towards the unemployed, after he returned in mid-November 1936 from a highly successful tour of the industrial blackspots of South Wales. 'Something must be done' was also the determination of Stanley Baldwin's Cabinet, now increasingly anxious about the prospect of Wallis Simpson as Queen. The Chancellor of the Exchequer, Neville Chamberlain, had already drafted a letter to the King threatening that his government would resign if he did not end his liaison with Mrs Simpson; the Prime Minister suppressed the letter, aware that too harsh a reaction from His Majesty's government would incline the public to the King's side. The Foreign Secretary, Anthony Eden, had his own misgivings about Edward VIII's pro-German sympathies at this critical juncture. The German Army had occupied the Rhineland in March — on Hitler's orders and apparently against the wishes of the German High Command which had given orders to pull back if Britain and France had responded strongly.

While the King had been consorting with miners and steelworkers, Wallis herself had not been idle. At lunch in Claridge's with Lord Rothermere's son, Esmond Harmsworth, she listened with interest to a proposition he put to her. Had she ever considered marrying the King morganatically — in other words, becoming his wife but not his Queen? As a consolation prize, she might even adopt the title of Duchess of Lancaster. The King, after all, was Duke of Lancaster. Constitutionally, the children of a royal morganatic marriage were commoners, but if she had no children, this drawback would not arise. The King had already pondered and rejected the idea of a morganatic marriage several weeks earlier, but now, on hearing of Wallis's interest, he was minded to follow it through. He asked Esmond Harmsworth to put the idea to the Prime Minister. To Baldwin, it was an unhelpful suggestion, borne by an unpopular messenger. Had the King not been so preoccupied, he would have recognised that Baldwin regarded both the Rothermere and Beaverbrook papers as 'the Devil's press', seeking 'power without responsibility, the prerogative of the harlot through the ages'. Curtly, the Prime Minister informed Esmond Harmsworth that the proposal of a morganatic marriage would have to be presented to Parliament, and that 'Parliament would *never* pass it.' Even so the King kept trying, and two days later, having received no formal answer from Baldwin, asked the Prime Minister to come to see him.

It was this meeting that sealed David's fate. If, like the Duke of York, Edward VIII had taken a more active interest in the constitution, or if at this point he had called on Winston Churchill or Max Beaverbrook to guide him, the Crown might have played a more politically astute game. As it was, David handed the advantage to Baldwin on a plate by allowing the question of his marriage to be made a constitutional issue. The wily Prime Minister merely reiterated what he had said to Harmsworth: that he would need to put the morganatic proposal to the Cabinet, and to the prime ministers of the Dominions. Implicit was the rider that the monarch, having formally asked his ministers' advice, was bound either to accept it or else face his ministers' resignation since they would no longer enjoy their sovereign's confidence. Was that what the King really wanted? With nobody to counsel him except Wallis, Edward VIII insisted that Baldwin take official soundings. By the time Beaverbrook was able to warn him that he was putting his head on the executioner's block, it was too late to pull back.

The Duke of York meanwhile was attempting to come to terms with the grim reality manifesting itself before him. 'I feel like the proverbial sheep being led to the slaughter,' he told his private secretary. He composed a letter to Godfrey Thomas, the King's assistant private secretary. 'If the worst happens,' he wrote, '& I have to take over, you can be assured that I will do my best to clear up the inevitable mess, if,' he added bleakly, 'the whole fabric does not crumble under the shock and strain of it all.' Elizabeth was more worried about Bertie crumbling under the shock and strain. She wrote a secret letter to the King — not for Bertie's eyes — which resonates to this day with the desperate anxiety that the rest of the family felt but could not put into words: 'Darling David. *Please* read this. Please be kind to Bertie when you see him, because he loves you, and minds terribly all that happens to you. I wish that you could realize how loyal and true he is to you, and you have no idea how hard it has been for him lately. I *know* that he is fonder of you than anybody else, and as his wife I must write to tell you this. I am terrified for him — so DO help him, and *for God's sake* don't tell him that I have written. We both uphold you always. We want you to be happy more than anything else, but it's awfully difficult for Bertie to say what he thinks, you know how shy he is — so do help him.'

It was a foregone conclusion that the morganatic marriage proposal would be rejected.

'The people won't 'ave it,' the Labour politician Ernest Bevin had told Baldwin, and the Cabinet agreed. So did the Dominions — Australia, Canada, South Africa and New Zealand — although New Zealand had been entirely unaware of the existence of Wallis Simpson. The Australian premier felt the impropriety so strongly that he advised abdication even if the King did not marry Mrs Simpson. Edward VIII's response, according to Baldwin, was mildly to remark, 'There are not many people in Australia.'

For her part, Wallis was feeling increasingly threatened and alone. She sensed that her dazzling reign at the summit of London society was over. 'Everything is wrong and going more wrong, and I am so tired of it all,' she confessed to her old friend 'Foxy' Gwynne who had been with Lord Sefton on the *Nahlin*. And to Sibyl Colefax she wrote self-pityingly, 'I am planning quite by myself to go away for a while. I think everyone here would like that — except one person perhaps — but I am planning a clever means of escape. After a while my name will be forgotten by the people and only two people will suffer instead of a mass of people who aren't interested anyway in individual feelings but only the workings of a system.'

But there was no time to plan a clever escape. She had become the victim of hate mail and bomb threats, even a threat to scar her face with vitriol. A brick crashed through a window of the house next door (courtesy of the *Daily Express*, whose proprietor, Beaverbrook, wanted to get Wallis out of London for her own safety) and menacing graffiti was chalked on walls with messages such as 'Down With the American Whore'. Nor was her position made easier by Sir Oswald Mosley and his Fascist henchmen parading in black shirts through the East End in support of the King — 'One, two, three, four, five; We want Baldwin, dead or alive!' On the same day that Baldwin's telegrams went out to his opposite numbers in the Dominions, Wallis fled Cumberland Terrace to the security of Fort Belvedere. She departed just in time: a few days after she left, the house was besieged by a stone-throwing mob. It was only a matter of weeks since an American biography had hailed Wallis as a heroine, 'the queen of romance, of glamour and the unfulfilled longings of a love-starved world'. Now, convinced that she was a target of hatred in the country, she took shelter behind the battlements of her knight errant.

As November gave way to December, the mood of crisis intensified. Queen Mary had reacted bitterly to the proposal of a morganatic marriage. As the descendant of such a union herself, she saw her life, until the blessed deliverance of her marriage, as ignominiously blighted by it. 'Really! We might as well be living in Rumania!' she exclaimed to Lady Airlie. North of the border, where the Duke of York had gone to be installed as Grand Master Mason of Scotland (a position his brother had held until he became King), Bertie and Elizabeth were being serenaded with enthusiastic renderings of 'Will Ye No' Come Back Again?' In conferring upon her the Freedom of Edinburgh, the Lord Provost saluted Elizabeth as 'Beloved Duchess, daughter of our northern land, gracious servant of the State, ambassadress of Empire' — praise which held a special significance in the uncertain times.

With David and Wallis at Fort Belvedere was Aunt Bessie who had valiantly journeyed over from America to provide moral support. By now the King was neglecting all matters of state except those directly affecting his emotions. 'I feared for him,' Walter Monckton was to say later. 'Outwardly he remained charming, polite. But he was like a man who had taken leave of the real world . . . *She* was the reality. We were shadows.' Tommy Lascelles said memorably of David at the time of his abdication that he was 'like the child in the fairy story who was given everything in the world, but they forgot the soul. He has no spiritual or aesthetic side at all. He did not know beauty when he saw it . . . He cared for nothing in nature.' Baldwin, too, marvelled to Harold Nicolson about the King's total lack of any religious sense.

When, in the early hours of 1 December, the old Crystal Palace south of the Thames on Sydenham Hill went up in flames, the symbolism was not lost on those caught up in the royal drama. As thousands watched, a great monument of Victorian tradition collapsed in burning ruins. 'We saw the smoke from my window,' commented Queen Mary baldly. 'What a pity . . . ' In fact, she was very soon going to have to face the fact that her own private world was going to be set ablaze. The same day, the Bishop of Bradford — a little-known churchman named Dr Blunt — took the King to task at a diocesan conference for not going to church more regularly. It was a mild and innocent admonition, but such was the pent-up frustration of the British newspapers that they chose to react to it like the Pope anathematising Henry VIII. Within forty-eight hours the 'Blunt instrument', as it came to be known, had broken open the floodgates. When Bertie and Elizabeth returned from Scotland on the morning of 3 December they were confronted, as they stepped off the train at Euston, with newspaper posters flagging 'THE KING'S MARRIAGE' in letters a full twelve inches high. Now at last, the British people could share the secret of their sovereign's affair with an American divorcee, a woman who, as Queen Mary commented, had two husbands still living. Overnight, Mrs Simpson became a household name. Children chanted new lines to the old carol:

Hark the herald angels sing,
Mrs Simpson's pinched our King!

A whole new genre of jokes sprang into being like the dragons' teeth. It was, said the wits over the breakfast table, the first case of a British Admiral who'd become third mate to an American tramp. The relationship was now seen for what it was — 'King Edward the Eighth and Mrs Simpson the Seven-Eighths'.

The Prime Minister hoped that so much evidence of public antipathy to his marriage might make Edward VIII appreciate the duty he owed to his subjects. But the press comment simply confirmed the King's belief that there was a conspiracy against him. 'They don't want me,' he railed at Stanley Baldwin when he read a critical article in the *Birmingham Post*. After forty-two years of generally unalloyed praise, Prince Charming was suddenly discovering what it meant to have the press turn against him. Yet he put the blame on Dr Blunt and the government. The King 'clearly thought [it] had been inspired by No 10,' Baldwin told his private secretary. Instead of a high-minded discussion on the sacrificial and solemn duties of kingship, which was what he had wished for, Baldwin was treated to the usual emotional justification of Mrs Simpson: 'Wallis is the most wonderful woman in the world.'

'Well, sir, I hope you may find her so,' the Prime Minister answered wearily.

David's family were also smarting at the harsh attitude taken by the press, the first overt criticism of the royal family since 1864, when the widowed Queen Victoria found herself rebuked for her extreme reclusiveness. 'Darling David,' Queen Mary made haste to write to her eldest son on the day the story broke, 'This news in the papers is very upsetting, especially as I have not seen you for 10 days — I would very much like to see you, won't you look in some time today?'

David did as she had asked him, later that

evening. During the day there had been more pressing matters to attend to. The morning's tidal wave of criticism had finally convinced him of the urgent need to get Wallis out of the country until matters were settled. He arranged for her to leave that evening for the villa near Cannes in the south of France owned by her old friends Katherine and Herman Rogers. His lord-in-waiting, Lord Brownlow, was to accompany her, driving her to Newhaven where they would be met by a Scotland Yard detective. They would then change to the royal Buick and take the ferry across the Channel. Tearfully, the King instructed Wallis to telephone him at the Palace wherever she ended up that night, no matter how late. White with apprehension, Wallis thrust her beloved Slipper ('Slippy-Poo') into David's arms, and left the Fort for the last time, without a word of farewell to the servants. Travelling light, she had nevertheless managed to find room in her luggage for jewellery valued at £100,000.

Before she left, she persuaded the King to broadcast an appeal to the nation, over the heads of his ministers. He must explain that his decision to marry her was final, and suggest that he left the country for a few weeks to give 'the people' time to decide what they wanted to happen next. That this plan was both impractical and unconstitutional never occurred to him, then or later, but it undoubtedly occurred to Bertie and Walter Monckton, whom the King saw that evening before returning to London to present the Prime Minister with the draft of his speech.

Baldwin, sensing the makings of an even deeper crisis, played for time and promised to put the King's suggestion to a special Cabinet meeting the following day. On hearing that Edward VIII had two aircraft waiting at Hendon Aerodrome to take him abroad, his Prime Minister quietly ensured that they remained grounded.

As Wallis and Brownlow drove south on the first leg of their journey, Edward VIII, that same night of 3 December, answered his mother's summons and presented himself for dinner at Marlborough House. There he found Queen Mary and his sister, with Bertie and Elizabeth. It had been a wretched day for all of them. Upset by the reports in the press and elsewhere, they had cancelled their public engagements. Even such a trouper as the Duchess of York could not bring herself to fulfil her scheduled visit to the Mothercraft Training Society. Elizabeth was in all probability tired from a restless night on the sleeper, but her distress had been compounded by the revelations in the morning papers. More than that, she was appalled by the way David was treating his family. His mother, in particular, had been kept in the dark about his plans for ten days or more. The Duchess of York had been unable to keep silent, and had spoken testily when she had been quizzed by journalists a month earlier. 'Everyone knows more than we do. We know nothing. Nothing!' she was reported to have said. Now she showed her anger by refusing to have anything to do with the ensuing family conference. To those who knew her well, it was the start of what was to become a familiar pattern. In future, when faced with a difficult or unpleasant situation, Elizabeth's prime tactic would be withdrawal.

Left alone with his family, David tried to brazen it out, explaining away his weeks of estrangement from them with the bland excuse that he had been trying to shelter them in a situation he felt he should handle on his own. He then appealed to their sympathy, telling them that he was going to marry Mrs Simpson because he could not live alone as King. The family plainly thought that, in his state of psychological collapse, David was more than a little mad. He was smoking incessantly — either a pipe or a cigarette — and (according to Beaverbrook) kept pressing his handkerchief to his head, or using it to wipe the sweat from his forehead. Day after day he repeated the same phrases like a mantra against reason — '*No marriage, no coronation*', he would repeat, or, to his mother's appeals, '*All that matters is our happiness.*' Alec Hardinge's wife Helen claimed that at the Fort he slept with a loaded pistol under his pillow, though on the night of 8 December, Walter Monckton and the King's valet, concerned about David's state of near-collapse, searched his bedroom and found no gun to hand.

Meanwhile Bertie started keeping a diary of events. 'When David left after making his dreadful announcement to his mother,' he recorded, 'he told me to come & see him at the Fort the next morning.' In fact it was not the next morning, but three days later, on the evening of Monday 7 December, when David finally spoke to Bertie. For four nerve-wracking days, the Duke of York, the heir presumptive and a pivotal figure in the drama, was kept completely in the dark about the latest developments. David promised meetings and then cancelled them. He failed to answer telephone calls. Watching her husband almost beside himself with worry, Elizabeth felt the humiliation acutely. A few weeks later she would give away something of what they had been through when she wrote to a friend, Victor Cazalet, 'I don't think we could ever imagine a more incredible tragedy, and the agony of it all has been beyond words. And the melancholy fact remains still at the present moment that he for whom he agonized is the one person it did not touch. Poor soul, a fearful awakening is awaiting his completely blinded reason before very long.'

However, there were others who were prepared to stand by Bertie and lend him their support that crucial weekend. The Prime Minister, with an eye to the increasingly probable succession, saw to it that the Duke of York was kept abreast of developments. Bertie had three or four secret meetings with Baldwin in Downing Street, slipping into No 10 unobserved through the garden entrance. This small subterfuge was well advised. Egged on by the Beaverbrook and Rothermere newspapers, voices in support of Edward VIII were beginning to be heard. For a moment, during those turbulent days, there appeared to be a real danger that a King's Party would form, and would divide the country down the middle, particularly if the King were to quit Fort Belvedere, come down to London and appeal to the populace, like one of his medieval predecessors. Small crowds gathered outside No 10 waving placards inscribed 'Hands Off Our King' and 'Abdication Means Revolution'. Others gathered outside Buckingham Palace, singing 'For He's A Jolly Good Fellow' or shouting, 'We want Eddie and his Missus!'

Among the politicos, Oswald Mosley was not the only one stirring the pot. Partly to get at Baldwin and partly out of romantic sympathy for a beleaguered monarch, Winston Churchill did his best to put some backbone into the King, counselling him to hold fast and play for time. 'We must have time for the big battalions to mass,' he urged, in the style of public oratory which would become familiar to the world in 1940. 'We may win. We may not. Retire to Windsor Castle! Summon the Beefeaters! Raise the drawbridge! Close the gates! And dare Baldwin to drag you out!' However, on the Monday, when he raised the matter in the Commons, the House turned on Churchill and shouted him down. The King's Party was submerged in the ensuing uproar.

Unable to communicate with each other, David and Bertie endured as best they could their private misery. Bertie was well aware that there were serious misgivings about his stammer and about his physical and mental ability to serve as King. A suggestion is supposed to have been put up to Baldwin, reportedly by the

King's adviser Walter Monckton, that the Heir Presumptive should step aside in favour of one of his younger brothers: but since that choice lay between the ineffably wooden Prince Harry and the scandal-ridden Prince George, the proposal, if it was ever made, was quickly scotched. David meanwhile was agonising in spirit with Wallis on her long car journey across France, during which she had to hide from the packhounds of the press under a travelling-rug in the footwell of the car. At one point, in order to escape her pursuers, she had had to be bundled through a restaurant kitchen window into a back alley where the Buick waited with its engine running. yet even at this distance, and with the terrible pressures on her, it was Wallis's sheer will-power that was prolonging the crisis by keeping Edward VIII on the throne. In a crisis in which Baldwin, Beaverbrook and Winston Churchill all played their part, it is noteworthy that the two strongest personalities, albeit behind the scenes, would turn out to be Wallis and her old adversary, Elizabeth.

For his part, David was wearying of the struggle. Walter Monckton, who was with him at the Fort until the end, later testified to the detrimental effect that Wallis's hectoring telephone calls, made 'on a bad line, at a long distance', were having on the already unbalanced King. The Cabinet was due to meet on Sunday 6 December. On the Saturday, David finally crumbled, and sent Walter Monckton to tell the Prime Minister that he was ready to quit and wanted to negotiate appropriate terms. These, insisted upon by Wallis, boiled down to a decent amount of money, a title for Wallis, along with the rank of Her Royal Highness and, rather astutely, a guarantee that her divorce would be allowed to go through.

This last idea was probably Monckton's, who rightly feared that proof of collusion might be produced, which would invalidate the Simpson divorce and wreck the king's most cherished plans. The King's Proctor was said at that very moment to be investigating two such allegations. To prevent this, Edward VIII and Monckton wanted a bill to pass through Parliament granting the Simpsons an immediate divorce, alongside the bill which dealt with the abdication. Without any real enthusiasm, Baldwin promised to put this to the Cabinet the next morning. It was not an unwelcome surprise to the Prime Minister when his ministerial colleagues on Sunday rejected the idea out of hand: but it was this which probably persuaded Edward VIII that he had to go. His supporters recognised the fatalism in him. Max Beaverbrook telephoned Churchill a few days later and said, 'Our cock won't fight.'

That Sunday evening Wallis finally arrived at her friends the Rogers' gloomy, part-medieval home in Cannes, the Villa Lou Viei. She was as emotionally exhausted as David. As she wrote later to Sibyl Colefax, 'If only they had said, let's drop the [abdication] idea now and in the autumn we'll discuss it again. And Sibyl darling in the autumn I would have been so very far away . . . ' The next day, over the telephone, she read David the statement she proposed issuing to the press. In it she said she was 'willing, if such action would solve the problem, to withdraw forthwith from a situation that has been rendered both unhappy and untenable.' The King allowed this statement to be released to the press on the grounds that it would help to divert criticism away from her on to him — and perhaps it did. The *Daily Express* published it under the headline 'END OF CRISIS'. What David actually said to Wallis on the telephone, after a long pause, was 'Go ahead, if you wish; it won't make any difference.'

Some historians have glossed this interchange as a cynical, face-saving ploy on Wallis's part. In the opinion of Baldwin and his ministers, and probably of the majority of the British people, the woman who had gained so much from (in Baldwin's phrase) 'bewitching' England's King, was an unscrupulous gold-digger. As Neville Chamberlain wrote in his diary on 7 December, 'She has already ruined him in money and jewels and it is thought that she can be squared when she realises that she has lost the game.' This attitude towards Wallis was what now persuaded the Prime Minister to send her solicitor, Theodore Goddard, out to Cannes to negotiate with her in person, under the guise of warning his client about the allegations of collusion in her divorce.

As Mr Goddard was to discover, the truth of the situation was more complicated. It was never a question of bribing Wallis to back down. As he reported by telephone to Baldwin's secretary, Wallis was in a 'terrified state of nerves; complete capitulation and willingness to do anything had superseded her former truculent self.' She was prepared to do anything, withdraw her petition for divorce, travel to China if it came to that, but the point was that it would make no difference. She knew that David would, in her words, follow her to the ends of the earth — he had told her so himself often enough. On or off the throne, marriage to David was a foregone conclusion: what mattered in the meantime was that he should go on fighting for his rights — not least over the size of the pension he would obtain on leaving the throne. The actual effect of Baldwin's unilateral decision to send Theodore Goddard out to Cannes was to galvanise the King into action. Rightly, he suspected Baldwin of trying to scare Wallis off at the eleventh hour, and decided there was no more time to be lost. In an audience with the Prime Minister he informed him that his decision to abdicate was final. Then, at long last, he rang Bertie at Royal Lodge in Windsor Great Park. 'Come and see me after dinner,' he requested. Having been kept waiting for so long, Bertie finally found the strength to face down his elder brother. 'No,' he replied firmly, 'I will come and see you at once.' He arrived at the Fort from Royal Lodge ten minutes later.

Elizabeth, with characteristic timing, had succumbed to a bout of flu, and taken to her bed at 145 Piccadilly. With Wallis also absent, the two brothers were alone, as they had been at the deathbed of their father. As it was, after days

251

of nail-biting tension, the encounter was almost an anticlimax. David had made his decision. As his heir, Bertie would become King-Emperor, he explained, and also take over as head of the House of Windsor. Beyond that brief statement of the facts, David seemed to have little else to say. There was no brotherly reminiscence, no acknowledgement of the momentousness of the occasion — the King was too preoccupied for that. Nevertheless Bertie, having made contact with his brother, had no intention of being dismissed back to the wings. He returned to Royal Lodge for dinner, and came straight back afterwards. He wrote later in his diary, 'I felt once I got there I was not going to leave. As he is my eldest brother I had to be there to try & help him in his hour of need.'

This was the familiar, selfless Bertie, without the stiffening provided by Elizabeth's implacable resolve. David, as it turned out, did indeed have a 'need', but there was nothing spiritual about it: he wanted to ensure that, after he quitted the throne, he and Wallis would continue to live in the style to which they were accustomed. This became painfully clear at subsequent meetings between the two brothers and their lawyers. In contrast to Bertie's sincere and heart-searching grief — grief felt for his brother as much as for himself — David's sole preoccupation was with what would satisfy Wallis.

Just as the government now wanted to settle the matter of the abdication as swiftly as possible (the uncertainty, so the Chancellor Neville Chamberlain informed his Cabinet colleagues, was depressing the Christmas trade), so the King, too, was determined to resolve things quickly. As a result, the final forty-eight hours of abdication week passed in a maelstrom of hurriedly convened meetings, backroom compromises, public expressions of noble sentiment, and private wranglings over money — all conducted in an atmosphere of growing mutual distrust and increasingly overwrought nerves. The resentment and hostility that this bred was to poison the relationship between Bertie and David for the rest of their lives. Throughout this period the long-suffering Bertie showed his errant brother what was, in the circumstances, an extraordinary amount of unreciprocated understanding and affection. The Duke of York knew better than anyone the magnitude of the task his older brother was foisting upon him, which he would now have to undertake to the best of his ability until his dying day. At home with his parents during long periods of wartime convalescence he, more than any of George V's sons, had come to recognise the heavy burden his father had shouldered in his solitary calling, and the unstinting devotion to duty first and duty foremost, which kingship always demanded. In spite of this, Bertie's devotion and admiration for his older brother did not falter. 'Isn't my brother wonderful, isn't he wonderful? No-one could carry off this dinner as he can!' he murmured to fellow guests seated round the table at Fort Belvedere on Tuesday 8 December. To Walter Monckton he whispered, 'And this is the man we are going to lose!'

Others present at that dinner at Fort Belvedere agreed that Edward VIII, dapper in his white kilt, was the life and soul of the party. Walter Monckton later wrote, 'In that quiet panelled room he sat at the head of the table with his boyish face and smile, with a good fresh colour while the rest of us were pale as sheets, rippling over with bright conversation.' Baldwin, who had driven up from London in a last attempt to change the King's mind, reassured another guest that — no — Bertie was not as dull as he looked, but was very like his father George V who 'by perseverance, reliability, example to his people and a sense of duty' gained for himself 'the much loved position he held when he died'. Baldwin was prescient and, in any case, he could afford to be magnanimous. In this, the trickiest passage of his premiership, he had seen off his enemies, Churchill and Beaverbrook. He had been a rock of stability throughout the crisis, the pivot upon whom history turned. He could afford a degree of self-glorification as he drove home at the end of his evening. 'This is making history,' he told his private secretary with unabashed glee. And then: 'This is what I like.'

For his part, Bertie drove back to London as if to his public execution. Throughout the next day, Wednesday 9 December, he held meetings about his new dual role as Head of State and head of the House of Windsor. With Baldwin and his political advisers he discussed the machinery for the abdication process, and for his own accession. In a discussion with

Monckton, he agreed that David after his abdication should retain his royal rank and have Fort Belvedere to live in when he returned to England. On such a fraught day, Queen Mary's diary entry was typically laconic: 'Rather foggy day. At 1.30 with Mary to meet David (on business) at Royal Lodge — Back before 5 — Georgie and Marina dined.' Knowing full well what her oldest son was going to say, Queen Mary had refused to go to Fort Belvedere to hear it. She wanted to be in the more familiar and comforting surroundings of Royal Lodge when she finally had to confront the 'business' of her son's abdication.

It was a harrowing day for the sixty-nine-year-old Queen Mary. After dinner, the Duke of York arrived to see her and talk her through the latest events. In doing so, the full import of what was about to happen dawned on him, and he broke down and sobbed for fully an hour in his mother's arms. It was perhaps the most intimate time that Bertie had ever spent with her. He was still composing himself when a message reached him that he was wanted at Fort Belvedere at ten o'clock the following morning to witness the signing of King Edward VIII's Instrument of Abdication. The Duke and his mother immediately summoned Walter Monckton, who arrived from Downing Street, bringing what Queen Mary described as 'the paper drawn up for David's abdication of the Throne of this Empire because he wants to marry Mrs Simpson!!!!!' Five exclamation marks denoted her conviction that this was an unparalleled catastrophe. 'The whole affair,' she wrote, 'has lasted since 16 November and is very painful. It is a terrible blow to us all and particularly to poor Bertie.' In the presence of Walter Monckton, a comparative stranger, she could not contain her humiliation and anger. 'To give up all that for this!' she exclaimed, distraught.

In the early hours of Thursday morning, the indefatigable Walter Monckton arrived back at Fort Belvedere to show the King the abdication documents in draft. Only a few hours later he was on call again, as the King's brothers arrived to witness the historic moment when David signed the papers declaring his 'irrevocable determination to renounce the throne for Myself and My descendants'. At the last, Edward VIII continued to rebel against the trappings of monarchy. Handed the royal quill to sign the Abdication document, he cried fretfully, 'There's no ink in the damn pot!' Upon which, this most untraditional of monarchs was handed a fountain pen.

In the House of Commons that afternoon, Stanley Baldwin gave his historic account of the abdication crisis to a packed and attentive audience of MPs: 'Let us look forward and remember our country and the trust reposed by it in this House of Commons, and let us rally behind the new King, stand by him and help him.' When he sat down, the first hostile shots were fired in the direction of the 'collaborators' who had supported the ex-King. 'People who have been licking Mrs Simpson's boots ought to be shot,' Nancy Astor yelled across the chamber at Chips Channon.

Late in the afternoon, when all the participants in the drama were emotionally and physically exhausted, David and Bertie sat down to what Bertie later described as 'a terrible lawyer interview'. The legal teams of the two brothers were still trying to thrash out a financial settlement for David and Wallis, and resolve the disagreement over George V's will which David saw as cheating him out of income which was rightfully his. The meeting opened with a speech from David warning how badly off he would be, and demanding a substantial allowance in return for surrendering his life interest in Sandringham and Balmoral. To emphasise the point, Edward VIII asserted that his entire fortune was no more than £90,000, and that in disposable income he did not think he had above £5000 a year.

He was deliberately covering up the truth. His true assets, not counting his property in Canada, were at least twelve times greater than that, exceeding £1.1 million in the values of the time. In truth, David, despite losing his throne, was still a very rich man, with an annual income by today's values in excess of £1 million. To Edward VIII's official biographer, Philip Ziegler, 'It was a suicidal lie, and could only be explained by the traditional charity of the coroner recording a verdict of suicide — that the deceased took his own life while the balance of his mind was disturbed.' Under great strain, and constantly bullied by Wallis on the telephone

257

from Cannes to extract as much money for them as possible, David ignored the fact that his brother would inevitably learn the true state of his finances. As it turned out, his greed and dishonesty would lose him the confidence of the two men whose support would most have mattered in the years of his exile: George VI and Winston Churchill.

Within three months Bertie learned the real worth of David's true fortune. 'You were under great strain and I am not seeking to reproach you or anyone,' the new King wrote to him three months later. 'But the fact remains that I was completely misled.' For all his mildness, Bertie did in fact feel profoundly let down and betrayed. David's behaviour had grievously undermined the trust and admiration with which he had looked up to his brother for over forty years. Edward VIII may have left the meeting on his final full day as King-Emperor with a guaranteed income of £25,000 a year, provided either by Parliament or directly by the Crown, but he paid the price for the rest of his life — a life spent cut adrift from his family, his country, and the brother who had once loved him so dearly.

The erstwhile Duke of York acceded the throne as King-Emperor eight minutes before two o'clock on the afternoon of Friday 11 December 1936. He had chosen to call himself George VI on the grounds that King Albert might have sounded too Germanic. The first act of his new reign was to give his older brother a new name as well. In this he displayed unexpected shrewdness and, given his previous saintly demeanour, at last a belated flash of royal spleen. David was scheduled to make a national broadcast that evening, and Sir John Reith was proposing to introduce him as Mr Edward Windsor. 'That is quite wrong,' Bertie snapped. His own proposal was a new royal dukedom. David had already reverted to being His Royal Highness, Prince Edward: he should also now be created Duke of Windsor. As a Royal Duke, David would not be able to stand for election in the Commons, or speak or vote in the House of Lords. He could, however, retain his rank in all the armed forces. It was an entirely sensible decision, and one bound to appeal to David since it gave him status without responsibility. But it left open the emotive question of whether the same status would be accorded to Wallis.

Before the new Duke of Windsor's broadcast and departure, there was the final ordeal of a family dinner at Royal Lodge. 'That last family dinner party was too awful,' Elizabeth admitted years later. 'Thank goodness I had the flu and couldn't go.' From her sickbed she had written the departing King a letter: 'Dearest David, I am so sad not to be with you today, as I wanted so much to see you before you go, and say 'God bless you' from my heart. We are all overcome with misery and can only pray that you will find happiness in your life. I often think of the old days and how you helped Bertie and me in the first years of our marriage. I shall always mention you in my prayers.' Having despatched this letter — avoiding any mention of Wallis Simpson whom she would never forgive — Elizabeth lay in bed for her first evening as Queen-Empress, listening intently along with the rest of the nation and much of the Empire, as her brother-in-law made his abdication broadcast from his suite in the Augusta Tower of Windsor Castle.

The actor in David rose to this occasion nobly, with the help of a script rewritten by Winston Churchill, who had thrown the King's first, self-serving draft on the fire at Fort Belvedere.

A few hours ago I discharged my last duty as King and Emperor, and now I have been succeeded by my brother the Duke of York, my first words must be to declare my allegiance to him This I do with all my heart . . . This decision has been made less difficult for me by the sure knowledge that my brother, with his long training in the public affairs of this country, and with his fine qualities, will be able to take my place forthwith, without interruption or injury to the life and progress of the Empire. And he has one matchless blessing enjoyed by so many of you and not bestowed on me — a happy home with his wife and children . . . I wish him, and you, his people, happiness and prosperity with all my heart. God bless you all. God Save the King.

If Elizabeth shed tears, she was not alone. Far away, in the Villa Lou Viei, Wallis was also lying on the drawing-room sofa weeping, her hands held over her eyes. Few of those who heard the abdication speech, in Britain and around the world, did so without a lump in their throats. Prayers were said for the former King, just as they would be said, equally fervently in the months to come, for his successor. In Royal Lodge, Queen Mary and her sons listened in silence, though there must have been a disturbance from the younger ones, because Bertie went up to them and said quite fiercely, 'If *you two* think that now I have taken this job on, you can go on behaving just as you like, in the same old way, you're very much mistaken. You two have got to pull yourselves together!' When Edward VIII, now Duke of Windsor, reappeared in the drawing-room of Royal Lodge, Queen Mary, true to form, was, in Monckton's words, 'mute and immovable and very royal', just as all her children had known her from their earliest recollections. Prince George burst into tears, exclaiming, 'It isn't possible! Is isn't happening!' when the time came for his eldest brother to take his leave. David said farewell to Bertie last, kissing him first as a brother before bowing to him as the King.

In the small hours of a foggy Saturday morning, HMS *Fury* left Portsmouth to take the former Edward VIII on the first leg of his journey into exile. Not one of his servants had elected to go with him. His change of status did not change the ex-King's regal ways. Busy sending messages via the ship's radio, he was outraged when they entered French territorial waters and the radio had to shut down. Immediately, he ordered the ship to sea again until he had quite finished. Nevertheless, his father's grim prophecy to Baldwin, that 'After I am dead the boy will ruin himself in twelve months,' had now been fulfilled. Edward VIII's reign as King-Emperor had lasted just 325 days; it would take him a great deal longer to come to terms with what he had relinquished.

Thus ended a reign which, in its mingling of gravity with farce, brought out the best and the worst from the British establishment. What began as a divisive and apparently insoluble drama of national morality was skilfully transformed by Stanley Baldwin into a political crisis which lent itself to a political solution. Underlying public sentiment in both cases was the issue of class: Mrs Simpson was an American woman from Baltimore, whose mother was widely believed to have taken in lodgers. The riposte was provided by the indomitable Aunt Bessie: 'It isn't as if the King were giving it all up for nothing,' she told an American acquaintance proudly as she left Fort Belvedere for the last time. 'After all, Wallis *does* have background.'

Nine hours after David had left the shores of his old realm, Bertie, looking 'pale and haggard' in his naval uniform, addressed his Accession Council in the Entree Room at St James's Palace. He spoke in a low and halting voice, which gradually gained in confidence. 'I meet you today,' he began, 'in circumstances which are without parallel in the history of our country . . . With my wife and helpmeet by my side, I now take up the heavy task which lies before me.'

Elizabeth, still confined to her sickroom where she lay reading the Bible, undoubtedly had mixed feelings about the task which lay before them. At no stage did she express any qualms about her own ability to fulfil the role of Queen-Empress, but she voiced deep misgivings about steering Bertie through a responsibility so much greater than that of being David's stand-in. 'Darling David, Please read this. Please be kind to Bertie when you see him,' she had pleaded a month ago, when hope still lingered that her husband might be spared. 'I am terrified for him, so DO help him.' Now Elizabeth had her answer. David, ignoring her pleas, had sacrificed her husband for the woman he loved. Settling that score could be set aside for the time being. At the moment, like the other intensely ambitious lady of Glamis who married Macbeth, she had to screw her courage to the sticking place, and concentrate on putting some of her own steel into the man who now had no choice but to call himself King George VI.

6

THE BROTHERS FALL OUT

Once the abdication was over, and the Duke
of Windsor had retired to the continent, most
people turned quietly to more pressing concerns.
Abroad, the Spanish Civil War was reaching a
climax. Adolf Hitler, who believed that with the
abdication of Edward VIII he had lost an ally,
was busy building aircraft carriers. At home, the
last of the Jarrow marchers, protesting against
widespread unemployment, had only recently
returned home after a Communist-organised
rally in Hyde Park. And besides, it was nearly
Christmas. 'In any other country,' wrote Queen
Mary, 'there wd. have been riots, thank God
people did not lose their heads.' On the day
that the abdication was proclaimed, Geoffrey
Dawson's reporters at *The Times* were sent
to scour London for evidence of popular relief
at Edward VIII's departure and enthusiasm for
George VI's arrival. Neither was to be found.
There were 'no demonstrations or signs of
marked popular feeling', and in Parliament
Square the announcement produced 'no change
in the demeanour of the crowds'. In fact, much
to the chagrin of *The Times*, 'no emotion
was perceptible' at all. Shares climbed on the
Stock Exchange. The King was dead; long live
the King.

Nevertheless, there were plenty of national pundits eager to make their voices heard. The Archbishop of Canterbury, Cosmo Lang was the first to the microphone, the day after the Duke of Windsor sailed into exile. He sermonised with an equal measure of sanctimony and tactlessness. The former King had never had any regard for him, and Lang did not forget this as he warmed to his theme. 'From God,' he intoned, 'he had received a high and sacred trust. Yet by his own will he has abdicated — he has surrendered the trust. With characteristic frankness he has told us the motive. It was a craving for private happiness.' It was even more strange and sad, Lang went on loftily, that he had sought this happiness, not only outside a Christian marriage, but 'within a social circle whose standard and way of life are alien to all the best instincts and traditions of his people'. The Archbishop then attempted to offer wise words of encouragement from the pulpit to the new King. In doing so, he managed to direct the nation's attention to Bertie's principal defect and source of public embarrassment, his stammer. 'In manner and speech he is more quiet and reserved than his brother,' is how the Archbishop began, thus obligingly underlining the difference between the royal siblings which had dogged Bertie since birth. He went on to highlight what he called 'an occasional and momentary hesitation' in the new monarch's speech. 'But he has brought it into full control, and to those who hear it need cause no sort of embarrassment, for it causes none to him who speaks.'

265

Cosmo Lang was roundly condemned for his intervention. Within twenty-four-hours 250 letters had arrived at Lambeth Palace, the majority of them highly critical. The Primate of all England found himself able to dismiss them on the grounds that they came 'mostly from lower-middle-class homes'. Besides, he had the support of the new court gathering round George VI, most particularly the new King's wife and mother. Elizabeth was pleased by the frank criticism expressed by Cosmo Lang about David's unsuitable friends and somewhat louche 'social circle'. 'I don't think you need feel the Archbishop failed to express the right thing,' she wrote a short time later, adding that her mother-in-law 'felt he said exactly what he should and was grateful to him'.

The vengeance of the two queens soon made itself felt, as the new court, led this time by the royal family, turned on the ringleaders of Edward VIII's coterie. The result was an unedifying scramble among David's erstwhile loyal supporters to deny their allegiance to him. 'Rat week', Osbert Sitwell dubbed it, in his unsigned poem of that name. It produced the absurd spectacle of Emerald Cunard, among others, blithely announcing that she hardly knew Mrs Simpson. The social columns of the last few months read otherwise, and Lady Cunard became an early casualty, decisively dropped from royal favour overnight. 'The other day in my presence, Bertie told George he wished him and Marina never to see Lady Cunard again,' Queen Mary wrote to Prince Paul of Yugoslavia, 'and George said he would not do so.' So far so good, only four days after the departure of their elder brother. Emerald Cunard was damned quite simply for 'being great friends with Mrs S. at one time', and, of course, for giving parties for her.

An even harsher fate awaited Perry Brownlow, who, as the King's lord-in-waiting, had been detailed to escort Wallis to the south of France. Brownlow, or 'the Lincolnshire Handicap' as Bertie referred to his Lord Lieutenant of that country with an uncharacteristic flash of wit, was doubly culpable in the eyes of the royal family. After safely installing Mrs Simpson behind the walls of the Villa Lou Viei, where he had helped with her public offer to withdraw from Edward VIII's life, he had travelled on to Austria. There he was the Duke of Windsor's first British visitor at his new home, Schloss Enzesfeld, Baron Eugene de Rothschild's country house near Vienna where the Duke was living until Wallis's divorce was made absolute and he could safely be reunited with her. Returning to London afterwards in the misguided conviction that Queen Mary would enjoy hearing about his trip, Brownlow was fobbed off with a curt refusal. Three days before Christmas, he read in the Court Circular that the Marquess of Dufferin and Ava had been appointed to his post. A telephone call to the Lord Chamberlain confirmed the fact that his resignation had been accepted — although he had never actually offered it — and that his name would not appear in the Court Circular again.

'Am I to be turned away, like a dishonest servant with no notice, no warning, no thanks, when all I did was to obey my master, the late King?' asked Edward VIII's late lord-in-waiting.

'Yes,' answered the Lord Chamberlain, Lord Cromer, who six weeks earlier had been seen hobnobbing with Mrs Simpson at the Royal Opera House.

As for the public, King George VI's newly acquired subjects still harboured understandable misgivings about his ability to hold down a job which to all outward appearances had been done with such flair by his elder brother. As time was to show, Bertie had qualities of character and resolve which David lacked. He was decent, disciplined and hard-working, with a knowledge of manufacturing and the industrial working classes far greater than that of any of his predecessors. But he was also shy, reserved, slow to learn and physically less robust than David. British and American journals carried rumours which proved false, that he had 'falling fits' — in other words that he was epileptic like his deceased brother, Prince John. These real or imaginary disabilities would have mattered less if the new King had possessed the confidence to shrug them off. But being suddenly thrust into the limelight only aggravated Bertie's natural diffidence. He felt like a schoolboy made to sit a public exam for which he alone was untutored. To his cousin Lord Louis Mountbatten, at Fort Belvedere on the day of David's departure, he had blurted out, 'This is terrible, Dickie! I never wanted this to happen. I'm quite unprepared for it. David has been trained for it all his life, whereas I've never even seen a State paper. I'm only a naval officer. It's the only thing I know about.'

When the new King took his family to Sandringham for Christmas, their send-off from London was hardly effusive. Even the *New York Herald Tribune* saw fit to report, 'There was a subdued murmur which might have been a suppressed cheer — or might not. In short, on his first public appearance after his succession to his brother, King George VI was given an extremely cold shoulder.' Anti-monarchy speeches had been made in the House of Commons — impulsive, hot-headed expressions of discontent, but hurtful to Elizabeth all the same, since the most vocal of them came from fellow Scots. There was no royal message of good cheer broadcast at Christmas 1936. By the time the Year of Three Kings ended, Bertie had hardly been seen in public since his accession, and even more rarely heard. His young daughters were pleasing enough. His mother still retained the magnificent remoteness and queenly reserve which had sustained her through life, and would accompany her to the grave. But it seemed likely to most observers that the success of the new royal family — indeed, the fortunes of the monarchy — would depend largely on the new King's wife.

Happily, Queen Elizabeth was revelling in the stardom that was finally hers, and settling into the brilliantly successful run she continued to enjoy for the rest of the twentieth century. Her husband's esteem for her was manifested three days after the accession, when Bertie gave her the Order of the Garter. Only a few months later, she would become the first Queen Consort to carry out royal business in the sovereign's absence. Her husband set a new style by allowing her to walk ahead of him on all but the most formal of public engagements. With the *annus horribilis* of 1936 behind her, the new Queen could prepare for a year of stabilising the monarchy, and settling some old scores while she was about it.

For David and Wallis, in their enforced separation across the Channel, the new year of 1937 brought mixed emotions. The Duke of Windsor oscillated between happiness and dejection. People who visited him in Austria immediately after the abdication commented on his mood of euphoria. To have given up the Crown in order to spend an uncomplicated life with the woman he loved was to him the best of all possible resolutions. The anxiety and tension which are evident in almost every photograph of King Edward VIII had fallen away from the newly-created Duke of Windsor. For the first time in his life there was nobody to make him do what he didn't want to do — not his dreaded father, nor versions of his father in the shape of pernickety old courtiers and boring government ministers. His new life seemed to open on a glorious vacuum in which there were no responsibilities and nothing much to do except travel, swim, play golf and cards, and go to dances and dinners with Wallis beside him. 'It's all so lovely Wallis and so dear and sweet and sacred,' he had written in his first post-abdication letter, 'and I'm really happy for the very first time in my life.' Meanwhile he slept in a room at the Schloss which, according to Lord Brownlow, was almost bare, except for a number of large photographs of Mrs Simpson and a little yellow pillow which used to belong to her.

But as winter turned to spring, the Duke grew tetchy. Isolation and rejection took their toll on both of the lovers. So preoccupied had he been with keeping Wallis happy before his departure that David had given little thought to where he would end up. It was Kitty Rothschild who had originally invited Wallis to spend Christmas at the Schloss Enzesfeld, and who had generously agreed to take the former King in her place for an unspecified length of time. Her husband the Baron tactfully moved out as soon as the Duke of Windsor arrived. To David's barely disguised frustration, and despite Wallis's mounting jealousy, Kitty stayed on to act as hostess. On New Year's Day, David wrote to Wallis, underlining the new date 1937 four times. 'Oh! WE will make it,' he reassured her, 'this separation but by golly it is hard and a terrible strain. If it wasn't for that unsatisfactory telephone then I really would go mad.' Even now David could see only too clearly how vulnerable they were, exiled from the centre of power, when so many details of their future life together still remained to be answered. 'I'll have to watch out for our interests in England like the dickens although we still have loyal friends,' he warned Wallis. 'Oh! how hopeless writing is when WE have so much to say and arrange about the future.' Over the coming months he would wear out the telephone lines and write screeds 'arranging the future', but to have to wrangle with his powerful adversaries in monastic isolation, and at such a distance, was hard for a man who had always prided himself on his zest for direct action.

The middle weeks of January saw temporary salvation. He was joined by his boon companion, Fruity Metcalfe, who had generously abandoned his winter holiday in Kitzbühel to keep his old friend company. Even more generously, he turned up with his suitcase, but without his wife; (with Kitty all too much in evidence, David had made it known that he wanted no more women in the house). Fruity was touchingly loyal, joining in marathon sessions on the ski slopes which left him aching and exhausted night after night, then staying up into the small hours to listen to the Duke's self-pitying ramblings. From the start, Fruity Metcalfe realised that David had quite failed to appreciate his change of status. Still, in his own mind, master of all he surveyed, he seemed unaware of the role reversal which was bound to be occurring between himself, an exiled Duke, and Bertie, a soon to be crowned and anointed King. Shortly after his arrival, Metcalfe witnessed a telling scene which he recounted to his wife in one of the letters he snatched time to write to her. 'Tonight he [David] was told at dinner that HM [Bertie] wanted to talk on phone to him,' Fruity wrote to Alexandra. 'He said he couldn't take the call but asked it to be put through at 10 p.m. The answer to this was that HM said he would talk at 6.45 p.m. tomorrow as he was too busy to talk any other time. It was pathetic to see HRH's face. He couldn't believe it! He's been so used to having everything done as he wishes. I'm afraid he's going to have many more shocks like this.' Fruity ended his letter 'PPS — He seems to only see one thing & has the whole thing out of proportion.'

The new King George VI's first nerve-wracking weeks on the throne were made more tense by the telephone calls his older sibling was putting through to him almost every day. These had started, from David's point of view at least, as brotherly offers of guidance and help. However, difficulties soon arose, almost all of them a direct result of David's other daily telephone calls, to and from Wallis in Cannes. Mrs Simpson was lonely, anxious and fretful. Hate mail continued to pour in to the Villa Lou Viei; she hardly dared to leave the house. The King's Proctor was still on the prowl, sniffing around for proof that her divorce was a sham. The King himself — 'York' as she continued disparagingly to refer to him — was, in her view, being manipulated by his mother, his wife and his government in order to stonewall their plans. The Duke's financial settlement still looked in jeopardy, as did the frequently invoked trinity — respect, dignity and position — all of which the ex-Mrs Simpson saw as her right.

Above all, Wallis, who not for nothing had been described as being 'clever as a cartload of monkeys', already had strong suspicions that she might be robbed of the consolation prize — her right to the title Her Royal Highness. 'It is plain that York guided by her [Queen Mary] would not give us the extra chic of creating me HRH — the only thing to bring me back in the eyes of the world,' she had warned David three days after the abdication. On 3 January she returned to the attack: 'One realises now the impossibility of getting the marriage announced in the Court Circular and of the HRH. It is all a great pity because I loathe being undignified and also of joining the countless titles that roam around Europe meaning nothing.'

Stoked up by Wallis's constant fretful nagging ('I feel so sorry for him, he never seems able to do what she considers the right thing,' observed Fruity), David began to let off steam in his chats with Bertie. The telephone was not the ideal medium of communication between them. Apart from the infuriating technical hindrances of international calls in the 1930s, the brothers' differing personalities contributed to their misunderstandings. David was articulate and quick-witted. Bertie had always been a slow thinker: under pressure he spoke slowly as well. The result was that David did nearly all the talking and Bertie most of the listening, and the calls invariably ended with frustration on David's part and emotional exhaustion on his brother's.

David not only treated his brother to a catalogue of Wallis's grievances; he also felt obliged to hold forth on current political problems, foreign affairs and the business of kingship. His advice was very often contrary to that given by government ministers, and his interventions left Bertie ruffled and confused. Whereas David's companions at the Schloss Enzesfeld noticed that he was often on edge after a telephone conversation with Wallis, Bertie's family and personal staff soon saw that the King's outbursts of temper ('gnashes', as they were familiarly known) invariably followed one of David's calls — all the more so if Wallis had been the principal topic of conversation. The truth of the matter was that David now had little else to do with his time, whereas Bertie was over-worked and as lacking in self-confidence in his new position as he ever had been. Walter Monckton, one of the few central figures in the abdication still trusted by both brothers, appreciated Bertie's predicament. Of the barrage of conflicting advice which rained down on the new King from all sides, but especially through a crackling telephone wire from Austria, Monckton was to write: 'This caused him trouble which no one would understand who did not know the extent to which before the abdication the Duke of Windsor's brother admired and looked up to him.'

The Queen, who saw the exasperating and demoralising effect his brother's calls were having on Bertie, was keen to eliminate his influence for good. Aided by Bertie's close advisers — in particular Alec Hardinge and Tommy Lascelles — she demanded that the calls should cease. According to David, it was Bertie who pulled the plug on him, telling his brother bluntly that he wanted the telephoning to end.

'Are you serious?' asked David.

'Yes, I'm sorry to say that I am,' responded Bertie. 'The reason must be clear to you.'

Whether it was or not, the ending of their regular telephone conversations signalled the beginning of hostility between the brothers. 'Our relations as brothers were, as far as I am concerned, severed,' David was to tell Bertie, shortly after the outbreak of the Second World War, when of necessity he was back in touch with George VI. By the end of 1937, they were no longer even on speaking terms.

The break with the King his brother, although by far the most serious, was only one of a succession of official snubs ('small hurts' the Duke called them to his mother), which, like the daily sacks of hate mail, followed Wallis and David into exile. For her, there had been the move by the Home Secretary Sir John Simon to take away the police escort guarding the Villa Lou Viei, though in her view it was now more necessary than ever. For him, there was the steady erosion of his royal status and the loss of official posts which he had taken for granted. He had assumed, for example, that he would automatically become personal ADC to the King, just as Bertie had been ADC to him. Bertie, however, had different ideas, claiming that it would appear unbecoming for David to step down from the throne and immediately take up the duties of a younger son.

'Well, I suppose I have no standing of any kind now,' the former Edward VIII railed at Fruity Metcalfe. 'I used to be a Field Marshal and Admiral of the Fleet — but now I'm nothing!' It hurt especially when the Welsh Guards, whose Colonel he had been, bowed to the overriding opinion in the mess that King Edward VIII had let the side down. The Colonelcy lapsed on David's abdication, and he was not invited to put his name forward. The words of an officer in the Royal Fusiliers, of which the Prince of Wales had been Colonel-in-Chief, summed up the feelings of many people: 'We loved him. We would have drawn our swords for him. And then by God, didn't he let us down!' A question mark was even raised about his membership of the Privy Council. One by one, the positions he had formerly held so lightly, and in some cases with a degree of wry contempt, assumed a poignant significance as they were stripped away. In their place came offers of a rather different sort. In Detroit someone was needed to open a nudist colony: would the Duke be interested? Hollywood approached him with the offer of the starring role in a 'stupendous historical film'. Rather less glamorous was the appeal from the townsfolk of Chippewa Falls, Wisconsin, who were on the look-out for a mayor. Inappropriate it might have been, but at least Wallis's native country could contemplate some sort of role in life for an ex-King.

Spurred by Wallis, and with nothing else to do, David now put all his efforts into his campaign to win an advantageous financial settlement. Coupled to his demands were strong hints that it was high time that the royal family accepted the woman he was going to marry, and gave her the status she deserved. The wranglings over money came to a head in the middle of February 1937, when Bertie finally learned the truth about the fortune that David had stashed away, and had then lied about so brazenly back in December. The fact of his brother's deviousness upset Bertie greatly, even before he came to realise fully the extent of the deception. Apart from anything else, there was the potential risk to the royal family's future income when the Civil List came up for discussion by Parliament. Now that word had got out about the Duke of Windsor's settlement, George VI feared that it might be viewed as tantamount to fraud.

Writing to David, he tried to explain the depth of feeling in the country against his proposed marriage, and the weight of opposition that was building against him personally in the wake of the abdication. Bertie's tactful choice of words — that people were 'a little sore with you for having given up being King' — may not have conveyed the real hostility with which a growing number of his former subjects viewed the ex-King. However, in the hothouse atmosphere of persecution then pervading Schloss Enzesfeld, the message got through. Walter Monckton was immediately dispatched to try and strike a bargain. Winston Churchill also tried to

278

intervene with the flint-hearted Chamberlain, who was still Chancellor of the Exchequer. The unseemly haggling continued over the next twelve months, until finally, in February 1938, there came confirmation that Bertie would after all grant David his £25,000 a year. By that time, his family's attitude towards Wallis herself had overtaken money as the Duke of Windsor's principal source of bitterness and recrimination.

It was perhaps unfortunate that the first visit made to David by any member of the royal family should have coincided with provocative reports in the *Daily Mirror* about the financial negotiations. In February 1937 the Duke's sister Mary, the Princess Royal, came to see him at the Schloss Enzesfeld with her husband, Lord Harewood. They would not have been David's first choice to relieve the gloom of his exile from home and Wallis, but at least the Harewoods brought with them a breath of England, for which the Duke pined, despite the kippers and Oxford marmalade shipped to him in Austria by Fortnum & Mason. Three weeks later more congenial company arrived in the person of David's youngest and favourite brother, George. Marina was not with him; Princess Alexandra had been born two months earlier, and the demands of motherhood spared Marina the embarrassment of having to join in the visit to her exiled brother-in-law, and thus offend her sister-in-law, the Queen.

Dickie Mountbatten wrote to Schloss Enzesfeld a few weeks later to offer his services as best man. He was returning the compliment David had paid him by acting as best man at his wedding to Edwina Ashley fifteen years earlier. 'This will be a royal wedding,' explained David as he politely declined his cousin's offer. 'My two youngest brothers will come over as supporters.' Less than twelve weeks away from the date of his wedding in France, the Duke of Windsor was still deluding himself that his family would come to their senses and cross the Channel to celebrate his union with Wallis. By the time the wedding day arrived, all his fond hopes had been exposed as self-delusion. During the drama of the abdication, Elizabeth had written to a friend of Edward VIII, 'Poor soul, a fearful awakening is awaiting his completely blinded reason before very long.' During the spring of 1937, the Duke of Windsor was finally and brutally shaken from his reverie.

The seeds of Wallis's enduring attraction for the Duke of Windsor were sown, did he but know it, in his childhood. Her hectoring and bullying represented familiarity and a tortured kind of intimacy to him, being all too reminiscent of his father's angry ranting. Now his growing apprehension that he was letting down the most important person in his life reinforced the sense of inadequacy and failure he had harboured since he was a child. It was a relationship made in the psychology textbooks. To David it was made to seem as if he had wooed and won his future wife under false pretences. Hoping to be able to offer her security of riches and status, as well as a place in the history books as his consort on the most prestigious throne in the world, he now found himself taking her with him into ignominious banishment, to the accompaniment of jeers from their enemies and cowardly silence from their erstwhile friends. It would take a lifetime to compensate Wallis for what he had made her endure, and David set about his lifetime's task by, first of all, trying to ensure that their marriage ceremony would be conducted with the dignity and decorum that befitted a royal bride. His difficulty was that none of his family was prepared to assist.

Early in April, the suggestion was made that a royal chaplain should officiate at the wedding, and that, at the very least, Harry and George should be there to see their eldest brother married. Clive Wigram and Alec Hardinge at court, backed by Chamberlain and Simon in the Cabinet (and Elizabeth herself in private) were quick to scotch the idea. If any member of the family turned up for the wedding, they argued, it would be seen publicly as an acceptance of Wallis into the royal family. This was the last thing either the Queen or Queen Mary wanted. The King saw strong religious objections to any member of the family joining in a service that could not be accepted by the Church of England. Fearful as he was of his older brother's reaction to the news, he wrote in the middle of April to tell him categorically that not one member of the royal family would be permitted to attend his wedding. Nor would any royal chaplain be allowed to take part. 'It would place us all in an impossibly false position,' argued Bertie by way of explanation, 'and would be harmful to the Monarchy.'

David was shocked to the core. He shot off a reply, the gist of which was that his brother was once again allowing himself to be controlled by others. His aggrieved tone reflected his continuing failure to grasp the reality of how people now perceived him. 'I shall always be sorry to remember,' he wrote, 'that you did not have the courage to give me the same support at the start of my new life, that I so whole-heartedly gave to you at the beginning of yours.'

When the word went out that no one from the royal family would be at the Duke of Windsor's wedding, other potential guests also fell by the wayside. Perry Brownlow lost his taste for European travel when it was hinted that he might also lose his position as His Majesty's Lord Lieutenant in Lincolnshire. Dickie Mountbatten, too, had to tell David that he could not attend. The signs had been there when he wrote to assure his old friend that he had not 'quite given up all hope yet' of being with him. With Harry and George also unavailable to stand alongside David at the altar, faithful Fruity Metcalfe stepped forward as best man. One by one the guest-list was whittled away, until all that remained of the glittering assembly Wallis had dreamed of was a motley collection of hangers-on.

The long-awaited news that Wallis's second marriage had been ended by the granting of a decree absolute reached her on 3 May 1937, one month to the day before she embarked on her third union. In the end the King's Proctor had failed to find any evidence of collusion, and the last legal barrier to her marriage to the former King of England was removed. David left Austria immediately to join her. The next day, the Orient Express made an unscheduled stop forty-five kilometres short of Paris to drop him off. After five months' separation, the Duke of Windsor and his future Duchess were reunited at the Château de Candé near Tours, where they had decided they would be married.

Wallis's favoured place to hold the wedding had been the Château La Croë, a villa on the Cap d'Antibes in the south of France. The substitution of this château in Touraine had been made by George VI, who considered that the raffish atmosphere of the Riviera lacked the essential gravitas that his brother's wedding required. The Château de Candé belonged to Charles Bedaux, a French-born naturalised American who had amassed a fortune through the creation and implementation of a system of industrial efficiency which had made him the bosses' friend and the workers' foe throughout most of the developed world. Bedaux had originally offered his French home to Mrs Simpson at the time of the abdication, thinking that it would provide her with a refuge from the press, who were beating on the doors of the Villa Lou Viei. He was surprised and delighted to be told that it had been chosen for the Windsor wedding. Bedaux was only vaguely known to Wallis's host in Cannes, Herman Rogers. The Duke of Windsor knew nothing about him, nor did Wallis, nor did the King. As subsequent events were to show, a little time spent investigating Bedaux and his background would have saved the British government and the royal family a good deal of embarrassment during the next few years. It may ultimately have even spared Charles Bedaux his life. However, no one at the time of the wedding saw fit to make enquiries about the Windsors' mysterious benefactor. Wallis had been in residence at the château for a couple of months by the time the Duke of Windsor arrived.

Now that they were together, final preparations could go ahead for what they were still determined would be the wedding of the year. Five days after David's arrival, Wallis changed her name by deed poll back to Mrs Wallis Warfield. With a stroke of the pen she cancelled out the infamous Mrs Simpson, and the ill-starred and long-forgotten Mrs Spencer. On the same day, the press statement announcing the wedding to be held at Candé on 3 June 1937 also had to make the best of it by adding that, 'Invitations to the wedding of the Duke of Windsor and Mrs Warfield will be confined to those who have been with them during the past months. There will be no member of the royal family present.'

Back in London, Bertie and Elizabeth were busy adding the finishing touches to their own great day, in which the King consecrated his union with his subject peoples. Preparations for the coronation, already fixed for King Edward VIII on 12 May, had been in progress for over a year. Now plans for the coronation of one king were seamlessly woven into the coronation of his successor. Nothing much was changed, save for the addition of an extra throne in Westminster Abbey for Elizabeth. The special vantage-point the ex-King had demanded for Wallis ('the Loose Box' as it had been dubbed), was no longer needed. Almost the only visible evidence of the swift change of cast was the array of coronation mugs and plaster busts of King Edward VIII to be seen at London souvenir stalls, marked '1/6 to Clear'.

In private, Bertie and Elizabeth were still busy wielding a new broom about the court. They were sensible enough to cultivate the loyalty of the few members of Edward VIII's coterie who might be of use to them. Royal favour and forgiveness smiled on Duff and Diana Cooper who, in spite of having joined the *Nahlin* cruise, were invited for a weekend of reconciliation at Windsor. The result could have been anticipated. Lady Diana (who confessed to George VI, 'I am a Rat, sir') came away with the impression that 'things would do a lot better under the new regime'. Edward VIII's reign at Fort Belvedere she now dismissed as 'an operetta', while the regime at Windsor Castle under the new King and Queen had the solidity of 'an institution'. Winning over Winston Churchill was an even shrewder move. Having on their side one of the former King's most eloquent supporters would enhance their standing and at the same time deny David one of his few remaining allies of any influence. As for those who had not yet been won over, Elizabeth and Bertie saw the day of the coronation as their chance to sway popular opinion in their favour.

That George VI should return to the royal tradition of the State Procession was itself seen as a symbol that old certainties could be renewed in a world which seemed bent on destroying them. Throughout the long day of ceremony and splendour, the new King carried himself with a shy composure. In some quarters, this brought huge relief. Six months into George VI's reign there were still those who doubted whether their new King could undertake an ordeal such as the coronation service without suffering some dreadful physical or vocal calamity. The Archbishop of Canterbury, Cosmo Lang, had taken the precaution of monitoring the newsreel coverage before it was released that evening, in order to censor out anything which showed the King in an unfortunate light. Such were the fears about his competence. About Elizabeth there were no fears. From his seat in the Abbey, watching Cosmo Lang place the Consort's diadem upon her head, Winston Churchill whispered to his wife Clementine, with tears in his eyes, 'You were right; I see now that the 'other one' wouldn't have done.'

Across the Channel in the Château de Candé, the 'other one' listened grimly to the service broadcast on the radio, restraining her tears as 'the mental image of what might have been and should have been kept forming, disintegrating, and re-forming in my mind'. By her side sat David, listening to the service that would publicly elevate Bertie above him for the first time in their lives. Whatever was going through his mind, the former King Edward's hands were busy knitting a jersey for the woman who was shortly to be his wife.

The Crown and the Consort's throne had been denied Wallis, but her marriage could surely still bring her the honours and dignity she craved. David continued to pin his hopes on obtaining the title of HRH as a wedding present for his wife. He had written again to Bertie asking him to announce formally that Wallis would be styled Her Royal Highness the Duchess of Windsor. The royal family might choose not to attend his wedding but, as he pointed out to his brother, 'Wallis's royal title comes automatically with marriage in our case.' And, indeed, Bertie had promised as much the day before the abdication. But six months had passed since then, and the new King was now back-tracking on an offer made, admittedly, when he was under great emotional strain. More to the point, Bertie had made this promise to his older brother without reference to his mother or his wife, both of whom were implacably opposed to any move that might dignify Wallis. In the royal household Mrs Simpson's name was taboo — not to be mentioned in front of Elizabeth and Margaret, the two young princesses. The King and Queen were occasionally heard to refer to her as 'the lowest of the low'. Queen Mary had promised her late husband King George that she would never ever receive Mrs Simpson.

The new Queen backed her up, making clear to her husband how adamant she was that Mrs Simpson, as she continued to call her, should be denied any form of recognition. Elizabeth's feeling was that, far from being rewarded for the ex-King's abdication, Wallis Simpson, as the responsible party, should be punished. Since Wallis had been publicly declared unfit to be a queen or even a morganatic wife, it surely followed that to let her become a member of the royal family would make nonsense of the abdication. Furthermore Elizabeth, for one, believed that there was every chance that the marriage might not survive, leaving Wallis free to rocket round the world with her HRH in her baggage, lending her royal title to books, charities, merchandise, as well as any number of unsavoury escapades. David had wanted a morganatic marriage when he was on the throne; now that he had disgraced his family, let him have one.

The difficulty the royal family faced was one of precedent. There was no precedent in history of a monarch voluntarily abdicating the throne: as a result, no one was entirely certain how to handle the ex-King and his wife. The nearest recent precedent, ironically, involved Elizabeth herself, who although the daughter of an earl, had been a commoner before marrying Bertie, as had Prince Harry's wife, Lady Alice Montagu Douglas Scott. In both cases, the official announcement of the marriage had confirmed the future royal status of the bride, who would take 'the title, style or attribute of Royal Highness in accordance with the settled general rule that a wife takes the status of her husband'. (When Princess Marina married Prince George, no such statement was required since she was already a Royal Highness as a member of the Greek royal family.) In the light of this settled general rule, which the future Lord Chancellor, Lord Jowitt, had already quoted to the Duke of Windsor as grounds for making Wallis HRH, what could legally be done to stymie Wallis's royal aspirations? It took all of Sir John Simon's ingenuity as a lawyer to concoct some sort of answer. The solution the Home Secretary came up with was to argue that the title HRH should only be borne by members of the royal family in the line of succession, from which David had removed himself and his descendants. David's own HRH, Simon determined, could be dressed up as a gesture of generosity on the part of the King, who as Fount of Honour was unilaterally in a position to confer the title of HRH on his brother, David having given up his right to that title when he gave up the throne.

It was a far-fetched and legally dubious argument, but it satisfied the King and those close to him, who saw the matter in far more personal terms. They needed a scapegoat in order to preserve the reputation of the monarchy and Wallis, who was already the popular scapegoat for Edward VIII's abdication, was the obvious candidate. 'Is she a fit and proper person to become a Royal Highness after what she has done in this country;

and would the country understand it if she became one automatically on marriage?' was the rhetorical question Bertie put to his Prime Minister. To cover their tracks, it was decided that the matter should be referred to the Cabinet and the Dominion prime ministers. In view of Mrs Simpson's almost universal unpopularity throughout the Empire, their response was comfortingly predictable.

On 26 May, the decision to deny Wallis the royal rank that had been automatically accorded to Elizabeth was ratified at the last Cabinet meeting presided over by Stanley Baldwin, before he resigned and handed over the premiership to Neville Chamberlain. The announcement was formally published two days later, on the eve of David's wedding. Even if Bertie and Elizabeth had foreseen the lifelong resentment and burning animosity which this decision was to generate in the Duke and Duchess of Windsor, it is unlikely that it would have changed their minds. Walter Monckton had warned that such a blow to the Windsors' pride 'would create an intense bitterness in the Duke that should not be underestimated', and when he arrived at Candé the day before the wedding he was able to witness that resentment for himself. With him he brought a personal letter from Bertie in which the King expressed the hope that his brother would not take this action as a personal insult. But this was, of course, precisely how David took it — as the latest and most grievous of the many slurs cast on him and injuries done to him since he left

Britain. 'This is a nice wedding present,' he commented bitterly and tearfully as he showed Monckton the letter. He immediately suspected another influence, probably his mother's and Elizabeth's. 'I know Bertie. I know he couldn't have written this letter on his own. Why in God's name would they do this to me at this time?'

None of this rancour behind the scenes was evident to the newspapermen and photographers who had been besieging the Château de Candé for days, nor were David and Wallis going to allow anything to spoil their wedding. Along with the Metcalfes, the Herman Rogers, Walter Monckton and Randolph Churchill, came Cecil Beaton who had been invited to take the official photographs. Charles Bedaux and his wife were also present. Like her bridegroom, Wallis was on edge, cool and brittle, although so exquisitely dressed she might indeed have been a queen on her wedding day. David, as always, appeared totally captivated by her. 'If only she showed a glimmer of softness,' noted Alexandra Metcalfe, Fruity's wife, 'took his arm, looked at him as though she loved him, one would warm towards her, but her attitude is so correct.' In London, the *Evening Standard* ran a David Low cartoon showing 'Guests to the Duke's Wedding' filing into the church: Romeo and Juliet, Abelard and Heloïse, Tristan and Isolde, Paris and Helen, and Antony and Cleopatra, all being filmed by Great Love Stories Inc.

The day itself, 3 June, was George V's birthday, and the prayer book David used for the wedding service was the one his mother had given him when he was ten years old. But the clergyman who was to officiate personified the tawdry depths to which the wedding had been reduced by the Windsors' adversaries. Ignoring the decision by the Archbishops of Canterbury and York that no Anglican priest would be allowed to officiate, the Revd J. A. Jardine, Vicar of St Paul's, Darlington and a rampant self-publicist, had offered his services. For want of any suitable alternative, he had been accepted. Standing in front of a carved wooden chest converted as a makeshift altar, he married David and Wallis 'without episcopal licence or consent' in the presence of a congregation of sixteen. Subsequently, Jardine was to exploit his brief celebrity by styling himself 'The Duke's Vicar' on his business card, and heading off on a well-paid lecture tour. Four years later he was to end up in Hollywood, the pastor of a small church in Los Angeles which he renamed Windsor Cathedral. Not to be outdone, an entrepreneurial citizen of Baltimore opened one of Wallis's childhood homes to the paying public as 'A Shrine to Love'.

The loving couple, now at last man and wife, left at once for a honeymoon at the Schloss Wasserleonburg in the Austrian Tyrol, where they found time on their hands to contemplate a life together very different from the one they might once have envisaged. The Duke of Windsor now had time to give voice to his pent-up rage. 'I am at a loss to know how to write to you,' he scribbled to his mother, after she had failed to send him a wedding present.

'You must realise by this time that, as there is a limit to what one's feelings can endure, this most unjust and uncalled-for treatment can have had but one important result: my complete estrangement from all of you.' Taking up the cudgels on Queen Mary's behalf, Bertie had written back to the Duke, 'Of course we don't mean to humiliate you. Everything I have done has been absolutely necessary for the sake of the country. How do you think I liked taking on a rocking throne, and trying to make it steady again? It has not been a pleasant job, and it is not finished yet.' The two of them should now work together for the future, 'and if you do want to let yourself go, do write to me and not Mama, as it makes her absolutely miserable.'

The Duke of Windsor wrote back to George VI in a storm of self-pity. 'I do not agree with your description of the throne as 'tottering' . . . I know it has not been easy for the Monarchy to adjust itself to the trend of the times, and I do not think that even my most vindictive enemy would deny that I have done a great deal to preserve the system . . . I have always felt that one of the sources of power of the Monarchy in Great Britain has been the fact that we were a united family, with no public discords and working together as one for the welfare of our people. What other motive had I in abdicating, except a patriotic one?'

The Windsors were still on honeymoon when David experienced once again the family hostility orchestrated by Queen Mary and her daughter-in-law. As George V's eldest son, David had given half the total cost of £8000 towards the monument to his father in St George's Chapel. Now, when the time came for it to be dedicated, he was not invited to the ceremony, nor, to his disgust, was any mention made of his substantial contribution. Later that summer, an irreconcilable rift developed with Prince George, the Duke of Kent, for some years David's favourite brother. The row began when Marina, primed by the two Queens, refused to accompany her husband to see the Windsors while in the vicinity of Wasserleonburg. When George finally appeared without his wife, Wallis, in her husband's words, 'properly refused to see him, and I gave him a brotherly lecture he wouldn't soon forget'. Having refused to be best man at the wedding of the brother he had once adored, and who had helped to cure his drug addiction, George had sent David a Fabergé box as a wedding present. That Christmas, the Duke sent it back, with a note saying that the only boxes he was collecting were those that could be delivered on the ears. When, five years later, the Duke of Kent was killed in an aeroplane crash, Marina received no word of condolence from the man who had once been her husband's inseparable friend. To give David his due, he claimed subsequently that he had written to her. He may well have done, and as it was wartime, the letter may well have gone astray.

From Austria the Windsors moved to Paris, where they took a suite in the Hotel Meurice. The Duke still had the notion that after a short spell abroad he would be welcomed home to take up a post in which his undeniable talents would be put to proper use, rather as if he and Bertie had simply changed places. In his abdication broadcast David has promised the nation, 'If at any time in the future I can be found of service to His Majesty in a private station, I shall not fail.' In almost the same breath he had announced his intention of altogether quitting public affairs, but nine months away from the centres of power and influence had convinced him that this would be impossible. Above all else, he needed to prove to Wallis that he still counted for something. Visiting the Windsors at Wasserleonburg, Walter Monckton recognised similar pressure coming from the newly created Duchess. 'She wanted him to eat his cake and have it. She could not easily reconcile herself to the fact that by marrying her he had become a less important person.' It certainly came as little surprise to his legal adviser when on 3 September 1937, a quasi-official communiqué was released: 'In accordance with the Duke of Windsor's message to the world Press last June that he would release any information of interest regarding his plans or movements, His Royal Highness makes it known that he and the Duchess of Windsor are visiting Germany and the United States in the near future for the purpose of studying housing and working conditions in these two countries.'

In the private apartments of Buckingham Palace and in the corridors of Whitehall, this announcement exploded like a bombshell. Housing and working conditions — it might have been a case study of the Windsors' own domestic predicament, but Bertie and Elizabeth were hardly disposed to see the irony of it. To some, the visit to Germany was confirmation of the Windsors' long-suspected pro-German sympathies. Wallis in particular was suspect on account of the armfuls of flowers said to have been regularly sent round by Hitler's Ambassador Joachim von Ribbentrop to Bryanston Court, the same man who this February had greeted George VI with a Nazi salute.

For a former King of England to visit Germany with the express interest of studying the social and commercial fabric of National Socialism was a major propaganda coup for Hitler and his ministers. Chamberlain's policy of appeasing the European dictators was under attack at home, and while the new King and Queen did not oppose it in public, there was no mistaking their private loathing of the Fascist regimes. Elizabeth was furious at what she saw as a blatant publicity stunt. She recognised Wallis's influence at work behind the scenes, manoeuvring David into the limelight, and trying to elbow Bertie back into the wings. But in fact, Bertie and Elizabeth had only themselves to blame. As shortly became evident, the driving force behind the Duke's proposed visits was Charles Bedaux, the Windsors' host at their wedding who was now calling in the debt.

When the Nazi government had come to power in Germany in 1933, Bedaux's lucrative business there had been shut down. He needed to curry favour with the party hierarchy to get it up and running again, and David unwittingly provided the key. And Bedaux had other plans for the Duke of Windsor: the visits to Germany and the United States were to be merely the overture. The Duke, he had decided, could be put to use as the figurehead of a worldwide peace movement. Excited by the possibility of a return to public life — this was to be the closest Wallis would ever get to a royal tour — the politically naïve Duke failed to recognise that the backers for this movement were a group of right-wing industrialists who would soon be investigated by Allied secret services for their strong pro-Nazi sympathies. It was a problem which was to recur in the royal family half a century later, that members of it who exiled themselves had no recourse to advisers who might prevent them from making embarrassing mistakes. In David's case, it would eventually take him perilously close to treason. Meanwhile, the Duke of Windsor insisted that he was travelling as a private citizen and was nobody's pawn — although he personally had no quarrel with Herr Hitler. In 1937 this was not yet an unforgivable attitude to take: Churchill himself had declared not long before that Britain could do with a man such as Hitler in time of peril.

Germany was a country which David had not visited since his Oxford days: he plainly had not the faintest idea how much it was changed. The royal progress got off to a disappointing start, when in mid-October the Windsors stepped off the train at Berlin's Friedrichstrasse Station. Waiting to greet them were Nazis by the score, but from the British Embassy only the lowly figure of the Third Secretary. He had been despatched to tell them that the Ambassador was away and that, in any case, he could 'take no official cognizance' of the visit. However, for the next two weeks their Nazi hosts rolled out the red carpet, while the King of England's brother and sister-in-law were wheeled out to meet all the principal thugs, war-mongers and architects of the Holocaust, who would soon be rolling their tanks over the frontiers of Europe. Their principal host was the unsavoury head of the German Labour Front, Dr Robert Ley, described by Mussolini's son-in-law as 'a drunkard who used to live in a Cologne brothel'. His idea of hospitality was to bundle the Windsors into a large open-top Mercedes-Benz, with black uniformed SS guards standing to attention on the running boards and drive at high speed with sirens blaring and the wireless thumping out German military music. Wallis, who was always a nervous passenger, dreaded these expeditions. Only the satisfaction of being addressed everywhere as Her Royal Highness (the German Foreign Ministry had made sure of that), and her husband's constant admonitions to the driver to slow down, kept her in her seat.

David did his best to make regal capital out of the visit. 'Heil Windsor!' shouted the well-drilled factory workers and well-housed citizens as they sped through the country. 'Heil Hitler!'

replied the foolish Duke, with an arm movement that might or might not have approximated to a Nazi salute. One afternoon, the Goerings invited them to tea. Frau Goering was impressed by the Duchess of Windsor, who was, as always, beautifully dressed. 'This woman would certainly have cut a good figure on the throne of England,' was Emmy Goering's opinion. She was slightly taken aback when her guests refused a drink, but then, she commented, 'one simply cannot believe everything one reads in newspapers'. Meanwhile, Hermann Goering had taken the Duke to see his nephew's magnificent train set. On the wall was a large map, showing Austria as part of Germany. The Duke, who had been back there very recently on his honeymoon, naturally questioned this, only to be told firmly that the Austrians would soon see the sense of joining forces with their northern neighbours. As he watched Goering play with a model aeroplane which crossed the room on wires to scatter wooden bombs on the trains below, David should perhaps have gained an insight into what the commander-in-chief of the Luftwaffe was planning.

There was another tea party at Berchtesgaden, where Hitler spoke to the ex-King alone. Wallis, with typical self-absorption, decided that the German leader 'did not care for women'. The Führer, on the other hand, concurred with Emmy Goering that Wallis 'would have made a good Queen'. The Duke drew his own conclusions from his chat with the Führer. 'And what did he have to say about Bolshevism?' was what Wallis wanted to know. 'He's against it,' was all the Duke could find to say in reply, and indeed, that was what mattered to him most. It did not escape their German hosts that the ex-King of England was broadly sympathetic to their cause. He might even be useful in their plans to create 'an English form of Fascism and alliance with Germany', which is how a briefing to the Foreign Office by the journalist Robert Bruce Lockhart put it. Charles Bedaux was rewarded with meetings in high places in Berlin. As the Duke and Duchess returned to Paris to compose themselves for their next trip, it was Bedaux, who had kept his head down during the German visit, who now took charge of the proposed tour of the United States. He proved not to be a happy choice as travel agent.

On a personal level, the King and Queen disliked the idea of the Windsors' forthcoming visit to America far more than their tour of Germany, diplomatically embarrassing though that had been. As Prince of Wales, David had been a runaway success in the United States. Furthermore, the American press had largely applauded the wedding of Baltimore's 'Queen of Romance', as she was known, to her Prince Charming-turned-King. In contrast, the new King and Queen were still unknown and unproven across the Atlantic, and with their own royal tour of North America still only in the planning stage, it seemed David and Wallis were deliberately intent on stealing their thunder. The British Ambassador, Sir Ronald Lindsay, was recalled from Washington, ostensibly to discuss how he should receive the Windsors in Washington. At Balmoral, however, he found himself sitting down to a council of war, in which, he recorded, the Duke of Windsor came across as 'a hated rival claimant [to the throne] living in exile', while the new King was like 'a medieval monarch' who 'does not yet feel safe on the throne'. Both Bertie and Tommy Lascelles told the Ambassador forcefully that David was 'trying to stage a come-back, and his friends and advisers were semi-Nazis'. The Queen spoke more guardedly 'in terms of acute pain and distress . . . all tempered by affection for 'David'. 'He's changed so much now, and he used to be so kind to us.' ' As for 'that woman', Elizabeth, 'with all her charity', was heard to make no mention of Wallis. The Balmoral meeting wound up with the agreement that the Windsors should be given a modest dinner-party at the Embassy, while President Roosevelt — who was said to be looking forward to meeting the Duke and Duchess — should be encouraged to offer them nothing more than a cup of tea when they called on him at the White House. In the event, neither engagement could be fulfilled: Charles Bedaux, perversely, saw to that.

American press reports about the Windsors' visit to Germany, where trade unions had been smashed by the Nazis, had already begun to stir up anti-Fascist feeling in the New World. Coupled with this, there was a widespread hatred among American workers for Bedaux and his efficiency programmes, which had been brilliantly satirised in the 1936 Charlie Chaplin film *Modern Times*. It all led to a hardening of public opinion against the Windsors' trip. Even in Baltimore, local trades union leaders branded Bedaux 'the arch-enemy' of the working man, and threatened to boycott receptions planned for the city's famous Duchess. David and Wallis had not helped matters either when, with a distinct lack of tact, they had booked their passage on the German-registered liner *Bremen*. American newspaper headlines declared 'New York Longshoremen Promise 'We'll Boycott Duke's Ship' ' and 'Baltimore Mayor Won't Receive Duchess'. Before long, the sustained public condemnation became too much for Bedaux, who made his apologies to David, before throwing in the towel and bolting back to safety in France. It was six years before he returned to America, and then it was on a charge of wartime treason, which eventually led him to take his own life with an overdose of sleeping pills. But that was in the future: for now, the growing outcry forced the Windsors to reconsider their journey. At the last minute — their luggage was already ticketed on the quay at Cherbourg — they accepted that they had no option but to call the whole thing off. The Duke issued a statement, emphasising 'that there is no shadow of justification for any suggestion that he is allied to any industrial system, or that he is for or against any particular political and racial doctrine.'

The anniversary of the abdication, now

302

approaching, found the Windsors living tax-free in France, with a great deal of money and nothing much to do with it. That is, besides play golf, buy jewellery, decorate their homes, garden, shop and shop again. Even David felt there had to be more of a contribution he could make. Above all he was homesick. Winston Churchill had encouraged him in the belief that he could expect to be able to spend a substantial part of the year in England, at his beloved Fort Belvedere, and the Attorney General had formally indicated that there was nothing to prevent the Duke returning. Only Walter Monckton's caution about the heavy taxes he would have to pay in Britain gave the Duke second thoughts about pushing for the right to settle permanently in what was, after all, his own country.

George VI's court and a significant majority of Chamberlain's government were opposed to the Windsors' returning. Bertie himself was torn between the affection he had once held for his brother, and his fear of David's crowd-pulling charisma. As it happened, Bertie was already winning the approbation of his government ministers, who found him as sensible and straightforward as his father George V, and more thoughtful, even if his natural reserve led him to play his cards close to his chest. But this same reserve still kept him at arm's length from his subjects, in a way that David, for all his self-centredness, had never been. His characteristic self-deprecation — *Time* magazine reported him as saying, 'According to the papers,

I am supposed to be unable to speak without stammering, to have fits, and to die in two years. All in all, I am to be a crock!' — disguised a continuing unease about where the nation's loyalty lay. He noted that a poll published in the *Daily Telegraph* indicated that 61 per cent of the British people wanted the Windsors to return to Britain; only 16 per cent were against. In the end it was Elizabeth who eventually persuaded Bertie to block his brother's return. The Queen wanted David kept away for as long as possible, while she helped Bertie earn the nation's loyalty and grow into his new role. Moreover, as she had no intention of ever receiving Wallis, it suited Elizabeth to have her kept out of the country as well.

In November 1937 the suggestion was revived that David should receive his allowance only on condition that he stayed overseas. Following this, Bertie wrote to him to say that he would have to clear any proposal with his ministers before David could think of returning home. The ex-King was furious both with his brother and with his brother's ministers. Wallis had had enough of France. 'Anything would be better than this,' she told Monckton, 'huddled in a rented house like orphans in a storm.' Austria would shortly be out of the question, even if she had fancied the idea: in April 1938, it obediently coloured itself according to Goering's map, when officially 99.75 per cent of Austrians balloted for union with Germany. She harried David to settle either for the United States or Britain — but it was unwise to visit America in the aftermath of the

Bedaux débâcle, and Britain was now closing its doors to them, as though the Windsors were criminals or stateless aliens.

In what can best be interpreted as a cry for help, the Duke gave an interview to a correspondent of the *Daily Herald* (which was not printed) in which he went as far as to say that if a future Labour government wished, and were in a position to offer it, he would consider returning to Britain as President of an English Republic. It was desperate stuff, but after a year of setbacks and humiliation, caution was no longer uppermost in his mind. 'The drawbridges are going up behind me,' he told Wallis, mournfully. 'I have taken you into a void.'

Friends from England who came out to see them found the bitterness very near the surface. After one such visit, Victor Cazalet in his diary recorded the Duke saying to him, 'If people want me to be Buddies with my brother he must recognise his sister-in-law — I want to be — I did everything I could during that last week not to make [a] King party. I want to help him. If he will grant me this — we never want to see them again.' To keep Wallis's mind off the HRH, David set about finding them a couple of homes in France, taking a lease on the house in which she had wanted them to be married, La Croë at Cap d'Antibes, and another lease on a house in Paris, 24 Boulevard Suchet, near the Bois de Boulogne. Even in this, he was not free of family machinations. Bertie and Elizabeth were booked in for a State visit to France in early summer 1938. When the Duke requested, through Monckton, that he and his wife be officially received, Bertie minuted discouragingly, 'Official invitation would help their position in French society. Recent reports show that no woman in Paris wishes to meet her. Their behaviour has not been polite to us . . . Much better for them to go away while visit is on.' The Duke and Duchess had no option but to leave Paris during the royal visit. Bertie's reaction, almost chilling in its animosity, is a yardstick of Elizabeth's success in detaching her husband from any residual family loyalty and affection towards his elder brother — much as Wallis, in the early 1930s had detached David from the rest of his family.

Five days before the State visit was due to begin, the Countess of Strathmore died at Glamis. Bravely, a privately grief-stricken Elizabeth put duty first, and crossed the Channel with her husband after a delay of less than a month. Ironically, the period of mourning for her mother presented Elizabeth with one of her most dazzling successes in all the many overseas tours she undertook as Queen. She opted for the royal prerogative of wearing white for mourning. Under the supervision of Norman Hartnell, who shared in her triumph, her entire wardrobe turned white overnight, from her furs to her shoes (fifty trunks of clothes went with her, along with £7 million of jewellery). The effect was spell-binding. Wallis's 'Dowdy Duchess', whom she commonly referred to as 'Cookie' for her mumsy figure and sad lack of chic, was suddenly being hailed as a fashion icon, and greeted with worldwide adulation, just as a future Princess of Wales would be half a century later. Wallis, who six months earlier had basked in being voted number one among the top ten best-dressed women in the world, followed her sister-in-law's regal progress in the newspapers, and realised, as she had not fully realised before, how great a task it would be to stage a comeback for David. Adolf Hitler, watching a newsreel film of the unveiling of an Australian war memorial, at which Elizabeth spontaneously scattered an armful of poppies given to her by a French child, also took the measure of a future adversary. Wallis might have made a good Queen in his eyes, but her sister-in-law, the one parading before him on the screen, was in the opinion of Germany's leader, 'the most dangerous woman in Europe'.

Hitler very nearly got a letter from Bertie that autumn. The King was troubled by the Führer's plan to march into the Sudetenland, inconveniently part of Czechoslovakia, if the Czech government refused to hand it over. He had given the matter considerable thought at Balmoral, between picnics and days on the moors shooting grouse, and concluded that what was needed at this time of international tension was a personal letter from him to Herr Hitler, as 'one ex-serviceman to another', pleading for peace. Neville Chamberlain was not keen on the idea, and Bertie's letter remained in his blotter. His elder brother had an even bolder plan. If Chamberlain had not beaten him to it with his infamous flight to Munich, the Duke had been all for offering his services as an international go-between, and jumping on the next train to Germany to 'expostulate with Hitler'. In spite of being pipped at the post, he was loud in his praise of the Prime Minister's bold step. Bertie, of course, could have the last word. He invited the Prime Minister and Mrs Chamberlain to join him and the Queen on the balcony of Buckingham Palace, from where Neville Chamberlain could wave to the grateful crowds whom he had saved from war — if only for one year.

Having sold the Czechs out to Hitler, while admittedly buying valuable time to replenish Britain's depleted defences, the Prime Minister found himself once again embroiled in the issue of when it would be appropriate for the Windsors to come home. Returning from Munich, he had stopped off in Paris to inform the Duke that, while he had no objection to his return, it was a matter in which the King's desires were paramount. Chamberlain then decided to test public opinion by suggesting to the Duke and Duchess of Gloucester, who had been on safari in Kenya, that they return home via Paris, so that they could call on the Windsors at the Hotel Meurice. The Duchess of Gloucester was less than thrilled at the prospect. She had almost nothing to wear apart from her travel-stained tropical clothes, in marked contrast to the Duchess of Windsor, who glided in for dinner in a shimmering purple sheath. Alice had the red dust of Kenya in her hair; Wallis, sleekly coiffed, sported diamond clips. Somehow the intimate get-together between two brothers and their wives failed to take off and win for Wallis the recognition from David's family that she craved. Without it, there would be no smooth homecoming.

Chamberlain had not fully taken the measure of the formidable opposition of courtiers, ministers and royal family ranged against the Duke and Duchess of Windsor. As Sir Ronald Lindsay wrote, 'the Palace secretaries are extremist, the Foreign Office still more so. All are seeing ghosts and phantasms everywhere, and think there are disasters round every corner.' In February 1939, deferring to this mood, Chamberlain wrote to the Duke to tell him finally that 'the time was not yet ripe' for any return. Bertie's promise before the abdication that David could come back to Britain was never formally withdrawn, simply postponed a little further each time his brother raised the subject. David had been angling for permission to come home in the spring of 1939, but once again he was told to wait, this time until Bertie and Elizabeth had completed their royal tour of North America. 'Of course, you know as well as I do,' David wrote angrily to Beaverbrook, 'that it is for no other reasons than for fear lest the attitude my mother and sister-in-law seem likely to adopt towards my wife may provoke some controversy in England and adverse criticism of them in America.'

In fact, the Prime Minister and Palace were right to be nervous about the threat the Windsors

309

might pose to the success of the royal visit. A recent article in *Scribners* had examined the problem of 'Selling George VI to the United States'. The writer had concluded that it was a tough assignment, because of the fact that 'a large part of the country still believes that Edward, Duke of Windsor, is the rightful owner of the British throne, and that King George VI is a colourless, weak personality largely on probation in the public mind of Great Britain, as well as of the United States.' Even the usually popular Elizabeth did not escape unscathed. 'By Park Avenue standards,' continued the article, 'she appears to be far too plump of figure, too dowdy of dress, to meet American specifications of a reigning Queen. The living contrasts of Queen Mary (as regal as a woman can be) and the Duchess of Windsor (chic and charmingly American) certainly does not help Elizabeth.' The conclusion was unequivocal: Anglo-American relations in the critical time ahead depended in large part on the 'enthusiastic purchase' of the new King and Queen by the American people. Sailing for Quebec on 6 May aboard the *Empress of Australia*, Bertie's frame of mind was not improved when, four days into their voyage across the Atlantic, his brother's voice came over the airwaves, making a broadcast for world peace on behalf of the American NBC network. Aimed principally at the American audience, its timing was, to say the least, unfortunate. At worst, the broadcast could be interpreted as a blatant attempt by the Duke to upstage King George and Queen

Elizabeth on the eve of their vital mission. At best, it was calculated to remind the world that the ex-King of England still remained a figure of international importance.

Nevertheless, the kernel of David's message was sincere enough. Speaking from Verdun, on the anniversary of one of the bloodiest battles of the Great War, he told his audience that he was speaking for no one but himself, 'a soldier of the last war, whose earnest prayer is that a cruel and destructive madness shall never again overtake mankind'. To his American collaborator on his memoirs, Charles Murphy, he would later justify his decision to broadcast by claiming that, through channels of communication he still maintained (with the Fascist governments as well as with Washington and Whitehall), he had become 'convinced that Europe was headed down the slippery slope to war. Only the Americans had the influence to arrest the slide.'

Letters of appreciation were sent to the Duke from the US and those parts of Europe where his talk was broadcast. The BBC refused to carry it (after asking advice from Alec Hardinge), as did radio stations in Nazi Germany. Bobbing across the North Atlantic, perilously close to the latitude where the *Titanic* had gone down twenty-seven years earlier, the new King and Queen had plenty of time to reflect on the speech and its implications for their tour. The extent to which it spurred their determination to score an even more impressive public relations triumph can only be guessed at, but the scale of their success must have come as a blow to the Windsor camp. 'That tour made us!' Elizabeth would later tell the Canadian Prime Minister, Mackenzie King. 'I mean it made us, the King and I. It came at just the right time, particularly for us.'

She was right. From the moment the royal couple stepped ashore in French-speaking Quebec to a warm welcome and amazed exclamations of *'Qu'elle est charmante!'*, *'Qu'elle est chic!'*, right up to their very public farewell at the Roosevelts' country home, where the President and his wife led the crowds that lined the Hudson River in the singing of 'Auld Lang Syne', there was, in the words of the *New York World Telegram*, 'only affection for the charming pair who visited us, smilin' through.'

Smiling was Elizabeth's department, and one in which few could rival her. Bertie was diffident, honest and serious, but not without a shy, boyish smile of his own. For the first time he was relaxed enough to allow glimpses of his evident sense of humour. In Canada, Elizabeth shrewdly stopped to chat to a group of building workers, fellow Scots, with whom she carried on a bantering conversation in full view of 70,000 onlookers. Then there was the unveiling of a war memorial, a chance for the King and Queen to mingle spontaneously with the 10,000 veterans attending the ceremony. It was a security-officer's nightmare but it helped to ensure, in the words of *The Times* correspondent, 'that there will be no neutrality for Canada'.

The risk of an American refusal to fight in

the war that everyone now realised was coming made their visit south of the 49th parallel of still greater strategic significance. George VI was the first reigning British monarch to visit the United States since the American War of Independence had freed them from the clutches of his distant ancestor, George III. A century and a half later many Americans backed the isolationist policy that was aimed at keeping them out of a European war. Glowing reports from Canada paved the way for a tour that was a tumultuous success. 'THE BRITISH RE-TAKE WASHINGTON' ran one newspaper headline the morning after their arrival in the capital. 'Elizabeth was the perfect Queen', according to *Time* magazine. In New York there was a ticker-tape parade, and no awkward Irish dissent to mar the proceedings. The *New York Times* claimed not to remember crowds of the size which gathered to greet the royal visitors. Elizabeth was nominated 'Woman of the Year', and Bertie was said to have developed 'a special relationship' with the President over cocktails and a fireside chat. Could the King and Queen have asked for anything more? Well, yes, as it turned out. It had been long in coming, but they found it on their return home.

During their absence in North America — indeed very possibly because of their rapturous reception there which made an anxious nation feel that it would have allies if another war broke out — there had taken place what can only be called a sea-change in British public opinion about the monarchy.

Seven weeks after setting out on the *Empress of Australia*, the King and Queen sailed back to Southampton on board the *Empress of Britain* to receive what *Time* described as a monster welcome home. The seventy-eight mile train journey to London was lined with people waving flags and cheering. In London the crowds along the route back to the Palace must have made Bertie and Elizabeth feel as if they had just been crowned all over again. Harold Nicolson was among those who left the Commons to join the throng in Parliament Square. 'We lost all dignity and yelled and yelled,' he wrote in his diary. 'The King wore a happy schoolboy grin. The Queen was superb . . . she is in truth one of the most amazing Queens since Cleopatra. We returned to the House with lumps in our throats.' The day ended with a crowd of 50,000 serenading the royal couple in front of Buckingham Palace. The following morning the *Daily Mirror* summed it up as 'the greatest of all homecomings'.

How those words would have stuck in his throat, had David read the paper that morning. It was 23 June, his forty-fifth birthday. The world was sliding inexorably towards a war he still maintained need never happen, while he was effectively banished from his home and his family. Now it looked as if his only way back would be as a refugee. Through the summer of 1939 he kept a careful eye on the deteriorating international situation. In similar circumstances the year before, when trenches had been dug in London parks, gas-masks were issued, and Mr Chamberlain had flown to Munich to collect a piece of paper, David had made it clear that it was the responsibility of the British government to get him and Wallis, along with all their goods and chattels, safely out of France. After all, it had been the British government who had forced them to live there in the first place. Now, one year on, and with war looking even more imminent, he was busy checking that this particular insurance policy still held good.

Meanwhile, Paris had its pleasures. That same day the Duke celebrated his birthday with a party in the restaurant on the first platform of the Eiffel Tower. Since it was also the fiftieth anniversary of Eiffel's monument, their guest of honour was the six-foot-three three Jacqueline Vialle, who had been chosen as Mademoiselle Eiffel Tower in a national competition of tall women. According to the *New York Times*, the military attaché of the Czechoslovak government-in-exile, Bedrich Benes, was balancing on a metal strut 186 feet up the Tower and gazing at the Windsors through a window, when he lost his footing with a loud cry, clung to a girder for an instant, and then in full view of the revellers fell to his death on the paving below. Wallis and several of her guests screamed in fright — then got on with the party.

On 22 August, Hitler and Stalin signed the German-Soviet Non-Aggression Pact and effectually began the countdown to the Second World War. Immediately both George VI and his brother the ex-King separately dashed off last-minute messages in a vain attempt to try to forestall the crisis. Bertie's idea was to make an overture as quickly as possible to Japan: his suggestion, made to the Foreign Office, was that he should send a friendly personal message, monarch to monarch, to the Japanese Emperor. The Foreign Office thought otherwise, and firmly vetoed the idea. David was not hamstrung by such ministerial disapproval. He took it upon himself to send a telegram directly to Herr Hitler. Recalling their tea-time get-together two years earlier, he wired his 'entirely personal, simple though very earnest appeal for your utmost influence towards a peaceful solution of the present problems'.

Hitler, who was making final preparations for the Blitzkrieg he was about to launch against Poland a week later, sent a prompt reply: 'You may be sure that my attitude towards England is the same as ever . . . It depends upon England, however, whether my wishes for the future development of Anglo-German relations materialize.' Implicit in this communication was Hitler's hope that — if not now, then sometime in the future — the former King could bring his own influence to bear on the development of Britain's relations with Germany.

On Saturday 2 September, Hitler received another message, one that took the form of an ultimatum from Britain and France either to withdraw his troops from Poland, whose border they had crossed the previous day, or accept a declaration of war. This time Hitler sent no reply. On the Sunday morning, Queen Mary went to morning service in the little church of St Mary Magdalene, near Sandringham, where she listened on the wireless specially installed by the rector in the nave to Mr Chamberlain's announcement that his country was at war with Germany. Bertie and Elizabeth were together in Buckingham Palace to hear the broadcast. David was called away from the Windsors' swimming-pool at La Croë in Antibes, to be telephoned the news by the British Ambassador. 'Great Britain has just declared war on Germany,' he returned to inform Wallis and Fruity Metcalfe, the only one of their guests still remaining. 'I'm afraid,' he went on, 'in the end this may open the way for world Communism.' With that, the ex-King of England dived into the swimming-pool.

On the day Germany invaded Poland, David had received a call from Walter Monckton to tell him that the King was prepared to send his own aircraft to fetch them the next day. Wallis had a phobia about flying, but this was not the reason why the offer from England was withdrawn almost as soon as it had been made. It turned out that, with Europe on the brink of war, David was nevertheless refusing to return unless there was a guarantee that he and Wallis were to be put up at Windsor, or in another of the royal residences. He got his answer four days later when a dishevelled Walter Monckton climbed out of an equally dilapidated Leopard Moth at Antibes. He brought the news that, first, there was no accommodation available for the Windsors anywhere in the royal household, and that, furthermore, they would only be allowed home on condition that David accept one of two jobs his brother was prepared to offer him:

Deputy Regional Commissioner in Wales, or Liaison Officer with the British Military Mission to the French GHQ. This time the Windsors appreciated that they did not have any choice. With Fruity Metcalfe's help, David and Wallis quickly packed and set off through France for the English Channel, with the chauffeur, Fruity Metcalfe, the Cairn terriers Pookie, Prizzie and Detto, and a second motorcar piled high with cardboard boxes. If they had to go home ignominiously, it certainly would not be in the rickety aeroplane that had brought Walter Monckton.

Things were looking up. Winston Churchill was now in charge at the Admiralty, and had sent Dickie Mountbatten with his destroyer HMS *Kelly* to meet the Windsors when they arrived at Cherbourg after the four-day journey across France. They cast off at tea-time and six hours later, in pitch blackness, edged into Portsmouth harbour to berth at the same quay from which David had left on the night he abdicated.

'I don't know how this will work out,' he told Wallis. 'War should bring families together, even a royal family. But I don't know.'

He was to find out as soon as they stepped ashore. Churchill had managed to lay on accommodation with the Commander-in-Chief, Portsmouth as well as a guard of honour in tin hats and gas masks, and a Royal Marine band. But at the end of the red carpet stood just two figures — Walter Monckton and Lady Alexandra Metcalfe, wife to the ever-loyal Fruity.

No royal escort or member of the royal family had come to greet them; there was no message of welcome from Bertie and not even a royal car. The ex-King had been away from home for just over a thousand days, but as far as his family were concerned, it looked as if he might as well have been consigned to oblivion.

7

WINNER TAKES ALL

The Second World War gave the Duke of Windsor his last and best chance to get back on brotherly terms with George VI and pave the way for his wife's acceptance by the royal family. The success of the King's North American tour should have meant that he no longer had any reason to regard his elder brother as a rival. Eight months before his death, George V had growled at Lloyd George that he would sooner wave a red flag in Trafalgar Square than see his country dragged into another war. However, now that this Second World War was upon them, the nation rallied around its own Union flag and the old King's two eldest sons were given the chance to recover in full the popularity and public esteem which had melted away from the royal family after their father died.

Bertie found himself Head of State and Commander-in-Chief of the combined armed forces of the largest empire in the world. However, despite his high military rank he was to suffer the frustration of being allowed no direct impact on the conduct of the war. Access to top-secret information, military briefings and War Cabinet minutes meant that he was almost uniquely informed on its day-to-day progress, but his constitutional position barred him from exercising anything but an advisory role. Just as sickness had prevented him from taking an active part in the First World War, so symbolic status barred him from the Second, when this time even Harry and George had the chance to serve their country in the field.

On his first night as King, when Bertie had expressed his anxiety about what lay ahead to his cousin Dickie Mountbatten, protesting that all he knew about was being a naval officer, Mountbatten had done his best to reassure him. 'My father once told me that, when the Duke of Clarence died, your father came to him and said almost the same things that you have said to me now,' Mountbatten replied, 'and my father answered: 'George, you're wrong. There is no more fitting preparation for a king, than to have been trained in the Navy.' ' And indeed, whereas George V had never seen action, Bertie could at least claim to have come under fire at Jutland, which gave him, in one field at least, a modest superiority over his father. His time on active service may not have been glorious, but it counted for a great deal in Bertie's self-esteem. The problem, as always, was David.

Despite his estrangement from his family, the call to arms had stirred the Duke of Windsor's latent patriotism and brought back cherished memories of his huge popularity with troops from all corners of the Empire during the Great War. He envisaged himself getting back in contact with the soldiers again, visiting the Military Commands and even — who knows? — taking back his Colonelcy in the Welsh

Guards. If his energies and talents had been harnessed effectively in this war, he might indeed have proved to be a valuable card in the royal hand. That this did not happen may have been due in some small part to the competitive friction between Bertie and David — the edge which exists between many brothers isolated together in their childhoods — but mostly it was due to the mutual suspicion and distrust engendered by the abdication and since then nurtured by Queen Elizabeth's vendetta and the Duchess of Windsor's obsession with her status.

In reaction to his diminished status, David had quite changed his insouciant attitude towards 'the princing business' and become as much of a stickler for royal protocol as his father. In their homes in Paris and Antibes, the Windsors' servants always had to bow and curtsey, and refer to Wallis as Your Royal Highness, and the Duke expected similar treatment in Britain. Travelling home on HMS *Kelly*, he had criticised Randolph Churchill for having his spurs on upside-down. As Walter Monckton drove them away from the Portsmouth quayside, that September night in 1939, he complained to Wallis, 'The short version, by God!'

'The short version of what, David?' Wallis wanted to know.

' 'God Save the King',' her husband explained. 'The monarch gets the full treatment, other royalty only the first six bars. I'd become rather used to the full treatment.'

Sadly for him, the full treatment was never in

evidence, no matter where they went during their short stay. The morning after their overnight stay in Admiralty House, Portsmouth, there was still no word from Buckingham Palace. As a matter of urgency, the ever-loyal Metcalfes opened their Sussex home, South Hartfield House, to the royal refugee and his non-royal wife, and made preparations to rent a house for them in nearby Ashdown Forest. But the Windsors preferred the Metcalfes' hospitality to self-catering and settled in with Fruity and Alexandra for the rest of their stay. Lady Metcalfe gave them the run of her town house, 16 Wilton Place, which Wallis and David consented to use as a London base, graciously allowing their hostess to drive them the forty-five-minute trip to and from Sussex virtually every other day. Friends came to see them, but no one else, in or out of the royal family, offered them hospitality.

It had taken all Walter Monckton's tact as an intermediary to arrange a meeting between the brothers, and this had only been agreed after the King had made it plain that Wallis was not invited. Bertie's resolve in this was no doubt stiffened by the support of the two queens, Elizabeth and Mary. The dowager Queen had retired with a retinue of fifty-five servants to spend the war out of harm's way at Badminton House, where she conducted her own private war on the ivy covering the house and garden. She was back at the Palace on the day of the Windsors' return — perhaps fearing that her second son might give in to David's persistent requests that he receive Wallis there — but left for Badminton before the Duke came up to London, and did not see him until after the war.

'So far as David's family or the Court were concerned,' Wallis was to comment later on what she described as her 'little cold war with the palace', 'I simply did not exist . . . Nothing was ever said. It was simply a case of being confronted with a barrier of turned backs, rigid and immovable. For the first time I saw David's face set itself into a mask barely concealing his deep-smouldering anger.'

These were hardly ideal circumstances for the first meeting between the two brothers in nearly three years. Elizabeth, like her mother-in-law, made sure she was out of London when David called. It was a pattern she would rigidly stick to whenever, in the years to come, her brother-in-law dropped in to see Bertie. Lord Plunket, one of the royal family's favourite courtiers, said that he 'could always tell when the ex-King was due to call on one of his London stopovers because of the sudden chill in the atmosphere — though nothing was said — and the way in which George VI's wife would 'drive out' of Buckingham Palace.' In the event, the meeting was formal to the point of being 'very unbrotherly' in Bertie's opinion, though given his own refusal to acknowledge the Windsors' return to England in even the smallest way, it was hardly likely to be otherwise. 'He seems very well,' George VI wrote afterwards to the Prime Minister, Chamberlain, '& not a bit worried as to the effects he left on people's minds as to his

324

behaviour in 1936. He has forgotten all about it.' On Monckton's advice, David stayed clear of contentious subjects, which ruled Wallis out of the conversation. The only matter of substance they did discuss was David's new job. He said he preferred the post of Deputy Regional Commissioner in Wales. Bertie noted this, and said he would confirm it with his government.

First Bertie had to confirm it unofficially with Elizabeth too — not just because it was David, but because the King nowadays tended to bypass his courtiers and discuss almost everything of importance with his wife. She was far from keen on letting David have the run of the country, even if the country was Wales. She still believed that the Duke of Windsor was capable of diluting the public appeal and popularity which Bertie would inevitably depend upon as the months of the phoney war ticked away, and the country braced itself for the onslaught to come. David had seen almost continual active service in the Great War: his presence might remind people of Bertie's sickly youth and lack of an heroic past. Besides, Wallis would probably make her home in London, and the last thing Elizabeth wanted was to have Wallis anywhere nearby.

Twenty-four hours after his meeting with the King, David presented himself at the War Office, to be told by Leslie Hore-Belisha, the Secretary of State for War, that there had been second thoughts on the Welsh post. The only job for him now on offer was that of Liaison Officer with the British Military Mission in France. This the Duke agreed to accept. However, before taking it up, he asked humbly if he could spend two or three weeks visiting the military commands at home, just as he had done in the Great War, but this time taking his wife with him. Hore-Belisha immediately sensed difficulties and stalled for time, promising to look into it. He did not have to look far.

Dickie Mountbatten had so comprehensively switched loyalties that he had seen fit to warn his ship's officers against being taken in by the Duke of Windsor's infectious charm. He had a point. According to Lady Alexandra Metcalfe, the Windsors were receiving between two and three hundred letters a day, only a handful of them hostile. There were reports of impromptu crowds surrounding the ex-King, and well-wishers coming up to him in the street. In Buckingham Palace it must have seemed as if the phantom of the stammering, self-conscious, inadequate Duke of York was beckoning George VI back into the shadows. It was evident to Hore-Belisha when he went to the Palace, that the idea of David visiting the troops and (in Bertie's words to the Duke of Kent) 'flaunting his wife before the British Army', appalled George VI. Hore-Belisha found the King pacing the room in what the Secretary of State later described as 'a distressed state'. 'The Duke,' Bertie declared, 'had never had any discipline in his life.' After Bertie had taken advice over lunch, Hore-Belisha and the Chief of the Imperial General Staff returned to the Palace to discover that the King's attitude seemed to have hardened. According to Hore-Belisha's diary, 'HM remarked that all his predecessors had succeeded to the throne after their predecessors had died — 'Mine is not only alive, but very much so'.'

It fell to the Secretary of State for War to inform the Duke of Windsor that, far from being sent north to address ranks of cheering troops, his presence on the Military Mission in France turned out to be so essential that he must lose no time in packing his bags to cross the Channel again. It was a blow which the Duke might have been able to see coming. Earlier in the day he had had a chill reception from Neville Chamberlain, who clearly did not relish his return, and reinforced the point by thrusting a handful of abusive letters about the Windsors under the Duke's nose. David, though, was not to be hurried. He, too, could be obstructive. He proceeded to spend the best part of two leisurely weeks collecting his uniform, adding to it his Great War decorations, commandeering Fruity Metcalfe as his equerry and visiting friends — though no family ones. The closest he came to reliving his life before the abdication was a visit he and Wallis made one afternoon to Fort Belvedere. It must have been painful for them. The Fort had been left untended. The lawn was overgrown; his beloved garden in which he had toiled for so many hours was a tangle of weeds. The house, his last tangible link with his old life, was shuttered, damp and decaying, a mournful symbol of his lost authority.

Shortly before the Duke's second departure

from these shores, Lady Alexandra Metcalfe, who was after all more favourably disposed to the Windsors than almost anyone apart from Fruity, recorded a conversation she had with the Duchess. 'Wallis said they realised there was no place ever for him in this country & she saw no reason ever to return.' Lady Alexandra had made no attempt to deny this, and in her subsequent record noted sadly: 'They are incapable of truly trusting anybody, therefore one feels one's loyalty is misplaced. Their selfishness and self-concentration is terrifying. What I am finding it difficult to put into words is the reason for his only having so few friends. One is so perpetually disappointed.'

Within a few months the wisdom of those words would be bitterly brought home to the Metcalfes themselves. For the time being, the Windsors expressed their thanks for Fruity and Alexandra's unstinting support, hard work and generous hospitality by presenting them with a pair of ice buckets. Fruity accompanied David and Wallis when they returned to Cherbourg on 29 September 1939, leaving behind his wife, who predicted 'endless trouble ahead with the job in France as I don't think it's big enough'. In this prediction also she was proved only too accurate. The truth was that there *was* no proper job for David to do. General Lelong, the French military attaché in London, had immediately realised that talk of such a post was a smokescreen to get the Duke out of the country. As a soldier he saw the posting as 'a matter of pure expediency', adding, 'They do not quite know what to do with this encumbering personage, especially in England.' They had even less idea what to do with the Duke in France. After a couple of weeks, he was spending more time in Paris, dining with friends or back with Wallis in their town house in the Boulevard Suchet, than at the British military headquarters at Vincennes, where in spare moments he would take out wool and needles and knit scarves for the French troops.

If the Duke of Windsor's presence in France had any purpose at all, it was to report on the Maginot Line, the French Army's much vaunted defence system designed to shield the country from German attack. What was intended as a token posting ironically turned out to have real military potential. The historian Michael Bloch, who studied the Duke's wartime reports, has made the point that the ex-King was allowed by the French High Command to visit sectors of the Line which were inaccessible to other British officers, and his observations, written up with expert assistance, enabled him to make valuable and accurate predictions of where the Germans would break through. Unfortunately, nobody back at the War Office bothered to take them seriously — 'I do not think you have seen this report by HRH the Duke of Windsor. You will not I think want to read it' was minuted on one. When the German attack came, GCHQ was less well prepared than it ought to have been.

Perversely, far greater notice was taken of a minor misdemeanour that the Duke committed in the presence of his brother Prince Harry,

Duke of Gloucester. Harry was also serving in France as Chief Liaison Officer attached to the staff of the British Commander-in-Chief, Lord Gort, and in October 1939 the two royal brothers — Harry the senior on this occasion — found themselves touring the British Expeditionary Force with the C-in-C. At several points, guards were turned out to present arms to the visiting dignitaries, whereupon David, who was walking with Lord Gort ahead of Prince Harry, took the salute himself. David repeated this faux pas at different places all along the line, chatting genially with the soldiers and generally enjoying himself so much that in the end he had to be politely led away. The top brass were annoyed. 'If Master W thinks he can stage a come-back he's mighty wrong,' snorted Gort's Chief of Staff, Lieutenant General Sir Henry Pownall. In the event, David's irrepressible charm and obvious desire to mingle with the troops, worked its magic, as it had done when he was Prince of Wales, and he was warmly welcomed as a boost to their morale by the men digging in to face Hitler's Panzer divisions.

The news of David's behaviour in France quickly reached his brother. Shortly afterwards, Bertie received a jocular letter from Prince George, who trampled mercilessly on the King's easily bruised ego: 'I see David and Harry went together to look at troops but the former seemed to get all the attention. Was that true?' George VI knew only too well that his elder brother possessed naturally and in spades a quality he could never aspire to:

mastery of the common touch. In both wars, stories were told of David's effortless rapport with the fighting men. These latest reports of the Duke's popularity with the ranks aroused in Bertie painful adolescent memories of having to kick his heels uselessly at home while his elder brother went to the Front and rallied the troops. He commanded that the Duke be given a dressing-down for failing to observe military etiquette, and that in future he should be kept well away from British troops, except with special permission. It was a petty and uncharitable reaction — even the Duke of Gloucester thought so — and since no one among the Army top brass was prepared to gainsay the King, it meant that no effort would be made to find a use for the Duke of Windsor's undoubted morale-boosting talents. The Duke did not learn the truth about this prohibition for some time. When he did, his immediate reaction was to fly home to have the matter out in person with the King.

Furious, David prepared notes of what he would say, accusing Bertie of duping him by persuading him to accept a post he would never have accepted had he known the limitations which would be placed on his movements. Bertie, his brother raged, had behaved like a coward. 'On the other hand, maybe you hate me and always have. You certainly disguised it very well in the past, especially when I was King.' Walter Monckton was asked to arrange a meeting urgently, but Bertie would not see his brother, except in the presence of senior

Army commanders who could not be spared from their duties. The Duke offloaded his anger on Winston Churchill instead, describing it as 'merely fresh evidence of my brother's continued efforts to humiliate me by every means in his and his courtiers' power'.

The wounds festered unhealed throughout the autumn. When grudging permission was finally given that David could visit 'British units for a definite purpose, and with prior approval', it came too late. For the rest of his time with the Military Mission the Duke went through the motions, but he could no longer summon interest in a job which had been so belittled. He told Monckton, 'I am really only carrying on because it's the [job] that suits the Duchess and myself the best.' As the phoney war lingered on from one week to the next, with no sign of significant enemy action, the brothers' own phoney war degenerated into disillusionment and frustration on David's side. Wallis summed up their resentment at the time with the 'Palace vendetta' as she called it. 'It seemed to me tragic,' she wrote later and with some accuracy, 'that his unique gift [of dealing with troops], humbly proffered, was never really called upon, out of fear, I judged, that it might once more shine brightly, too brightly.'

As Christmas 1939 approached, it was Wallis who was busy working for the war-effort. The chic uniform of the French Red Cross's *Section Sanitaire* suited her, as did the world-wide press coverage that followed from the photographs of her wearing it. She drove medical supplies to the Front, once spending a night within sound of artillery fire. The approach of winter had found her packing food parcels and appealing for donations of warm clothing. All manner of garments poured into the *Section Sanitaire* headquarters. Shortly before Christmas, Bertie himself crossed over to France to tour the front, and David once again was told to absent himself. 'My brother-in-law arrives in France tomorrow,' Wallis wrote to Aunt Bessie, 'but competition still exists in the English mind — so one must hide so there is no rivalry.'

The third anniversary of the abdication found the Windsors sullen, dispirited and pessimistic, not only about their own future but about the future of the war against Hitler. All dressed up, they had nowhere to go. The contrast between their sore-headedness and the mood of cheerful endurance on display at Buckingham Palace could not have been greater. Where Wallis had been heard to speak disparagingly about the 'Bore War', Elizabeth threw herself into her role enthusiastically, relishing centre-stage and 'the proud privilege of serving our country in her hour of need'. Her wardrobe took on a deliberately jaunty air, with broad-brimmed hats which clung to the side of her head, apparently indifferent to the laws of gravity. It was at that 1939 Christmas that Bertie delivered his best remembered broadcast, a rallying cry to those allies abroad and waverers at home who, after four anxious months in which the war appeared to have been put on hold, were beginning to display defeatism by calling for peace talks with Hitler. The broadcast went out live, with the King speaking slowly, sometimes painfully slowly. But the sincerity of his tone and the lines he chose to conclude his address, echoed throughout the free world, steadying nerves, and summoning up steadfastness as Britain and its forces in France prepared for the German attack: 'I said to the man who stood at the Gate of the Year, 'Give me a light that I may tread safely into the unknown.' And he replied, 'Go out into the darkness and put your hand into the Hand of God. That shall be to you better than light, and safer than a known way.' May that Almighty Hand guide and uphold us all.'

The uniform of Admiral of the Fleet gave Bertie an undeniable air of authority, authoritative enough evidently to register with a sergeant from the BEF hurrying home on leave, who mistook the King, on a visit to Dover, for a ticket collector and thrust his travel pass at him as he raced for a train. While Bertie was getting used to being back in uniform, David was being urged to shed his. In London in January 1940, he met up with Max Beaverbrook, who shared his old friend's view that the war should be brought to an immediate halt and peace terms offered to Hitler. Wickedly, Beaverbrook tried to encourage the Duke of Windsor that it was his duty to give up his job in France in order to come home, rally support in the City, take the country by storm and sue for peace, thus saving the nation. It was an idea that might have attracted David, had Walter Monckton not reminded him that such a course of action would make him liable to pay UK income tax. There was no question that protecting his country took second place in the Duke of Windsor's mind to protecting his fortune. When Beaverbrook had gone, Monckton also had to remind the Duke that in discussing these things, he and his guest 'had been speaking high treason'. The Duke's reaction is not recorded: but he seems to have been unable to grasp this concept, then or later.

While he was still King, questions had been raised in high places about the security risk posed by David and Wallis. No evidence has ever been found to support the persistent rumours that Wallis Simpson was a Nazi agent, although George VI's official biographer, Sir John Wheeler-Bennett, offered his private belief that she was 'used' by Ribbentrop when he was Ambassador in London. The problem for British officials was that David, as King and as Duke of Windsor, had no conception of playing by the rules. As the elderly Lord Crawford minuted, when he heard that the Duke had been seen emerging with Churchill from the Secret Room at the Admiralty where all naval positions were plotted, 'He is too irresponsible a chatterbox to be entrusted with confidential information which will all be passed on to Wally at the dinner table. That is where the danger lies — namely that after nearly three years of complete obscurity, the temptation to show that he knows, that he is again at the centres of information will prove irresistible, and that he will blab and babble our state secrets without realising the danger.'

Six months later, the concerns were rather different. The Duke's outspoken comments around the dinner-table at the Boulevard Suchet, or at La Croë, where the Windsors now spent their wartime weekends, had reached the ears of German Intelligence, who began to take an interest in the former King of England and his Anglophobic wife. The German Minister to the Netherlands was one of many who reported back gossip of the Duke's pessimism about the British war effort. At the same time, the Duke and Duchess appeared to have patched up their differences with Charles Bedaux, whose sinister figure reappeared in Boulevard Suchet as the storm clouds of invasion massed over Europe.

The storm broke in April 1940, when Denmark and Norway were over-run in less than three weeks. Bertie and Elizabeth found themselves opening their doors to King Haakon, who led the exodus of European royals. The Low Countries fell next, the Germans invading on 10 May. On the same day in London, Neville Chamberlain resigned the seals of office. George VI pressed for Lord Halifax to form the next government, but Halifax was uncertain about his support in the House of Commons. With considerable reluctance the King had to call on David's staunch supporter Winston Churchill, a man whom neither Bertie nor his father had ever really trusted. Yet as it turned out, with Churchill as his wartime Prime Minister, Bertie was to forge one of the closest and most trusting relationships of his reign.

Only a few days later, the Duke of Windsor's

misgivings about the Maginot Line were proved disastrously well-founded. The German advance, side-stepping it completely, brushed aside the Allied defences, and made straight for Paris. David, transformed by anxiety for Wallis into a man of action, rushed his wife down refugee-choked roads to the safety of Biarritz. To give him credit, he then hurried back to Paris, where he fussed about ineffectually, pining for the Duchess like a dog without its master. His only useful efforts were on behalf of himself, his wife and their belongings. One unflattering account has him ordering Fruity Metcalfe to take the Cairn terriers to the safety of the Riviera, leaving them at La Croë. Lady Alexandra Metcalfe's version of events is more damning. Far from giving Fruity any instructions, David is said to have left them completely in the lurch, cutting and running from Paris as soon as orders had been issued to the British Military Mission to destroy its papers and retreat to the nearest port. Fruity Metcalfe apparently asked the Duke that evening in Paris what it was he wanted him to do, and was told to ring for instructions the following morning. When he did telephone, Metcalfe was astonished to hear that the Duke had left at six o'clock that morning for La Croë, taking all the cars, stripping the house of anything of value, and leaving Fruity with no money, no instructions, not even a farewell note. 'Plainly,' commented Lady Alexandra, 'Wallis had told him, 'I'm leaving now. You follow!' ' And so, as what remained of the British and French forces retreated to await their fate at the beachhead at Dunkirk, the Duke of Windsor answered a different call to arms and hurried south to rejoin the woman he loved.

In the fury of the moment Fruity wrote to his wife. 'After twenty years I am through — *utterly* I despise him . . . He deserted his job in 1936; well, he's deserted his country now.' This last accusation was stretching the truth. The Duke had reached an agreement with his senior officer, Major-General Howard-Vyse, who wanted nothing more than to have him safely out of the way, that he would go and 'have a look at the French troops on the Italian front', conveniently close to the Riviera. What is undeniable is that he was not told to make his way there via Biarritz in order to collect Wallis, and that in doing so he left his closest friend to fend for himself as best he could, hitchhiking up to the west coast of France to try and get across the Channel. As his cousin Dickie Mountbatten observed when he heard about it, 'David would never have behaved like that in the old days. He was brave to the point of rashness in the Great War, but now something — I won't speculate *what* — something had drained away his courage. He was a totally different man.'

A month after David's ignominious departure, the British press was to report laconically that he had been absent from his 'purely nominal job' for over four weeks, and had 'relinquished' his appointment as liaison officer between the British and French armies. On 10 June, the entertainer Maurice Chevalier was lunching with the Duke and Duchess of Windsor at La Croë when the Italians decided it was time to join what looked like the winning side, and declared war on France. This time there was no destroyer to take them home. David, who had already prophesied, 'This is the finish. Europe is lost,' when King Leopold III surrendered Belgium to the Germans, now swiftly made arrangements with the British Consul General in Nice to join his convoy escaping across the south of France to Spain. Wallis explained why it was quite the bravest thing to do: 'If [the Germans] had overflowed the Riviera and caught us, people would say we had deliberately given ourselves up.'

Back in Britain, fugitive European royalty were pouring into Buckingham Palace, where Elizabeth treated them with characteristic hospitality, blended with a hint of asperity. To make her point, she began to learn to shoot with a revolver, taking lessons each morning. She declared, 'I shall not go down like the others,' and, with more ringing defiance, 'The Princesses would never leave without me, and I couldn't leave without the King, and the King will never leave.' The family followed her lead. Lilibet stopped learning German and took to reading American history instead. Bertie, having sharpened up his marksmanship by practising with a rifle in the grounds of Buckingham Palace, now armed himself with both rifle and revolver whenever he was being driven out in his car. As with his older brother, people began to recognise that the King was a changed man. But where David had become withdrawn and bitter, Bertie was more expansive and self-confident than he ever had been. Harold Nicolson noticed it when he lunched with the King and Queen, writing afterwards to his wife, Vita Sackville-West, 'What astonished me is how the King is changed. I always thought him rather a foolish loutish boy. He is now like his brother [David]. He was so gay and she so calm. They did me all the good in the world.'

Few in the country would have disagreed during that summer of 1940. Although they are best remembered for their wartime contribution to raising morale during the Blitz (still several months away), Bertie and Elizabeth had already begun to establish themselves as a symbol of Britain's defiance, undaunted at the very heart of the nation. It was an achievement which, by the end of the war, would restore the monarchy to a place at the centre of British life. Winston Churchill's celebrated words to his fellow-countrymen applied to his King and Queen as much as to every other civilian on the Home Front: 'Let us therefore brace ourselves to our duties and so bear ourselves that if the British Empire and its Commonwealth last for a thousand years men will still say, 'This was their finest hour.' '

At La Croë, Wallis's forty-fourth birthday on 19 June was occupied in packing up as many valuables as the royal refugees could take with them. The George II salt cellars rescued by David's comptroller from the Boulevard Suchet, the dogs, a mound of hastily-packed suitcases, an enormous cheese — all were piled into a three-car caravanserai, which swung out of the gates of La Croë on the first leg of the flight to neutral Spain. As they approached the French military controls, manned by French veterans of the Great War, the Duke opened the door of the Buick, stood on the running-board and called out, *'Je suis le Prince de Galles. Laissez-moi passer, s'il vous plaît!'* The men doffed their berets, and on the evening of the following day the caravanserai finally crossed the border into Spain. Weary and travelsore, they spent the night in an hotel in Barcelona. From there, David sent a curt telegram to Churchill, 'Having received no instructions have arrived in Spain to avoid capture. Proceeding to Madrid. Edward.'

The Prime Minister now had to turn his attention from the conduct of the war at its most critical stage, and confront the problem of what to do with the ex-King and his wife. Winston Churchill was no longer prepared to champion the ex-King as unreservedly as he had done in the past, largely because, since stepping into Chamberlain's shoes, he had been shocked to discover the extent to which the Duke had misled the government and his brother about his finances at the time of the abdication. But he remained sympathetic to the Windsors' predicament. The difficulties of bringing them home had already been well rehearsed, but to leave them in Fascist-controlled Spain risked the possibility of their falling into German hands. Franco, though ostensibly neutral, was pro-German in his sympathies. Churchill chose the lesser of two evils, and telegraphed David at the British Embassy in Madrid, requesting him to come straight back to England.

A separate telegram, sent to the Ambassador, David's old friend, Sir Samuel Hoare, explained that two flying-boats were being sent to Portugal to pick up the royal party, and invited 'Their Royal Highnesses to proceed to Lisbon'. In the heat of the moment it was a small enough slip, but the Palace was on to it in a moment. Alex Hardinge sent off a stiff note of rebuke, pointing to the King's 'extreme displeasure' that Wallis had been momentarily elevated to royal rank in this way by the use of the term 'Their Royal Highnesses'. 'This appellation was false and utterly impermissible,' Hardinge warned sternly. The war with Hitler may have been hanging in the balance, but the Palace still had its priorities.

Hoare went to see the Duke at the Ritz in Madrid where the Windsors were staying, and told him that Saighton Grange, a country house near Chester belonging to the Duke of Westminster, could be made available to him. Meanwhile, the German Ambassador in Madrid, Baron Eberhard von Stohrer, was in close contact with Berlin and with his superior, Joachim von Ribbentrop, now the German Foreign Minister. The Spanish were asking whether the Germans wanted the Windsors kept in Spain, and if they had an interest in making contact with the Duke. Ribbentrop, who knew Wallis well from Bryanston Court days, was cautious. Detaining the Duke and Duchess for a couple of weeks might very well prove useful, but it was imperative that the Nazi interest in the couple was kept concealed unless and until the Reich was in a position to take advantage of the situation. Meanwhile von Stohrer could perhaps persuade the Spanish to delay issuing the Windsors an exit visa.

Telegrams were also flying between Madrid and London. In a salvo of them fired off at the hard-pressed Prime Minister, the Duke of Windsor chose this of all moments to dig in his heels about returning home. His treatment by his family during the previous September still smarted. He was determined to prove to Wallis that he could exploit the current situation to his advantage. If the British government wanted him and Wallis safely back in Britain, this time it would be on his terms. They would not move, David informed London, unless Wallis was given equal status with the wives of his brothers, and until he knew that a suitably important and prestigious job awaited him. Churchill tried to dodge both issues by maintaining that they could be better sorted out once the Windsors were at home, 'when everything could be considered'. But David would have none of it. According to the Duchess in her memoirs, he said to her, 'Whatever I am to be, I must be with you; any position I am called on to fill I can only fill with you.' For once, it looked as though he might have the upper hand.

In Madrid, unlike London, the Windsors were receiving a royal welcome in all but name. Staying in the luxury of the Ritz, David and Wallis held court to a string of influential visitors. The Infante Alfonso, one of David's cousins by marriage, called in to discuss Britain's impending defeat. The Duke of Alba's sister greeted the Duke with a flamboyant Fascist salute. Then there was another old intimate from Bryanston Court days, the dashing diplomat Javier Bermejillo, known to his friends as Tiger, who had mysteriously appeared at the border to escort the Windsors to Madrid. Now he was acting as their unofficial aide. It was all very gratifying and so different to the situation at home — as the Duke and Duchess never tired of saying, not only to their Fascist flatterers, but to would-be allies such as the American Ambassador. He, like others, reported back how outspoken the former King of England was, that in his opinion, 'the most important thing now to be done was end the war before thousands more were killed or maimed to save the faces of a few politicians.' It was surely time for a negotiated peace, he told everybody who would listen. Germany, according to the Duke, had been gearing itself up for this war for ten years. Countries which had not made the same preparations should not embark on 'dangerous adventures', by which he presumably meant defending their sovereign independence and preserving their liberty. Wallis was even more forthright. She took the view that France had been defeated because she was 'internally diseased'. In her decided opinion, 'a country which was not in condition to fight a war should never have declared war'.

Completely opposed to the Duchess of

Windsor's brisk and selfserving pragmatism, was Queen Elizabeth's very public display of patriotism, a patriotism which in time of war she was willing to extend even to the French. Elizabeth was enraged when she learned what Wallis had been saying. When France fell, she had broadcast to the women of that beleaguered country, speaking in French and assuring them: 'I share your suffering today and feel it . . . A nation defended by such men and loved by such women must sooner or later attain victory.' With two such entrenched positions there could be no meeting of minds between the brothers or the sisters-in-law. Sir Samuel Hoare was given the unenviable ask of trying to demonstrate to the Duke that in supporting the idea of a 'Peace Cabinet', and openly speculating on the defeat of his country, he was doing more harm than good. He eventually persuaded the Duke to drop his demand for a worthwhile job, and told Churchill that in the matter of Wallis's status, 'it boiled down to them both being received only once for quite a short meeting by the King and Queen, and notice of this fact appearing in the Court Circular'. All that was needed, if George VI would agree, was a 'once-only' meeting for just 'a quarter of an hour'. Whether or not Churchill took these much more humble proposals to the King, it made no difference: the Palace remained implacable. However much David climbed down, there was no question of Bertie, let alone Elizabeth, agreeing to let Wallis set foot inside Buckingham Palace.

The outcome of Ribbentrop's request that the

Windsors be encouraged to tarry in Spain was a visit from 'Tiger' Bermejillo suggesting, on behalf of the Spanish government, that they move into the Palace of the Moorish Kings down south in Andalusia. Although they knew it was one of the most beautiful small palaces in the whole of Spain, the Duke and Duchess reluctantly allowed themselves to be convinced by Hoare that their best interests would be served by moving to Lisbon. Lingering only to request through the Spanish Foreign Ministry that the enemy governments of Germany and Italy be asked to protect their homes in Paris and on the Riviera, David, Wallis, Pookie, Prizzie and Detto left the Ritz and arrived in Lisbon on 3 July.

Waiting there were a pair of flying-boats, moored in the Tagus, ready to fly them back to England. Churchill's exemplary patience by now had run out. He sent the Duke what he himself described as a very stiff telegram, reminding him that 'Your Royal Highness has taken active military rank, and refusal to obey direct orders of competent military authority would create a serious situation. I hope it will not be necessary for such orders to be sent. I most strongly urge compliance with wishes of the Government.' When this communication went to the Palace for approval, Hardinge was supportive: 'The King thinks that the Prime Minister's telegram would have a very salutary effect.'

Have an effect it did. Churchill's telegram implicitly threatening him with court-martial immediately prompted David to resign all his military ranks. The impasse continued. By now Bertie, too, had lost patience. If David could make life so difficult for everybody from Lisbon, how much worse might it be in London? As long as his brother was out of danger, Bertie did not much mind where David went, but he was now firmly of the opinion that he could not return to Great Britain. Attention in Whitehall switched to finding something for the Duke of Windsor to do anywhere else in the Empire. None of the Dominions would accept the Duke and Duchess, that was certain, but could a post as Governor perhaps be found in one of the colonies? Lord Lloyd, the Colonial Secretary, who was supposed to know about these things, ran his finger round the globe and stopped at a small pink dot sitting in the Atlantic just to the east of Florida. The Bahamas — would they do?

Churchill was taken by the idea. The islands were as safe as anywhere from German occupation and had as much sunshine as the Riviera, even if they were somewhat less chic.

'Do you think he'll take it?' the Prime Minister anxiously quizzed Beaverbrook, who was now a minister in his government in charge of aircraft production.

'Sure he will, and he'll find it a great relief.'

'Not half as much as his brother,' remarked Winston Churchill.

The suggestion drew heavy flak, even before it made its way by motorbike courier to the Windsors in Portugal. Elizabeth expressed her opinion that Wallis — 'that woman' or 'Mrs S' as Queen Mary continued to call the Duchess — would not be suitable as a Governor's wife, and indeed could set a precedent for a general lowering of standards. She took the same view as the Countess of Athlone, who had dreaded the prospect of the Windsors turning up on her doorstep at Government House in Ottawa: 'If David could not be King because of that wife, how can he be the King's representative?' Queen Mary refused to believe that any official appointment had been intended at all. In her view, it had all been a dreadful mistake: David had asked Bertie if he could find him a house in the Bahamas in which to sit out the war. Bertie had misunderstood and had made his brother Governor.

The prospective Governor and his wife were not exactly enthusiastic about the proposal either. David described it, disappointedly, as 'a small governorship and 3000 miles from the war'. Wallis, with typically mordant wit, christened it 'the St Helena of 1940'. Even so, David, who had promised in his abdication speech to be of any service that the King saw fit, felt that he had no alternative but to accept the appointment. As Governor of the Bahamas, Wallis would for the first time have equal status with him — which could be seen as demonstrating that his family had finally accepted her as his wife. He cabled Winston Churchill to thank him for having 'done your best for me in a difficult situation'. To the Dominion governments, Churchill now sent a telegram out which read: 'The position of the Duke of Windsor on the Continent in recent months has been causing His Majesty and His Majesty's Government embarrassment, as, though his loyalties are unimpeachable, there is always a backwash of Nazi intrigue which seeks to make trouble about him. The Continent is now in enemy hands. There are personal and family difficulties about his return to this country.' Although this was a toned-down version of the original draft from the Colonial Office, there was no disguising the threat that the Duke and Duchess continued to pose, so long as they persisted in making the subversive remarks that were being reported back to both London and Berlin.

The house in which the Duke and Duchess were now living, west of Lisbon in Cascais, belonged to a rich banker and known Nazi sympathiser, Ricardo Espírito Santo. A large 1920s seaside villa in pink stucco, set in walled gardens with a swimming-pool, it looked out over the Atlantic. Nearby was a deep cleft into which the waves dashed violently, and this gave its name to the house — Boca do Inferno, or Mouth of Hell. It was here, on the westernmost extremity of continental Europe, that the final drama between the two camps was to be played out.

The news that the Windsors were planning to go to the Bahamas spurred Ribbentrop into action. Both London and Berlin were getting reports that the Duke was still publicly declaring that the war should be ended and peace made with Hitler. More damning was his apparent view that prolonged bombing would force Britain to the peace table. In a conversation with the American Minister in Lisbon, the Duke reportedly speculated that, before this happened, the Churchill government would fall and a Labour government would negotiate peace with the Germans. In these circumstances he foresaw George VI abdicating — and the Duke added that if *he* went back he would have Britain lead a coalition of France, Spain and Portugal, thus leaving Germany free to march on Bolshevik Russia, from which the real threat came.

Such off-the-cuff remarks do not indicate that the ex-King was a traitor, or that he would have considered for one minute doing anything treasonable: but they do display the extreme extent of his political naivety and of his alienation from the British establishment — both qualities which Berlin was keen to exploit. On 11 July, the German Ambassador in Lisbon informed Ribbentrop that the Duke was intending 'to postpone his journey to the Bahamas for as long as possible' in the hope that events might swing in his favour. Late that same night, the German Foreign Minister, Ribbentrop, sent von Stohrer in Madrid a long cable, marked 'Top Secret. Special Confidential Handling'. It is worth quoting at some length.

According to the telegram from Lisbon, the Duke wishes to postpone his journey to the Bahamas until August. We are however convinced that he is surrounded by British agents who will try to get him out of Lisbon as soon as possible, if necessary even by

350

force. In our opinion, speed is therefore called for . . . After their return to Spain, the Duke and Duchess must be persuaded or compelled to remain on Spanish soil. For the latter eventuality we would have to secure the agreement of the Spanish government to the internment of the Duke under the neutrality regulations, for as a British officer and a member of the British Expeditionary Force the Duke could be arrested as a deserting military refugee . . . At any rate, at a suitable occasion in Spain, the Duke is to be informed that Germany wants peace with the English people, that the Churchill clique stands in the way of peace, and that it would be a good thing if the Duke were to hold himself in readiness for further developments.

What the Nazis clearly had in mind was the installation of the Windsors on the British throne as puppet monarchs. Hitler, who would have had to approve Ribbentrop's strategy, had intimated as much in his triumphant speech to the Reichstag on 19 July, in which, after predicting that Mr Churchill would shortly flee to Canada, he appeared to be ready to offer peace terms to Great Britain — terms which would be discussed, not with the existing British government, but with a British leader prepared to negotiate an end to hostilities. Meanwhile, Ribbentrop was prepared to offer the Windsors a substantial bribe, if only the Duke was 'prepared to co-operate in the establishment of good relations between Germany and England'.

A king's ransom was his for the asking: all it required was an act of treason. To make their prospective quisling even more favourably disposed, the German authorities in control of Occupied France now generously allowed Wallis to dispatch her maid to Paris in order to retrieve some of her precious belongings.

But Ribbentrop's anxieties were well-founded. Unlike Spain, the governing regime in Portugal was strongly pro-British: there were now probably as many British agents keeping an eye on the Windsors as there were German. None of this affected the Duke's determination to continue to delay his departure for the Bahamas. He had been pushed around enough: now he was getting his own back. In late July 1940, while Churchill and the British nation stared invasion in the face, the Duke of Windsor campaigned by cable and by personal envoy to have two of his former servants released from the Armed Forces to travel with him to the Bahamas. There were also his travel plans to consider. Instead of going directly to Nassau in the Bahamas, David wanted to stop off in New York so that they could go shopping and Wallis could visit her doctor. By the time Whitehall got wind of this, David had already booked their passage on board the SS *Excalibur*, and it cost the British government the best part of $20,000 to have the ship diverted via Bermuda, where the wayward Prince could be dropped off to pick up a connecting ship to his proper destination. Neither Bertie nor Churchill had any intention of letting the Windsors break their journey in the United States, where, for all anybody knew, they might suddenly decide that Wallis had a wasting disease which required them to stay in New York for medical treatment into the indefinite future. Besides, the Duke of Windsor was still calling for a 'Peace Cabinet' to enter into negotiations with Adolf Hitler, and the *New York Times* had just reported him as saying that he might elaborate his views if he came to the United States.

David was furious when he learned of the change to his travel arrangements. He threatened to reconsider his position, if his plans were not supported. Churchill weighed up the situation and concluded that the least damaging way out was to give David one of the soldier-servants he had asked for. The new Governor of the Bahamas accepted that this concession was the best he was likely to get and signalled to London that at last he was ready to go.

Now was the time for Ribbentrop to show his cards. First to be played was Don Miguel Primo de Rivera, the son of the former Spanish dictator, a cheerful, garrulous socialite who was well known to the Windsors. He was sent to Cascais to convince the Windsors of the benefits of returning to Spain, and the dangers that lay in wait in the Bahamas. If his despatch is to be believed, David told him bluntly that he was more distant than ever from the King and the present British government. He described Bertie as completely stupid ('*reiclich töricht*') and said that Elizabeth was skilfully intriguing against them both, particularly against Wallis. In a final flourish he also let slip that he was toying with the idea of making a public statement to assert his opposition to current British policy and to break with his brother. In a further despatch, Don Miguel describes his attempt to dissuade the Windsors from going to the Bahamas on the pretext that they might be needed on the throne of Britain. Even with his hazy understanding of the constitution, David apparently suggested that the abdication might make that unlikely. In answer to which came the reply that if Britain was defeated, even the British constitution could be amended to suit the needs of the time. Hearing this, according to Don Miguel, 'the Duchess in particular became very thoughtful.'

Whatever the truth of these reports — and the Duke, shown them in Downing Street after the war, marked 'Correct' against his judgements of Bertie and Elizabeth and 'No' against making the public statement — Ribbentrop took them sufficiently seriously to set in train the next phase of his plot. On his orders, Walter Schellenberg, a bright and ambitious young intelligence officer in the SS, was sent to Lisbon to devise a means of getting the Windsors back into Spain by hook or by crook. The plan he came up with was a complicated ruse which required the Duke and Duchess to join a hunting trip with friends in the north of Portugal, whence they could be ushered back over the Spanish border. Meanwhile Schellenberg was also to offer the Duke a down-payment of at least 50 million Swiss francs — cunningly to be deposited in a Spanish bank — if he was prepared to make some official gesture dissociating himself from the British Crown and government.

By 26 July everything was in place. The Spanish secret service had been briefed, and German commandos were on standby to deal covertly with any British or Portuguese resistance that might be encountered when the Duke and Duchess were whisked over the border. A final touch was the wholly unexpected return of the Duke's passport, which had been temporarily impounded in the British Embassy, and had now been handed back with a new Spanish visa. To Ribbentrop in Berlin, the plot looked foolproof. Schellenberg, cleverer than his master, was not so sure. Once he arrived in Lisbon he realised that for Ribbentrop's scheme to succeed, the Duke of Windsor would have to be seen to have returned to Spain entirely of his own free will. Hiding German complicity in his escape would be simple enough, but if the Duke chose not to go to Spain — as seemed probable — what would be the point of trying to compel him? Ribbentrop continued to argue for 'forceful action'. Schellenberg concluded that the only way to smoke the Windsors out of Portugal would be by terrifying them back to Spain.

As it happened, David and Wallis were feeling increasingly alone and besieged at Boca d'Inferno. There were Portuguese guards around the house. If the Windsors went walking beyond its grounds, it had to be within sight of one of the patrols. Schellenberg's tactics were to make them feel more vulnerable still. He bribed some of the Portuguese officers to help. He arranged for a stone to be thrown through a window at Boca d'Inferno at night. Rumours reached their ear that a bomb was going to be planted on the SS *Excalibur*, on which they were due to sail in a few days' time. A bouquet was delivered with a note reading, 'Beware of the machinations of the British Secret Service — a Portuguese friend who has your interests at heart'. Today such tactics seem laughably melodramatic, the result of Schellenberg reading too many of 'those amazing novelettes which filled the reference library of the Gestapo', as Hugh Trevor-Roper writes in *The Last Days of Hitler*. But they were unnerving. Wallis, in particular, hated the feeling of being watched and spied upon all the time: it was like being a prisoner.

She wanted to move back into Lisbon; but Don Miguel, in on the plot, now sent an emissary with a letter to warn the pair of them that they were seen as a danger to Churchill's government, and that there were many British secret agents around who might be seeking to assassinate the Duke, either in Lisbon or in the Bahamas. Spain was safe, and he himself was willing to shepherd them across the Spanish border, after which they could choose between remaining in Spain and travelling to England or to a neutral country. All His Royal Highness had to do was to choose a date, and everything would be arranged.

Considering his wife's paranoia, it says something for the Duke of Windsor that he kept his head. He was frightened and confused. Who were his guards protecting him from: the

Germans or the British? It was impossible to know any longer who his friends were; yet now, when it was most needed, an instinct of duty came to his rescue. A royal Duke, he was also a soldier who had been given his orders, and perhaps he should obey them by going to the Bahamas on the *Excalibur*. Instead of immediately accepting Don Miguel's offer of sanctuary, he temporised and said that he would think it over.

There was, thankfully, enough British Intelligence activity in Lisbon for word to get back to London that attempts were being made to persuade the Duke to go to Spain. As a result, Walter Monckton was called upon yet again. For the best part of five years he had acted as the essential intermediary between Bertie and David, without whom all trust between the two brothers might have broken down. (George VI had recognised this service by knighting Monckton even before he moved to Buckingham Palace — remarking with characteristic modesty, as he put the sword down on the table and Monckton rose from the footstool, 'Well, Walter, I didn't manage that very well, but then neither of us had done it before.' The Duke of Windsor, whose obligations to his old friend and adviser were far greater, rewarded him with a pair of cuff-links and a silver cigarette box with his name, misspelled 'Monkton', inscribed on the front.) This was to be his sternest test. On the evening of 28 July he landed in Lisbon and drove straight to the Boca d'Inferno. His wise counsel proved an essential counterweight to the conspiratorial

357

threats of the Spanish and Portuguese. Where was the evidence for the British plot against the Duke and Duchess? What purpose would his assassination serve? Would it not be better to leave quickly to minimise any risks? If they were worried about the SS *Excalibur*, he could always provide a Scotland Yard detective to accompany them on the journey. And by the way, what were these suggestions that Britain should sue for peace? Britain was determined to carry on fighting, and in the end it would be victorious.

Bertie, in London, was smoking heavily and showing signs of the strain and weariness which were to contribute to his early death. For the King, who for so long had lived in the shadow of his brother, everything now hinged on whether David was ready to accept that the wheel had turned full circle, or whether he would succumb to the fantasy of his own importance, and take the road to Spain and to the inevitable treason which would drag him and his whole family down to disgrace. Elizabeth, watching her husband age visibly in front of her, blamed David for Bertie's suffering. The anger and resentment she had felt towards both David and Wallis now developed into an unyielding hostility towards the Windsors which after the war was largely responsible for ensuring their permanent exile from these shores.

With only forty-eight hours to go before the SS *Excalibur* was due to depart, the Duke and Duchess were still torn between following Walter Monckton's advice to get out while the going was good, and being gulled by Primo de Rivera into hanging on a little longer in Cascais until the facts of the 'British plot' against them could be established. Wallis's maid had not yet arrived back from Paris with her linen; (nor would she: the Germans had detained her in Paris in order to increase the pressure on the Windsors to delay.) Meanwhile, at Walter Monckton's behest, the *Excalibur* had been searched from top to bottom, three times. But the Duke was still in two minds about leaving. He told his host Espirito Santo that it might have been better for him to have stayed in Europe, 'so as to be able to step in at the decisive moment' — although he believed he would still be able to do this from the Bahamas if the need for mediation arose.

The next day, the last day of July 1940, David sat down and wrote a letter to Churchill, 'I naturally do not consider my appointment as one of first-class importance, nor would you expect me to. On the other hand, since it is evident that the King and Queen do not wish to bring our family differences to an end, without which I could not accept a post in Great Britain, it is at least a temporary solution to the problem of my employment in this time of war.'

At 3 p.m. on the afternoon of 1 August — only an hour late — the Duke and Duchess of Windsor walked up the gangplank of the American Export Line steamer SS *Excalibur*. Carrying the cairn terriers, they bade a cursory farewell to Walter Monckton, waving from the quayside, and embarked with a motley crowd of American ambassadors and rich refugees, for the New World. On board, Wallis dashed off a letter to Aunt Bessie about the Duke's new job in the Bahamas. 'I have awful reports of the house — small, hideous, hardly any furniture — all unsatisfactory. It is very hard to have just finished two houses and now going to one with nothing in it and I was unable to get *anything* from either of the French houses.' This was hardly true. Packing for the journey, the Duchess recalled that she had left her favourite swimsuit behind at La Croë, and requested the American Consul in Lisbon to ask the American Consul at Nice to retrieve it for her. It was, she said, Nile green. Although the house was shuttered and barred and in enemy territory, the mission was accomplished. The story swiftly went the rounds of the American Foreign Service, where the Duchess's request was dubbed the Cleopatra Whim.

Shortly after the abdication Tommy Lascelles had lunched with Harold Nicolson, and the diarist recorded for posterity Lascelles' unforgiving analysis of the monarch he had served. 'Even nature meant nothing to him . . . and his gardening at the Fort meant nothing to him beyond a form of exercise . . . he had no friends in this country, nobody whom he would ever wish to see again . . . He hated his country since he had no soul and did not like to be reminded of his duties.' Lascelles was hardly an impartial commentator, but his conclusions about the effect of David's childhood on his subsequent behaviour were prescient. David had indeed been given every gift — except one, the most important one — the open love and support of his parents. Inevitably, given his position as heir to the throne, he came to associate his parents' strictures and demands with their constantly-reiterated mantra: his duty to his country. He came bitterly to resent it, but did not have the opportunity to show his resentment until he was independent and free of parental control. Now that he had finally found a soulmate, now that his country seemed happy to turn its back on him, he was perfectly content, provided he had sufficient money and status, to go his own way and let the country be the loser.

EPILOGUE

As he sailed westward, the Duke of Windsor had every reason to assume that he and Bertie had drawn a line under the events of the past. In voluntarily dispatching himself to a small British colony halfway across the world, in order to employ himself usefully in the service of the Crown, David felt he had done what had been asked of him. He and Wallis had humbled themselves: they now deserved to be accorded the respect that was their due. Not for a moment did he appreciate that the Palace vendetta had only just begun, and that its consequences would have the effect of condemning the Windsors to a life of rootless exile, trailing back and forth between France and the United States. Any hopes that his Governorship of the Bahamas would end the Palace feud with Wallis were shattered when the Duke stopped in Bermuda on his way out, to find a telegram sent by the Lord Chamberlain for the guidance of Government House officials: 'You are no doubt aware that a lady when presented to HRH the Duke of Windsor should make a half-curtsey. The Duchess of Windsor is not entitled to this. The Duke should be addressed as 'Your Royal Highness' and the Duchess as 'Your Grace'. Ends.'

Constantly, during the war, the Duke badgered Winston Churchill to find him employment where his talents could be put to better use; the best Churchill could offer was the Governorship of Bermuda, which the Duke regarded as insulting.

At the end of the war, the Palace blocked any suggestion that the Duke should be given any public employment, coming up with ingenious reasons why it would rock the diplomatic boat to make him an Ambassador or Governor abroad. As for living in Britain, that could never happen while Wallis remained *persona non grata*, although as David sardonically wrote to Churchill about Bertie and Elizabeth, 'Having been given to understand that they are by now so well and firmly established in the hearts of their people, I would not have thought that my presence in their midst could any longer be considered so formidable a nuisance to the solidarity of the monarchy.'

The Duke flew to London in October 1945, leaving Wallis in Paris, to see Bertie about a job. On the surface, all was sweetness and light. Queen Mary rediscovered maternal feelings for her eldest son. George VI let it be known that his meeting with David had gone well, that relations were on a better footing and the bitterness of the past was over. But the bitterness was not over. On his return to Paris from London, the Duke wrote to the King:

Dear Bertie,
I was very glad to see you in London after so long an interval and to find you looking so well and vigorous after the strain of the last six

years of total war. No one realises better than I do all that you have had to endure along with the people of Great Britain in the front line against the Germans, and my admiration for your fortitude knows no bounds. On the other hand, although in another sphere and under quite different conditions, my life has not been easy-going either, and without any desire to seek praise I am satisfied that the job I undertook as your representative in a third-class British Colony was fulfilled to the best of my ability.

... Now that all the shooting is over and postwar problems emerge in all their complexity ... [my] desire to offer my services to you is sincere and genuine ... The truth of the matter is that you and I happen to be two prominent personages placed in one of the most unique situations in history, the dignified handling of which is entirely yours and my responsibility, and ours alone. It is a situation from which we cannot escape and one which will always be watched with interest by the whole world. I can see no reason why we should not be able to handle it in the best interests of both of us, and I can only assure you that I will continue to play my part to this end ...

There was silence from Bertie for more than three weeks. When he did reply, it was to the effect that there was no question of official work for his brother in peacetime, but that everything would be done to facilitate any plans he might have to leave Europe for good and spend the rest of his life in America.

David did not give up. In March 1946, hearing that Fort Belvedere might be sold or leased by the Crown, David suggested that he might buy it back and spend the spring and autumn of each year in England. Fort Belvedere was promptly taken off the market, and remained without a tenant until a ninety-nine-year lease was sold in 1955. The idea of some representative post in the United States was mooted, and this time supported by George VI, but the smoothly powerful combination of Alan Lascelles and Lord Halifax, now serving as British Ambassador in Washington, put a stop to that. Bored and restless, the Duke was thrown back on his own pitifully limited resources.

At the end of the 1949, David made another direct approach to Bertie to win recognition for Wallis — the last occasion he was ever to see his younger brother. The gulf between the two of them had never been greater. Once more, Bertie pointed out that for him now to accept Wallis as a fully-fledged member of the royal family would be to make nonsense of the past. Once more, David accused Bertie of hatred and vindictiveness. But never again would the Duke of Windsor believe that he could win this battle. It meant that in the eyes of the woman on whom he had lavished clothes, jewels, houses and his utter devotion, he had abjectly failed to provide the one thing she really wanted.

The Windsors had not been invited to their niece's wedding to Prince Philip in 1947.

365

After the premature death of George VI, worn down by duty, in 1952, Wallis was not invited to his funeral either. David went and had polite, inconsequential conversations with the two 'ice-veined bitches', Queen Mary and Queen Elizabeth, now the Queen Mother. It never seems to have impressed itself upon the Windsors that Elizabeth had not forgiven, and would never forgive, the two people who had forced upon her husband the 'intolerable honour' of being King — an honour which he had borne with doggedness and courage but which had finally killed him.

Wallis was not invited to the coronation in 1953. Instead the Windsors went to a coronation party in Paris and the Duke commentated on the TV pictures for the other guests. The Queen Mother did finally consent to recognise Wallis in 1967, at the unveiling of a memorial to Queen Mary. The two women met again at the funeral of the Duke of Windsor five years later, the last time that the Duchess of Windsor set foot on English soil before her death in Paris in 1986.

Wallis returned to their house in the Bois de Boulogne, enfeebled and increasingly disorientated, and there she stayed, rarely venturing out and seeing fewer and fewer people. From 1980 until her death she was in a pitiable state, almost blind and having to be fed intravenously. She told one of her nurses, Elvire Gozin, that God was punishing her for taking England's King away from his people. Yet she kept England's King in her possession to the very end. His suits were in their cupboards; his pipes were in their rack; the inkwell on his desk was full — everything was as it was the day the Duke died. And in her own bedroom, framed in gold on the wall, hung the lines of seventeenth-century poetry which David had inscribed to her in his own hand.

My friend, to live with thee alone
Methinks were better than to own
A crown, a sceptre and a throne.

SELECT BIBLIOGRAPHY

AIRLIE, COUNTESS OF:
Thatched With Gold (1962)

ARONSON, THEO:
The Royal Family At War (1993)

BIRKENHEAD, LORD:
Walter Monckton (1969)

BLOCH, MICHAEL:
The Duke of Windsor's War (1982)
— *Operation Willi* (1984)
— *Wallis and Edward, Letters 1931 – 1937* (1986)
— *The Secret File of the Duke of Windsor* (1988)
— *The Duchess of Windsor* (1996)

BRADFORD, SARAH:
George VI (1989)

BRYAN, J. III and MURPHY, CHARLES V.:
The Windsor Story (1979)

BUXTON, AUBREY:
The King in His Country (1955)

DE-LA-NOY, MICHAEL:
The Queen Behind the Throne (1994)

DONALDSON, FRANCES:
Edward VIII (1974)

DUFF, DAVID:
Queen Mary (1985)

FORBES, GRANIA:
My Darling Buffy (1997)

FRIEDMAN, DENIS:
Inheritance (1993)
GODFREY, RUPERT (ed):
Letters from a Prince (1998)
HARDINGE, HELEN:
Loyal to Three Kings (1972)
HIBBERT, CHRISTOPHER:
Edward VIII (1982)
HIGHAM, CHARLES:
Wallis (1988)
HOWARTH, PATRICK:
George VI (1987)
LONGFORD, ELIZABETH:
The Queen Mother (1981)
MORTIMER, PENELOPE:
Queen Elizabeth (1986)
MOSLEY, DIANA:
The Duchess of Windsor (1980)
NICOLSON, HAROLD:
Diaries and Letters 1930 – 1939 (1966)
— *King George V* (1952)
POPE-HENNESSY, JAMES:
Queen Mary (1959)
RAYMOND, JOHN (ed):
The Baldwin Age (1960)
RHODES JAMES, ROBERT (ed):
Chips: The Diaries of Sir Henry Channon (1967)
ROSE, KENNETH:
King George V (1983)
SINCLAIR, DAVID:
Two Georges (1988)
SITWELL, OSBERT:
Rat Week (1986)

SPOTO, DONALD:
Dynasty (1995)
THORNTON, MICHAEL:
Royal Feud (1985)
TOMLINSON, RICHARD:
Divine Right (1994)
VANDERBILT, GLORIA and FURNESS, THELMA, LADY:
Double Exposure (1958)
WHEELER-BENNETT, JOHN W.:
King George VI (1958)
WILSON, EDWINA H.:
Her Name was Wallis Warfield (1936)
WINDSOR, H.R.H. THE DUKE OF:
A King's Story (1951)
WINDSOR, THE DUCHESS OF:
The Heart Has Its Reasons (1956)
ZIEGLER, PHILIP:
Diana Cooper (1981)
— *Mountbatten* (1985)
— *King Edward VIII* (1990)

THE SOLACE OF SIN

Catherine Cookson

As soon as she saw the isolated house on the moors north of Hexham, Constance Stapleton was attracted to it. With her marriage collapsing, she had decided to sell the large flat she and her husband Jim shared. Connie understood that she must negotiate with the nearby O'Connors, but she was somewhat surprised by Vincent O'Connor's abruptness. Afterwards, when the house was hers, Connie was to discover that mystery was a way of life with Vincent O'Connor. Even so, she realised she was beginning to rely on him more and more. But then, out of the blue, revelations about the man with whom she had shared a life for many years came to light and put her new life under threat . . .

LIGHTNING

Danielle Steel

As a partner in one of New York's most prestigious law firms, Alexandra Parker barely manages to juggle husband, career, and the three-year-old child she gave birth to at forty. Then lightning strikes — a routine medical check-up reveals shattering news. Almost overnight, her husband Sam takes his distance from Alex, and they become strangers. As lightning strikes them again, Sam's promising career in Wall Street suddenly explodes into disaster. With his future hanging in the balance, Alex must decide what she feels for Sam, if life will ever be the same for them again, or if she must move on without him.